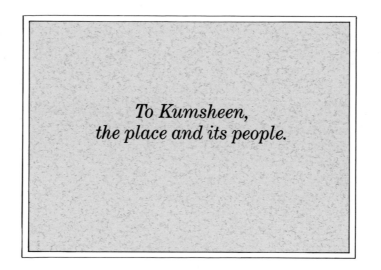

To Kumsheen,
the place and its people.

STEIN
The way of the River

MICHAEL M'GONIGLE AND WENDY WICKWIRE
Foreword by David Suzuki

TALONBOOKS
Vancouver, British Columbia

Canadian Cataloguing in Publication Data

M'Gonigle, R. Michael.
    Stein, the way of the river

    Includes bibliographical references.
    ISBN 0-88922-258-4

    1. Stein River Valley (B.C.). 2. Logging -
Environmental aspects - British Columbia -
Stein River Valley. 3. Nature conservation -
British Columbia - Stein River Valley. I.
Wickwire, Wendy C. II. Title.
QH77.C2M46 1988   333.78'16'0971141   C88-091488-2

Published with assistance from the Canada Council

Talonbooks
201 - 1019 E. Cordova St.
Vancouver, British Columbia
Canada V6A 1M8

Designed by Ken Seabrook; Production by Seabrook & Bobolo
Limited; Typesetting by Leading Type, Victoria, B.C.; Colour
separations by Color Graphics, Alberta Ltd.; Printed in
Edmonton, Alberta by Quality Color Press Inc.

Printed in Canada

First Printing: September 1988

CONTRIBUTORS

The following individuals contributed to the production of this
book:

Project Associate/**Richard Chester**
Research Assistant/**Chris Arnett**
Maps/**Peggy Frank**
Paintings/**Stephen Fick**
Natural History/**Richard Chester** and **Ken Lertzman**
Pictographs/**Chris Arnett**
Photograph Collection/**Richard Chester** and **Jeff Gibbs**

Lillooet boy in Native dress. (Photo: Bryan K. Evans)

The mouth of the Stein at the Fraser River. (Photo: Pat Morrow)

The meandering river in the central valley floodplain, dominated by cottonwood and aspen. (Photo: Robert Semeniuk/Gary Fiegehen)

TABLE OF CONTENTS

ACKNOWLEDGEMENTS

We would like to express our thanks to the many people who have helped in the preparation of this book. Over the seven years that we have been involved with the Stein, individuals too numerous to mention have guided and assisted us. In particular, we would like to thank Becky and Merritt Mundall of Earlscourt Farm, who offered us every consideration during the year we lived in the Lytton area. Many Native elders, especially Louis Phillips, Hilda Austin, Willy Justice, and Andrew Johnny have been a continuing source of inspiration and insight. Over the years members of the Save the Stein Coalition, especially David Thompson and Roger Freeman, have offered us invaluable expertise on the Stein Valley.

The early research on which much of the present book is based was undertaken under the auspices of the Institute for New Economics which was supported by the Laidlaw Foundation and, especially, the Donner Canadian Foundation. Their support is gratefully acknowledged, as is that of the Nlaka'pamux and Lillooet Tribal Councils which endorsed the Institute project.

While the authors are solely responsible for the views expressed in this book, the draft of the manuscript was read by Wendy Hilliard, Dana Lepofsky, Robin Fisher, Nils Zimmerman, David Thompson, Trevor Jones, and Blanca Chester. Gary Fisher of Talonbooks gave us invaluable editorial commentary. Rachel Kuropatwa and Nils Zimmerman provided reliable and timely secretarial assistance. Pat Morrow, Bob Semeniuk, and Gary Fiegehen made special photographic expeditions through the valley with the authors. We would like to thank them all for their generous assistance.

Three people deserve special mention. Dr. A.C.R. M'Gonigle spent many days reviewing the draft in each of its stages, and was unfailing in his excellent criticisms and suggestions. Richard Chester, our project associate, worked selflessly for many months on every aspect of the project. Without his participation, the manuscript could not have been completed. Karl Siegler of Talonbooks had the faith to undertake this project, and the patience and good humour to see it through. To them all, our gratitude.

Finally, to the several individuals who contributed their skills in the preparation of the manuscript, to the Western Canada Wilderness Committee for the use of many photographs from their collection, and to the Stein Wilderness Alliance which made the project financially possible, we acknowledge our debt.

Old ways still persist on the west side of the Fraser River. Here Sam and Josie Williams ride to Lytton. (Photo: Michael Mundhenk)

The old Winch mansion at Earlscourt Farm. (Photo: Pat Morrow)

We live in a remarkable period of human history, when the most predictable characteristic of our lives is *change*. It is easy to forget that this is a radical departure from the way our species has lived for 99.9 percent of our biological existence.

Homo sapiens evolved some 600,000 to 800,000 years ago; for almost all of that time, we lived in a state of nature—deeply embedded in and dependent on the rest of the natural world. Our numbers were small and our technology simple, as small family groups of hunter-gatherers lived lightly on the land. Nature was vast and endlessly self-renewing. People depended on their accumulated knowledge of seasons, plant cycles, and animal behaviour to avoid predation, to find nourishment, and to meet their medical and physical needs.

Around the world, land was sacred. Land meant much more than just a place, an area—it represented the spiritual and physical source of life itself. The land included the air, water, animals, rocks, plants, one's ancestors and the generations yet to come. The very definition of one's identity and purpose came from the land. Aboriginal people around the world maintain a radically different relationship with the land around them than do members of western technological societies.

Native people speak of their kinship with all creatures, of their brothers and sisters: the ravens, eagles and killer whales of the finned and the tree people. We tend to think of this as quaint metaphorical speech, but molecular biologists have begun to show that these relationships are grounded in physical reality. There is a unity of all life forms that goes to the evolutionary origin of life. So all living organisms are made up of the same seven major atoms, the same macromolecules, the same basic cellular structure. And all life is formed in accordance with a universal genetic code residing in DNA, the blueprint of life. Over 70 percent of the DNA in a wolf or seal, for example, is identical to that in our cells.

These remarkable scientific insights come at a time when the planet's biosphere is changing cataclysmically under the impact of the deadliest predator ever known—modern technological man.

Next to the threat of nuclear war, biologists agree that the most dire crisis facing the planet today is the loss of biodiversity. Species extinction is occurring at an alarming rate, primarily through habitat destruction in the great forests of the world. An attitude that sees all of nature as a potential resource has been given great muscle-power by science and technology and the delusion that we have sufficient knowledge to *manage* and sustain the likes of what we are "harvesting." The record of modern science has been astonishing, yet the gap between the frontiers of research and our manipulative powers remains immense. Nevertheless, the brute force of technology enables us to satisfy our immediate demands for profit and material wealth by extracting "resources" from the land.

This century has witnessed an unprecedented achievement of longevity and material wealth that has resulted in an explosive growth of human population. Today, *Homo sapiens* is the most ubiquitous and numerous large mammal on the planet. But we

Typical rock painting in the Stein Valley. (Photo: Chris Arnett)

David Suzuki addressing the 1988 Stein Voices for the Wilderness festival. (Photo: Greg McIntyre)

The Stein Rediscovery site in the heart of the valley. (Photo: Thom Henley)

are like no other species that has ever existed—because of science and technology. Nothing illustrates this increase in muscle-power more clearly than logging. Where it once took the Haida of the Queen Charlotte Islands over a year to cut down a single large tree, contact with Europeans brought steel saws which enabled two men to accomplish the same task in ten days. Today, one man and a chainsaw can do the same job in *minutes*.

By simply extrapolating along curves, it is possible to see that our current rate and growth of technological activity will result in the virtual loss of all wilderness (except for small islands of park or reserves, in which extinction will continue) in the next thirty years. We are the last generation to have any say about the future of wilderness because it will be gone within our lifetime. In the same way, it appears that in 150 years, 50 percent of all animal and plant species will be extinct while 200 years from now, only 20 percent will remain. Of the estimated 30 million species of organisms on the planet, biologists have only identified 1.7 million, barely over 5 percent. Our ignorance of the complexity of their life cycles and basic biology, to say nothing about their interdependence and interactions, is vast. We know next to nothing about the impact of massive removal of large pieces of the biosphere such as tropical rainforests or entire watersheds.

We—one species out of 30 million—now corral some 40 percent of the net primary productivity of the planet for our use. We have lost all sense of biological place. We are out of balance with the rest of nature, and like a malignancy in the biosphere, we consume far too much of the planet's resources. We seem driven by a need to sustain growth in profit and material consumption, and appear blinded by an illusion that we lie outside of the ecosystem and have become empowered to dominate and manage it. Most people in the world live in urban settings, or the human-created landscape of farms. It is easy to forget that the air we breathe, the food we eat and the water we drink all carry the debris of our activity. But, like all other living beings, we are affected by this debris.

Not long ago, coal miners took canaries into the pits with them to check for pockets of bad air. When the birds keeled over, the men abandoned the mines. Today, canaries are falling all around us. But we pay little heed because we are no longer aware of what the world once was. Yet if we listened to the elder citizens of society, we would hear of the vast changes that have taken place within the span of a single human life. The fish, the trees, the water, the air, the soil have been changed beyond recognition, but these changes are written off as "the price of progress."

As a biologist, I believe we have to change the destructive path we are on. We have to see with sharp clarity the consequences of what we are doing now. And we need a radically different perspective on our place in the natural world. Miraculously, there exists such an alternative within our own society. In spite of the depradations on their land and people, pockets of Native culture survive, a priceless potential for all of us. But that alternative perspective depends on the maintenance of the land as their forebears knew it for millennia. The destruction of the land through logging, mining, agriculture, and development means the end to the distinctiveness of Native people.

This book is a crucial document for a society desperately in need. It enables us to get a glimpse of the timelessness and endless bounty of a wilderness area. The Stein Valley has not only nourished Native bodies for thousands of years, it has fed their souls. The Stein reminds us that wilderness has sustained rich and flourishing cultures for countless generations while the "multiple use" of the same area may support a few hundred people for two or three decades.

It has been a privilege for me to walk the lower canyon of the Stein river, climb the hills of the headwaters, and fly over the valley's entire breadth. The Stein is a treasure beyond price that should be preserved forever.

David Suzuki

A several hundred year-old Douglas-fir tree. (Photo: Leo deGroot)

Forested slopes of a Stein side valley. (Photo: Adrian Dorst)

PREFACE

One would think that after 10,000 years, the Lytton and Mt. Currie Indian people would be thoroughly accustomed to the difficulties of the Stein Trail. No matter how old the "Stein Issue" is, however, the continuously unfolding path toward sustainable land use in this valley has in recent years become unbearably steep and rocky.

It sometimes seems as though I, personally, have a tremendously heavy pack on my back as I toil up the Stein Trail in the hot summer sun. Every time I begin to get used to its weight and I finally find my stride, someone or something puts another rock in my pack, and I stumble.

Nonetheless, the responsibility to protect and nurture the Stein Valley, passed on to me by my ancestors, is a load I'll never put down. Nor will I fall, no matter how heavy my burden, no matter how far the Stein Trail seems to stretch toward the horizon.

Our monumental task is made the easier because, as our elders are fond of telling me, the river nurtures us in return. There will always remain those unexpected twists and turns in the long Stein Trail which reveal that surprising glade where sunlight streams onto a profusion of wildflowers, the deer browse unalarmed, and one can rest a while. This book is one such glade.

Chief Ruby Dunstan,
Lytton.

A family of young Northern Saw-whet owls. These forest owls hunt by perching on low branches and logs, preying on deer mice, their favourite meal. (Photo: Richard Canning)

Chief Ruby Dunstan of Lytton, addressing the 1988 Stein Voices for the Wilderness festival. Chief Leonard Andrew of Mt. Currie looks on. (Photo: Greg McIntyre)

Elton Lake on the southwestern ridge of the Stein watershed. (Photo: Kevin Oke)

INTRODUCTION

It is late May and the snow has been gone from the valley floor for a couple of months now. The foliage is full, and the birch and aspen sway in the warm breezes, their fresh leaves glowing a light, almost pastel, green. With the bright sun beating down, the river sweeps silently by a sandbar, past fallen logs, and disappears around the next bend. The Stein rose almost a foot last night, its colour changing from emerald green to brown. The beaver ponds are full. Spring is very much alive in the Stein Valley.

We have returned to the river again, and are surrounded by a luxuriant vitality. Following the path of the river many kilometres from its mouth to Scudamore Creek, we walk silently, our moods alternating between wonder and sadness. For this may be the last spring for the Stein River Valley. The bulldozers stand ready, waiting only for the government go-ahead.

The Stein would change quickly then—blasted rock and eroded hillsides sliding into the river, the forests cut down and turned to slash, the animals dislodged from their homes and pursued by men and machines—ancient patterns of wood, water and wildlife gone forever. This would now be the valley of the engineer and the chainsaw.

Today the Stein is whole—a major river, long large tributary side creeks, a varied forest, high alpine meadows, glaciers and mountain peaks. It is an intact watershed, 1060 square kilometres (430 square miles), surrounded on all sides by high ridges which overlook a sweeping, unscarred forest carpet below. The Stein is the last large wilderness valley in southwestern British Columbia. And it is remarkably close—160 kilometres or 100 miles—to Vancouver's 1 1/2 million inhabitants.

It is also a place of history, its groves and crannies woven into the many-thousand-year-old tapestry of Native life. The river has been fished and the valley hunted in for millennia; its

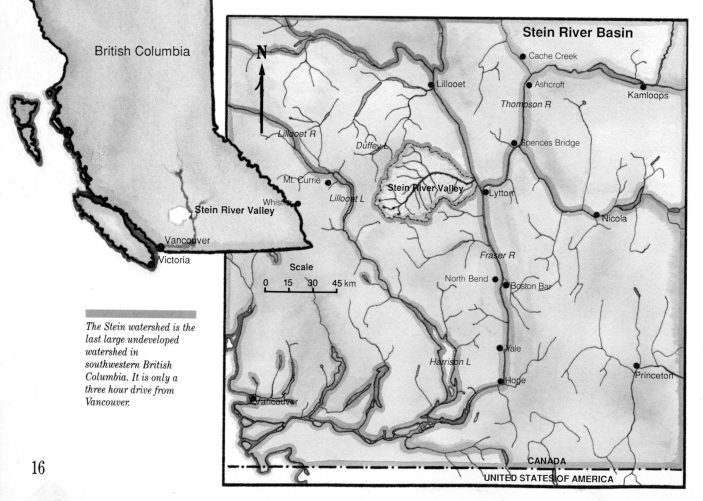

The Stein watershed is the last large undeveloped watershed in southwestern British Columbia. It is only a three hour drive from Vancouver.

The smooth-flowing waters of the central valley. (Photo: Robin Draper)

16

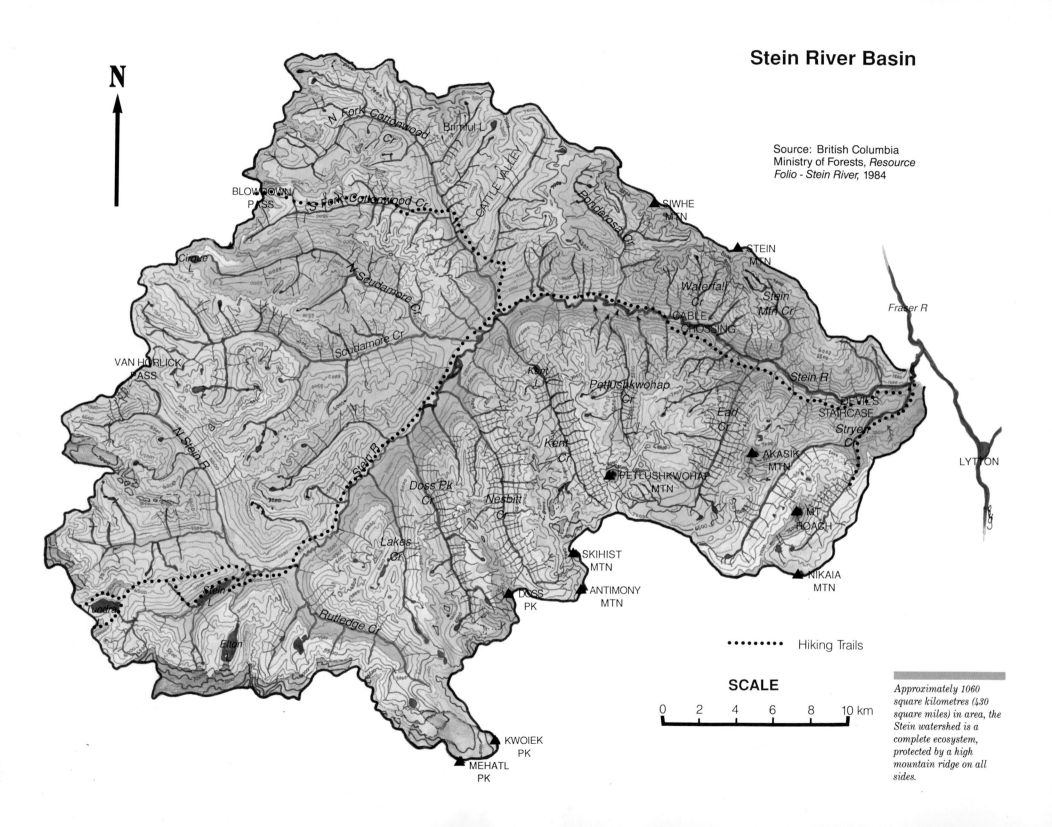

Stein River Basin

N

Source: British Columbia
Ministry of Forests, *Resource
Folio - Stein River,* 1984

BLOWDOWN PASS

N Fork Cottonwood Cr

Brimful L

CATTLE VALLEY

S Fork Cottonwood Cr

Ponderosa Cr

SIWHE MTN

STEIN MTN

Cirque L

N Scudamore Cr

Waterfall Cr

Stein Mtn Cr

Fraser R

CABLE CROSSING

Scudamore Cr

VAN HORLICK PASS

Kent L

Petlushkwohap Cr

Stein R

N Stein R

Stein R

Kent Cr

Earl Cr

DEVILS STAIRCASE

Stryen Cr

AKASIK MTN

LYTTON

Doss Pk Cr

Nesbitt Cr

PETLUSHKWOHAP MTN

MT ROACH

Lakes Cr

Stein L

SKIHIST MTN

Tundra L

DOSS PK

ANTIMONY MTN

NIKAIA MTN

Rutledge Cr

Elton L

KWOIEK PK

MEHATL PK

18

·········· Hiking Trails

SCALE

0   2   4   6   8   10 km

*Approximately 1060
square kilometres (430
square miles) in area, the
Stein watershed is a
complete ecosystem,
protected by a high
mountain ridge on all
sides.*

spiritual power has motivated and sustained countless generations. In turn, it has given its Native inhabitants a natural knowledge that those of us who dwell in the city today can scarcely even imagine. The Stein is a rare surviving microcosm of both nature and history—of grizzly bear and Native shaman, of old trapper and clear running river.

How can one convey the meaning of wilderness—the purpose and value of a wild thicket, remote from the everyday world, accessible only on foot and with patience? To a society perpetually rushing to the next appointment, wilderness is an antidote for our self-absorption. In wilderness is perfection without self-consciousness, a rich complexity of life woven into a dynamic wholeness that pulsates with vitality, yet is quiet to behold. In the flow and dance of a running stream is the movement of life itself. In the United States, wild rivers are officially recognized and protected by federal law. Although Canada and its commerce were built on the country's rivers, this country has remained blind to that heritage.

The Stein is a small river. It is, though, a powerful river; in late spring, it can be intimidating. But it is still of a manageable size, almost personal. Many hundreds of people, now perhaps thousands, feel that the Stein Valley is theirs. They have walked it, listened to it, drunk from it, slept beneath its stars. It is theirs, not because they own it, but because it is a source of strength and calm in their lives. It is their refuge and their source of power. For those who have not had this experience, wilderness may be an abstraction, even a threatening and hostile one. But the Stein could be an important valley for them too, for the valley is accessible, easy to walk, a willing teacher.

We discovered the Stein quite by accident a half-dozen years

ago. Car-camping on the west side of the Fraser at the Stein's mouth, we realized that there was no road along this river, just a trail through a canyon. We asked the Forest Service officer tending our campsite about this unknown valley. He shook his head in dismay, telling us of the logging plans, and of a small lobby, then just a handful of people, trying to preserve the watershed.

On that first visit we spent several days by the river. We walked upstream with some local children from the Indian reserve, and watched them fish their favourite pools. We had picnics on the bluff at the first side creek, Stryen Creek, and wondered what was depicted in the rock paintings above us. We feasted on ripe Saskatoon berries and drank the cool water of the river. Since then, like many others who have visited the Stein, we have been drawn to explore the valley further. For us too, the place has become an inspiration and a cause.

Unknown to us at the time was the extensive role the valley played in the culture of the Nlaka'pamux people who have wintered by its mouth for thousands of years. We have since seen the rock paintings which line the river for miles upstream, and learned of the stories of spirit training by Nlaka'pamux youth and Indian doctors (shamans), stories confirming the White visitor's own feeling that there is something magical about this valley.

The Stein cannot be appreciated fully except in this total way—as a wild river, complete watershed, place of spiritual power, and root of Native culture. In the chapters which follow, we hope to convey that sense of the valley's wholeless and why it must not be lost.

The Stein today is the centre of a struggle between private industrial interests seeking to road and log the valley, and public environmental and Native interests which are trying to preserve its historic and natural character. At stake is the

heart and mind of "SuperNatural" British Columbia. To understand the debate and how it can be resolved, we must also see the Stein as part of North American history since the arrival of the White man. The evolution since then of the community at the junction of the Fraser and Thompson Rivers, a place traditionally known as "Kumsheen," is a fascinating, though often painful, story.

The effort to preserve the Stein is also an effort to build a diverse and fulfilling foundation for that community of Kumsheen. It is one struggle among many. As fewer and fewer Stein valleys are left on the face of our planet, a global movement is emerging. This movement seeks, in part, to preserve what we still have and, in part, to transform what we will become. Places like the Stein offer opportunities—cultural, economic and political—which we are only beginning to understand.

Today we are approaching the third millennium of our Western calendar and, as we do, there exists a need for us to develop a new accommodation with the earth which supports us. To achieve that accommodation, we have much to learn from the way of this river and its community.

Michael M'Gonigle and Wendy Wickwire
May 1988

1987 Stein Voices for the Wilderness festival. (Photo: Thom Henley)

Cattle Valley, in the upper Cottonwood drainage. The Hance family still runs their cattle here, bringing them into the valley from over the northern ridge. (Photo: Terry Hale)

Press conference amid demonstration outside the head office of British Columbia Forest Products, 1985. In foreground, from left, are Chief Perry Redan, then Chairman of the Lillooet Tribal Council; John McCandless, then Environmental Co-ordinator of the Lillooet Tribal Council; Michael M'Gonigle, author. In the rear, looking on, are David Thompson of the Save the Stein Coalition, and Jessoa Lightfoot, currently co-ordinator of the Stein Rediscovery Programme. (Photo: Pat Morrow)

PART

SEVEN THOUSAND AND SEVENTY YEARS

The river in the lower canyon of the Stein Valley. (Painting: Stephen Fick)

This rock carving, or petroglyph, is located on the banks of the Fraser River just downstream from the junction of the Fraser with the Stein. (Photo: Adrian Dorst)

25

Like Ants About An Ant Hill

The old people say that forty or fifty years ago, when travelling along the Thompson River, the smoke of Indian camp-fires was always in view. This will be better understood when it is noted that the course of the Thompson River is very tortuous, and that in many places one can see but a very short distance up or down the river. The old Indians compare the number of people formerly living in the vicinity of Lytton to "ants about an ant hill . . ."

In 1858, when white miners first arrived in the country, the Indian population between Spuzzum and Lytton was estimated at not less than two thousand, while at present it is probably not over seven hundred. If that be correct, and assuming that the number in the upper part of the tribe was in about the same proportion to those in the lower as now, the population of the entire tribe would have numbered at least five thousand.

James Teit, "The Thompson Indians of British Columbia," *Memoir of the American Museum of Natural History*, 1900, p.175.

In 1808, Simon Fraser was the first White man to explore the river which now bears his name. As he paddled the rapids downstream to the Pacific, he passed through a wild, seemingly untouched land. Yet along the river banks, he came upon village after village of Indians whose ancestors had lived for millennia in the "wilderness" around them. At Kumsheen, where the Fraser River joins the Thompson, Fraser was conducted by his host "up the hill to the camp where [the chief's] people were sitting in rows, to the number of twelve hundred; and I had to shake hands with all of them."[1] In retrospect, this seems a strange contradiction: a river and a land that retained their wilderness character despite thousands of years of intensive human use and occupation.

A mere seventy years later the terrain through which Fraser had passed had been transformed. Forests had been cleared of timber to build boom towns; haulroads and settlers' farms spread across the hillsides; Native fishing stations by the river had been blasted to make way for the railroad; riverbeds had been dug up and sifted for gold. A new, very different society now flourished. To the settlers, these visible transformations of the landscape were proud evidence of a new civilization, but to the Native population, they were signs of a new and uninhabitable "wilderness" now spreading over their ancient land. The Native inhabitants, like the environment with which they had co-existed "from time immemorial," had changed too. Sick and much depleted in numbers, they believed that they were doomed to extinction.[2]

Who Lived By The Stein?

Simon Fraser's journal entry of June 19, 1808 identified his hosts at Kumsheen as being of the "Hacamaugh nation."[3] Almost a century later, the ethnographer James Teit noted that this name was a corruption of the word **NLak á pamux**.[4] As he explained it, "'Lākāp' [means] 'reach the bottom or base,' with reference to passing or [going] through a narrow place to the bottom or base, as [in] a canyon, for instance, [and] the suffix 'mux' or 'Emux' [means] 'people'".[5] This name, wrote Teit, "was applied to Lytton and the people there in a general sense and extended to embrace the whole tribe or people speaking the Thompson language."[6]

The Nlaka'pamux are one of four linguistic groups of the so-called Interior Salish people who have, according to modern archaeologists, inhabited the Interior Plateau of British Columbia for at least 7,000 years. These groups are associated today with their geographic regions—Thompson, Lillooet, Shuswap, and Okanagan.

The Thompsons (or Nlaka'pamux) were also known to neighbouring peoples like the Lillooets as the Knives or Knife People. This name is often associated today with the violent contact between the Nlaka'pamux and the miners in the 1850s, but it is a traditional name which predates this encounter, deriving from the story of a knife thrown to the Nlaka'pamux by a mythical monster when it was killed.[7] The first traders of the Hudson's Bay Company picked up the name in the early 1800s and called them, in French, the Couteau or Knife Indians.

Wilderness And Home

The word **wilderness** is a beautiful word. It's fitting that a beautiful word be used to describe a beautiful land. However, the idea of wilderness belongs to the "white man." To the native people, the land was not wild. It was home. It was where they lived, not a hostile environment they had to "tame." It was the "white men" who saw the land as a dangerous place, one that had to be battled, and made to resemble, as much as possible, distant homelands. Today the land, to a great extent, has been "tamed."

Bill Mason, *Path of the Paddle*, Toronto: Van Nostrand, 1980, p.191.

Lower Stein Valley looking up river from the Fraser Canyon. (Photo: Richard Chester)

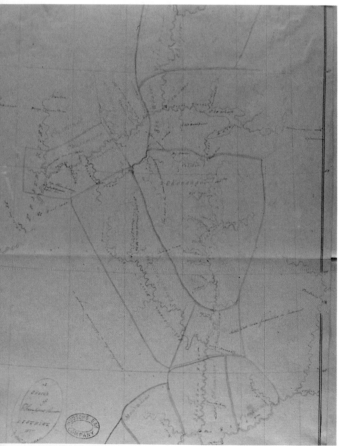

This 1827 sketch of "Thompson's River District" was made by Archibald McDonald, the clerk in charge of the Hudson's Bay Company's post at Kamloops. It roughly indicates the Native boundaries and shows the lower Stein River. (Photograph courtesy of the Hudson's Bay Company Archives, Winnipeg, Manitoba)

Stein, Styne . . .

"Stein" is one of many spellings for the name of the river. It has also appeared since the 1870s in various documents and maps as Staine, Stayin, Strain, Steyne, Stryne, Styne, Stine, Stain, and Styen. Annie York, a Nlaka'pamux elder from Spuzzum, translates Stein as "hidden place." The first name recorded for the river was "Last Chance Creek" in 1860 but, in later years, the name "Last Chance Creek" was transferred to the first side creek on the river's south bank (Stryen Creek).

The Country Was Rich

The country of the Thompson Indians was rich before the whites came. There was an abundance of all kinds of foods. Salmon were very plentiful in the rivers and great numbers were caught at many places. Deer were everywhere; and bear, elk, and mountain sheep abounded. Dressed skin was cheap and plentiful, and nearly everyone wore skin clothes. The people were numerous, healthy, strong, and happy. Now the people are few, sick, poor, and dejected. Game and salmon are now also scarce.

We are as in prison, and our lands and nearly everything we had have been spoiled or stolen from us . . .

Nlaka'pamux woman, 1900.

James Teit et al., "Folk-Tales of Salishan and Sahaptin Tribes," *Memoirs of the American Folklore Society,* Vol. XI, 1917, p.49.

All The Country To The Headwaters

One post up the Fraser at [La Fontaine]*—one down the Fraser at Spuzzum—one up the Thompson River at Ashcroft—one up the Nicola River at Quilchena—one down the Similkameen River at Tcutcuwīxa**. All the country between these posts is my country and the lands of my people. At Lytton is my centrepost. It is the middle of my house, and I sit there. All the country to the headwaters of all the streams running into the valleys between these posts is also our territory in which my children gather food. We extend to meet the boundaries of the hunting territories of other tribes all around over all this country I have spoken of, I have jurisdiction. I know no white man's boundaries or posts. If the whites have put up posts and divided my country, I do not recognize them. They have not consulted me. They have broken my house without my consent. All Indian tribes have the same as posts and recognized boundaries, and the chiefs know them since long before the first whites came to the country.

Cixpē'ntlam (or Spin'tlam), Head Chief of the Nlaka'pamux, 1858.

James Teit, unpublished fieldnotes, (1898-1918). American Philosophical Society, Philadelphia.

*Teit left this place blank in his footnotes. In a later publication, however, he noted the place to be "La Fontaine [Fountain]" near Lillooet.

**"Tcutcuwīxa," according to Teit, was a "main settlement close to Hedley."

During the years of White settlement, the Nlaka'pamux became known in anglicized terms as Thompson or Thompson River Indians after "the river in the neighbourhood of which they have their homes."[8] The Native people themselves set out their territories according to the natural boundaries suggested by the valleys and watersheds, and this association was a natural one for the White newcomers to make as well. River valleys became the major means of identifying each group. For example, there are the Upper Fraser Indians, the Stein Indians, the Nicola Indians in the next major river valley to the east, and the Coldwater Indians in yet another river valley. The territorial boundaries of the Nlaka'pamux were defined in this way in 1858 by David Cixpē´ntlam, a renowned Lytton Chief. His delineation includes the Stein River Valley.

Other groups used the Stein as well, including the Lillooet from the Lillooet Lakes area. Its use as a trail from Lillooet Lake to the Fraser River at Lytton is especially well remembered today. One account from 1906 notes that "a very long time ago, relations between the Lillooet and Thompson Indians were good" and, despite occasional disappearances in these boundary areas, Lillooet men and women were known to hunt and dig roots "in the mountains toward the Thompson country." In turn, small parties of Nlaka'pamux "came to the country around Lillooet Lake and paid friendly visits there."[9]

In these early days, people moved on foot with speed and ease, particularly along established trails. One group from Lytton travelling to the Lillooet Lakes was said to have gone by "the usual route up Styne Creek and across the mountains to the Lakes. On the third day they reached the mountains overlooking the country above the falls of the Lillooet River."[10] This is a remarkable rate; about twice as fast as a fit hiker would travel today. With its gradual incline following the river to the Coast Mountain divide, the Stein trail provided a direct route to the coast. For much of the year, it was more readily passable than the steep-sided and deeply indented canyon of the Fraser River going south. Used for many purposes, the Stein trail was part of an ancient network of trails through the mountains.

Where Did These People Come From?

The Native people occupying the south central interior of British Columbia had no writing system. Like other tribal peoples, theirs was a world of telling and remembering, their history and legends passed down, generation to generation, through stories and myths, songs and ritual dances.

Their own stories tell them that the Nlaka'pamux occupied their homelands for a very long time, and they consider Western explanations of their origins to be ludicrous. Many bristle at one explanation in particular—the idea that their earliest ancestors migrated some 12,000 to 40,000 years ago from Siberia via the Bering Sea Land Bridge, and then down the coast of British Columbia, or along an ice-free corridor between two large ice sheets on the east side of the Rockies. Whatever the scientific basis for this hypothesis, it tells us less about the Nlaka'pamux than do their own creation myths.

In Western religion, a single account explains the creation of the world and its inhabitants. With that view of life, Western culture has historically moved and expanded its territory. In the process, that culture has also developed a linear vision of history since creation as "progress." In contrast, the Nlaka'pamux lived for thousands of years in a dynamic balance with a relatively small, local environment. For them, life existed in timeless cycles of perpetual renewal, not in an historical line of expansion and conquest. Not surprisingly, no parallel concept of progress exists in their

Man posing in Nlaka'pamux battle dress, 1915. (Photograph courtesy of the Royal British Columbia Museum, Victoria)

Creation of the Earth

A long time ago, before the world was formed, there lived a number of people together. They were the Stars, Moon, Sun, and Earth. The latter was a woman, and her husband was the Sun. The Earth-woman always found fault with her husband, and was disagreeable with him, saying he was nasty, ugly, and too hot. They had several children. At last the Sun felt annoyed at her grumbling, and deserted her. The Moon and Stars, who were relatives of the Sun, also left her, and moved over to where the Sun had taken up his abode. When the Earth-woman saw that her husband and his friends had all deserted her, she became very sorrowful, and wept much. Now Old-One appeared and transformed Sun, Moon, and Stars into those we see in the sky at the present day, and placed them all so that they should look on the Earth-woman, and she could look at them. He said, "Henceforth you shall not desert people, nor hide yourselves, but shall remain where you can always be seen at night or by day. Henceforth you will look down on the Earth." Then he transformed the woman into the present earth. Her hair became the trees and grass; her flesh, the clay; her bones, the rocks; and her blood, the springs of water. Old-One said, "Henceforth you will be the earth, and people will live on you, and trample on your belly. You will be as their mother, for from you, bodies will spring, and to you they will go back. People will live as in your bosom, and sleep on your lap. They will derive nourishment from you, for you are fat; and they will utilize all parts of your body. You will no more weep when you see your children."

James Teit, "Mythology of the Thompson Indians," *Memoir of the American Museum of Natural History*, 1912, p.322.

traditional mythology. Instead, a variety of explanations is given for the creation of the sun and earth, animals and human beings, life and death. Some state that a great being, Old One, also known as the Old Man, Chief, Great Chief or Big Mystery,[11] lived in a world above this world, and created the Earth from the soil of that upper world.[12] In other accounts, Old One created the Earth through the transformation of a woman.

The Earth and its inhabitants have subsequently undergone a number of transformations involving various characters other than Old One. In one such account, three brothers, **Qoā′qLqaL**, travelled throughout the country creating mountains and lakes, introducing salmon and animals, and causing them to multiply. **Qoā′qLqaL** taught the first people or **spê̄tākl** (animals in human form who were gifted in magic) how to survive, and transformed bad-natured animal-people who preyed on good people into rocks, boulders, heavenly bodies, and even real animals.[13] Many rock formations are held as living testimony to these mythological occurrences, including two rocks at the mouth of the Stein and others a short distance upriver on the north bank.

The greatest of all these "transformers" was Old Coyote. He was the first ancestor of many Nlaka'pamux, Shuswap, Okanagan, and Lillooet peoples, who have often been called "Coyote people."[14] Crafty and deceitful, Coyote always pulled pranks and got himself and others into trouble. He had magic powers and nothing could kill him. Though he repeatedly tried to exceed his power in his mischievous pursuit of women, pleasure and wealth, the natural order of things always limited his success, without ultimately defeating him.

Kumsheen — Centre Of The World

The centre of the Nlaka'pamux world is the junction of the Fraser and Thompson rivers a few kilometres south of the Stein at the present site of Lytton. Today, we race by it on the Trans-Canada Highway, perhaps remarking that, on many a summer's day, the town of Lytton is "the hottest spot in Canada." Not long ago, it was a place of great reverence and power in Native mythology. It was called **Lkamtci′n** (in today's spelling, Kumsheen), meaning "the forks" or "confluence,"the place where two large rivers join.

Throughout the entire southern Interior, Kumsheen was known as the centre of the world. An ancient Coyote story is still told attesting to this. Ever the prankster, Coyote tricked his son and sent him to an Upper World. When the son finally

Transformers Come To the Stein

Two Transformers, Sesulia'n and Seku'lia, came down the Fraser River from the Shuswap country. They were good men, and taught the people many arts. They transformed those who were proud, while they helped those who were grateful for advice and instruction. They reached Styne Creek at dusk. A number of people were living in an underground lodge just north of the creek, and their dogs began to howl when the Transformers approached. A man went out to see who was coming. When he saw the Transformers, he made fun of them. Therefore they transformed him, the house, and the people into stone.

When leaving this place, Sesulia'n left the mark of his right foot on a stone, and a little farther down the river Seku'lia left the mark of his left foot. Both these impressions of human feet may still be seen in the woods near Styne.

James Teit et al., "Folk-Tales of Salishan and Sahaptin Tribes," pp. 13-14.

Confluence of the clear waters of the Thompson River with the silt-laden waters of the Fraser. This place, Kumsheen, is the site of present-day Lytton. (Photo: Key Lay)

made his way back to this world, he landed on a flat rock close to what is now Lytton Creek.[15] After the arrival of the White man, the people tried to keep this transformation site hidden, but during the surveys for the construction of the transcontinental railroad, a path was staked right through the rock and it was blown up.[16]

In many tribal societies, the landscape is seen as a house, with its own rituals and routines, the observance of which allows the community to keep order. A prominent landmark, in this case the confluence of two mighty rivers, is the centre of power which supports the "roof" over the Nlaka'pamux community. Since the environment which this community inhabits is seen as a house, in which one finds refuge and kinship and belonging, one looks after it for the benefit of all the members of the community, its children and its grandchildren. Such a community returns home, secure in its abundance, rather than leaving home in search of its fortune. As Chief Cixpē´ntlam, in his 1858 delineation of the territorial posts of the Nlaka'pamux, declared: ". . . at Lytton is my centrepost. It is the middle of my house and I sit there."[17]

Digging Up The Past

To the modern technological mind, the Native mythological understanding of the world is disconcerting. White society has had its own mythological age, of course, though it has all but been erased from our collective memory, surviving largely in a few written records such as the Bible. To reconstruct the past, we turn instead to scientific means, most notably to archaeology. By scientific standards too, the people of Kumsheen have a venerable heritage.

Archaeological evidence of human habitation in south central British Columbia dates back approximately 9000 years. The first evidence is found at the so-called Milliken Site, just

Old fire pit. (Photo: Dennis Darragh)

These seated human-figure bowls were found in a burial mound near the Stein in 1937. (Photograph courtesy of the Royal British Columbia Museum, Victoria)

north of Hope in the Fraser Canyon. Closer to the Stein, the earliest evidence of human activity dates back 7500 years. It is at Drynock Slide, just south of Spence's Bridge on the east side of the Thompson River. An 8600-year-old burial site exists at Gore Creek near Kamloops. Two other sites have been excavated close to the mouth of the Stein. One is the Lehman site halfway between Lytton and Lillooet on the east bank of the Fraser River, which is approximately 6650 years of age. The other is at Nesikep Creek on the west side of the Fraser opposite the Lehman site, and is about 5600 years old.[18]

Archaeologists know little about the earliest peoples who occupied the southern Interior except that they had a diverse hunting and gathering economy utilizing several resources, especially game. Even with only limited artifactual remains available for study, some interesting inferences have been drawn about the people of this early period. Writes one archaeologist: "[They] occupied a rich land that probably offered reasonable assurance of a happy, healthy life . . . the apparent scarcity of major changes in the archaeological record for thousands of years suggests that the interior people had found a stable comfortable niche."[19]

For the more recent period—the last 4500 years—evidence points to the existence of a relatively settled culture based on intensive use of salmon, combined with seasonal hunting and gathering in the river valleys. Stone sculpture blossomed during this period. Though small in size, in artistic quality this sculpture "rivals any on the Coast."[20] Over this enormous span of time, life was similar to that described in the ethnographies of the late 1800s and early 1900s.

The winter village provided the central focus of life during that period. The remains of numerous large flat-bottomed houses built deep into the ground, some complete with hearths, storage areas and cooking pits, have been discovered

Art And The Shaman

The number of known seated human figure bowls is about 60; they are the most numerous and widespread of the southern forms of stone sculpture . . . [T]hey represent the culmination of an evolution of bowl forms, which become increasingly complex in image and also, presumably, in meaning. They are made predominantly of steatite (soapstone), which occurs as natural boulders in the Fraser River above Hope . . . The artists who made the best ones seem . . . to have been upriver people, and the style seems to have reached its high point in a number of small and complex bowls from the vicinity of Lytton.

Wilson Duff, *Images Stone B.C.*, Seattle: University of Washington Press, 1975, p.50.

At the end of the puberty ceremonies the shaman led the girl back from seclusion in grand procession. He carried a dish called **tsuqta'n**, which is carved out of steatite, in one hand. The dish represents a woman giving birth to a child, along whose back a snake crawls. The child's back is hollowed out and serves as a receptacle for water. In the other hand the shaman carries certain herbs. When they returned to the village the herbs were put into the dish, and the girl was sprinkled with the water contained in the dish, the shaman praying at the same time for her to have many children.

Franz Boas, on the Nlaka'pamux at Yale, 1890. Quoted in *Images Stone B.C.*, p.50.

Rear view of seated human figure bowl. (Photo courtesy of Royal British Columbia Museum, Victoria)

This soapstone pipe was found near the Stein in the 1930s. (Photograph courtesy of the Royal British Columbia Museum, Victoria)

Deer blind on banks of lower Stein. With a salt lick directly across the river, this blind made hunting easy and reliable. (Drawing by Mike Rousseau. Courtesy of the Heritage Conservation Branch, Victoria)

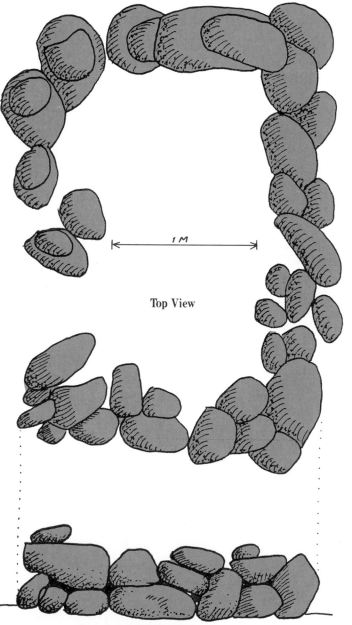

Top View

← 1 M →

Side View
(SOUTH WALL)

throughout the Interior Plateau.[21] The oldest date back 3500 to 4000 years. Abandoned throughout the 1800s, they appear today as large circular depressions in the ground. Approximately seventy of these so-called housepits near the mouth of the Stein have been recorded at the British Columbia Heritage Conservation Branch. Dozens of smaller depressions, scattered in and around the housepits, are the remains of storage pits used for dried foods.

Because of its general similarity over time, archaeologists classify this period as a single archaeological unit, the so-called Plateau Pithouse Tradition. This pithouse tradition, note archaeologists Stryd and Eldridge, "may indicate a four millennia antiquity for the ethnographic cultures of the Fraser-Thompson drainage."[22] Four thousand years of habitation and exploitation—but the land still revealed almost no trace of its use to the European eye of Simon Fraser.

Although there is much evidence of intensive occupation at the river's mouth, archaeological research in the rest of the valley has been patchy. The initial work in the area was undertaken by Harlan Smith in 1897 under the auspices of the Jesup North Pacific Expedition. At the Stein's mouth, Smith discovered an ancient village and a burial place complete with human bones, fragments of shells and soapstone pipes, and wedges of antler scattered by the wind. On the lower terrace close to the river, he found the remains of huge winter homes which measured 50 to 60 feet in diameter.[23] Upriver, Smith sketched and photographed many of the Native rock paintings, or pictographs, which line the Stein.

Despite Smith's findings, it was 60 years before another archaeologist, David Sanger, returned to the area in 1961. He also was greatly impressed by the richness of the Stein's Native heritage, and concluded that "[s]everal seasons could be spent conducting investigations in this area, which has a

36

Head of Van Horlick Pass at the end of the North Stein drainage. (Photo: June Ryder)

The ethnographer, James Teit, pursuing one of his many interests, big game hunting and guiding, seen here with a large mountain goat. Illustration in Frantz Rosenberg's Big Game Shooting in British Columbia and Norway (London: Martin Hopkinson 1928)

concluded in 1980, of 350 sites recorded in the approximately 150 kilometres between Chilliwack and Texas Creek, just under half were recorded in the vicinity of Lytton. The Study also noted that the Lytton area sites are the best preserved and most important.[27]

New sites are constantly being found, eight having been recorded in the short study undertaken by Ian Wilson in 1985, as part of the impact assessment along the proposed logging haulroad corridor up the valley to Cottonwood Creek.[28] One of the most dramatic discoveries was a cave, 900 metres above the valley floor, literally covered with some 65 rock paintings, discovered by the authors during a photographic helicopter tour of the valley in January 1986. At least one other, larger cave is known to exist. And culturally modified trees (CMTs) have been found along the valley all the way to Scudamore Creek, some of which date from the early 1800s. One of these trees has several pictographs on its scar.[29]

Older sites have not been found within the higher reaches of the valley because of the nature of the terrain and the temporary nature of the old hunting and gathering sites which would have left few remains for the modern archaeologist to uncover. In the valley bottom too, the shifting back and forth of the river's floodplain has likely obscured much of what was originally there. Even recent foot-trails have been lost to overgrowth. Only a large-scale archaeological study prepared to undertake the ordeals of wilderness travel over extended periods through dense underbrush, might give us a fuller understanding of the uses of this vast watershed beyond the main river. But we already know one thing with certainty. With at least 36 sites identified along the river, including 11 recorded and three unrecorded pictograph sites, as well as the major pithouse and burial sites at the mouth, the Stein River is a heritage treasure.

potential exceeding any area in the interior known to me."[24] Twelve years later, archaeologist James Baker led a third study team that surveyed the west bank of the Fraser. Of a total of 122 sites recorded by Baker's team, 49 were on the banks of the Stein River, mostly around the mouth where more sites were found than in any other area.[25] A short survey conducted in 1979 by archaeologist Mike Rousseau for the British Columbia Heritage Conservation Branch followed the existing Stein trail up to Cottonwood Creek and identified eight previously unrecorded sites.[26]

These studies to 1979 resulted in an inventory of some 72 archaeological sites at the mouth and in the lower valley of the Stein. As a **Lillooet-Fraser Heritage Resource Study**

Early Chroniclers Of Another World

For the Westerner, history is writing stored in a library and studied by experts. This is very different from a history which consists of stories told and retold from one generation to another—a history which is held by the people themselves. The idea of oral history is for us a contradiction in terms. We call anything before writing came into use pre-history. But for the Nlaka'pamux before contact, history was oral. Memories were strong, and story-telling was at the centre of social life. The coming of the White man rapidly undermined the community rituals and traditions which kept this history alive.

Fortunately, there was one man who took an active interest in recording that oral history. In 1883, in his late teens, James Teit left his home in the Shetland Islands to travel to Spence's Bridge east of Lytton along the Thompson River, where his uncle, John Murray, had settled some years earlier.[30] Teit married a local Nlaka'pamux woman, and grew to love her people and their land. He felt the gravity of the changes that were taking place, and the loss which these changes entailed. He soon made it his life's mission to record in writing the many myths and rich traditions of the

Harlan Smith in the field. (Photograph courtesy of National Museums of Canada, Ottawa)

Eastern Stein River Basin   Known Archaeological Sites

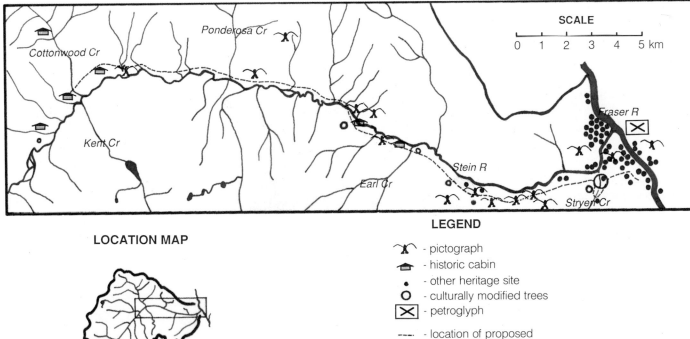

LOCATION MAP

LEGEND

- ↑ - pictograph
- 🏠 - historic cabin
- • - other heritage site
- ○ - culturally modified trees
- ☒ - petroglyph
- --- - location of proposed logging road

This map situates the Stein archaeological sites in relation to the route of the proposed logging haul-road. Note the density and extent of sites recorded as of 1987.

Native culture. In the process, he developed a perceptive eye and a remarkable narrative skill. And he was meticulous in detail.

When Teit arrived in the 1880s, the Indians of the area were already far removed from their pre-contact way of life. Almost 60 years earlier, their ancestors had participated in the Fur Trade as trappers and middlemen. Some had participated in the Gold Rush of 1858. Their population had been decimated by the smallpox epidemic of 1862-64. Only a fraction of the original community was left. Many had left their traditional subsistence activities to work as labourers on railway and highway construction gangs. By the time of Teit's work—after 1898—many were already Christians, worshipping an omnipotent God and indoctrinated in the cultural and moral panoply taught by the missionaries.

The many decades that separated these people from the time before the arrival of White settlers were not, however, enough to eradicate their link to the old ways. Compulsory formal schooling had not yet been introduced. The adults of the day had been raised by grandparents who had themselves seen the first White strangers arrive on the river. In these people, a rich and precious heritage still lived. Teit recorded this culture almost single-handedly but with financial support from some of the most famous anthropologists of this century: Franz Boas of Columbia University in New York, as well as Edward Sapir of the Anthropology Division of the Geological Survey of Canada in Ottawa (now the Canadian Museum of Civilization).

Teit lived with, hunted alongside, and listened to the most knowledgeable and skilled members of the tribe. He explored many dimensions of their oral tradition—origin myths and spiritual songs, use of wild plants for medicine, basket design and construction, and body painting. He was fluent in the language and served as an interpreter in Native struggles over both the allocation of reserve land and Indian conscription during the First World War. He was an advocate of human rights and justice for Native peoples long before it became fashionable to take notice of such things.[31]

Another British immigrant who worked with Native groups was Charles Hill-Tout. A contemporary of Teit, he also spent time in the area documenting the Native way of life. His ethnography lacks the depth of Teit's because, unlike Teit, he neither lived in the area nor was he a part of the Native community by marriage.[32] Nevertheless, his work contains good specific information on the lower Stein. He assisted Harlan Smith in his archaeological work on the west side of the Fraser in the summer of 1897, and worked with the old and knowledgeable Nlaka'pamux Chief Mischelle of Lytton.

Because of the work of Teit and Hill-Tout, some of the vast oral history of the Plateau Native people has been set down. From their work, we have a better understanding today of everything from their creation stories to the cycles of their daily lives. Especially since the historical ethnography so often echoes what contemporary elders tell us, the detailed writings of James Teit are an invaluable part of a culture still living, still evolving.

James Teit, back row centre with a delegation of Interior Chiefs in Ottawa in 1912 to air concerns regarding land and treaties. In the photograph, Chief John

Tetlenitsa is to the left of Teit. (Photograph courtesy of National Museums of Canada, Ottawa)

Okanagan pipe carrier, Napoleon Kruger, at the entrance to a cave located high above the Stein River. It contains over 60 individual rock paintings. (Photo: Jacques Andre)

Stein Archaeological Record

The archaeological record in the Stein is unique in what it adds to our scientific knowledge of past lifeways in B.C.'s Interior. Because the Stein sites still remain in their original natural setting, there is a great deal that can be learned from them about traditional native interaction with the land. The high diversity of site types which span the prehistoric and historic eras is a valuable scientific resource. The unusually high density of pictograph sites (including at least two pictograph caves in particular) makes the Stein archaeological record stand out from other areas in the Province.

Dana Lepofsky, "Archaeological Summary," A report prepared for the Lytton and Mt. Currie Indian Bands. *Stein River Heritage: Summary and Evaluation*, Vancouver: Institute for New Economics, 1986, p.60.

Ours is the age of the urban individual. Living without community in a synthetic world, society has become a collection of self-seeking individuals, getting and spending without much thought for the natural world around them. Among tribal societies, such individualism is unknown. From birth to old age and death, family and village provide a supportive context for the actions of its individual members. The natural environment provides an even larger context for the physical and psychological nurture of the community as a whole. More encompassing still are the spiritual values which permeate all aspects of life. To the Native before the White man, the human body was powerless without spiritual training. Every dimension of traditional Native culture—from birth and adolescence, to storytelling and social games, to hunting and gathering—celebrates the unity of individuals, society and nature within a spiritual world.

Cycles Of Life

For most so-called "primitive" peoples, individuals achieve status within the community through long-established processes of initiation and ritual. This social moulding of identity is the only way to become fully human. Every station in life has its ritual. When a mother ascends the mountains with her new-born baby for the first time, she performs a special ceremony to ensure good health and prosperity for her child. These rituals and training continue throughout childhood. Bathing in cold creeks year-round is a typical exercise in discipline as well as a useful practice for the development of a strong cardio-vascular system. The time spent in the sacred sweat-lodge, perhaps the most renowned of the rituals, similarly has spiritual significance and contributes to good health.

The most critical point in the life of a Nlaka'pamux boy or girl was puberty, a period of physical change and psychological uncertainty as a child's identity shifts into adulthood. To the contemporary Western adolescent, puberty is a gawky period to be suffered through, with as little attention given to it by adults as possible. To the Nlaka'pamux, puberty was a time of opportunity. Like the ancient Greeks, they saw this as a time to develop those qualities of strength and awareness essential to a life of maturity and wisdom. Puberty demanded intense training in both physical skills and spiritual values. At the end of this period, the young person became an initiated member of his or her tribe's spiritual and ancestral worlds. This collective process of **individual** character-building was ultimately as well a conscious process of **cultural** self-constitution. It stood as the most important goal of the Native community.

Achieving this goal demanded a close relationship with nature. An essential part of the training process was isolation in the wilder parts of the mountains for long periods lasting anywhere from four months to a year or more. For girls, much of this time was spent running as fast as possible to build strength required for rigorous travel; digging trenches in preparation for root-digging; and, making miniatures of every article they would be expected to make as adults. Boys practised shooting with bows and arrows; purged themselves with medicine; sweatbathed and performed gymnastics.

The Features Of Aboriginal Civilization

If one were asked to state briefly and succinctly what are the outstanding positive features of aboriginal civilizations, I, for one, would have no hesitation in answering that there are three: the respect for the individual, irrespective of age or sex; the amazing degree of social and political integration achieved by them; and the existence there of a concept of personal security which transcends all governmental forms and all tribal and group interests and conflicts.

Paul Radin, *The World of Primitive Man*, New York: Dutton, (1953) 1971 edition, p.11.

Nlaka'pamux girl in traditional puberty attire. (Photograph courtesy of National Museums of Canada, Ottawa)

The River Speaks

You wanted to be Indian Doctor. If you want to be a big chief or a powerful man you go to the creek and then you use that fir bough and you talk to the morning and to the creek. So as you'll talk to them—you ask them for guidance, so as you live a long time in this world and you wouldn't get old so quick, and you ask for their guidance to help you so as you become an Indian Doctor. Then you'll become a man—if you want. You'll go to the big mountain and you'll prepare yourself to become whatever you want to be.

Excerpt of speech by Chief Tetlenitsa to boys about to undergo their training, 1912. Running translation by Albert Seymour, Shackan, B.C.
(Recording courtesy of Canadian Centre for Folk Culture Studies, National Museums of Canada, Ottawa)

The True Man

The true man—the spiritual man—is not **given**, is not the result of a natural process. He is "made" by the old masters, in accordance with the models revealed by the Divine Beings and preserved in the myths. These old masters constitute the spiritual elites of archaic societies. It is they who know, who know the world of spirit, the truly human world. Their function is to reveal the deep meaning of existence to the new generations and to help them assume the responsibility of being truly men and hence of participating in culture.

Mircea Eliade, *Rites and Symbols of Initiation*, New York: Harper and Row, 1958, p.132.

Painted Cave
This cave is high up on a
cliff on the north bank of
the Stein about two
kilometres upriver from
the cable crossing.
(Photo: Brian Molyneaux)

Night was the time for spirit-training. At dusk, the boy or girl travelled alone to a prominent place such as a mountain peak or a ledge above a river, lit a fire there, and sang and danced until daybreak. The initiates implored the spirits of these places to look kindly on them, to give them strength and protect them throughout their lives.[1] In song, they appealed to the spirit of the Dawn to assist them in making contact with their individual spirit helpers. Eventually, exhausted from physical exertion, the young person fell asleep beside the dying embers.[2]

While asleep or in a semi-conscious state, an animal, bird, or other natural being appeared in a dream and spoke and sang to the young person. The song was left with the young person, enabling that person to call up his or her nature "partner" later. This song was the basis for the life-long alliance with a **sna7m** (pronounced "shna-am") which could put one into a powerful state known as **xa7xa7** (pronounced "hah-hah"). While in this state, one had special abilities such as clairvoyance, great endurance and strength, immunity to danger, and the capacities to transform oneself into other forms. An especially strong **sna7m** enabled one to cure illnesses and to see the power of an individual who was spiritually weaker. "If a boy wanted to develop into an extraordinary man," wrote Teit, "the ceremonial isolation and practice were extended over years, which he spent alone with his guardian spirit in the mountains, fasting and praying, until he gained the desired knowledge."[3]

Acquisition of power through a nature helper was the culmination of the puberty experience. After such an

A Mysterious Power Pervades All Nature

The religion of the interior tribes may be described as a sort of animism, or nature-worship, based largely on the belief that a certain mysterious power pervaded all nature, its manifestations varying in different objects as to kind and degree. It was the effort of the Indians to obtain as much as possible of this power from those animals and objects in nature that appeared to possess it in the greatest degree or that manifested the type of power considered the most valuable. Thus the sun and day-dawn were among the chief objects of veneration and supplication, as were certain mountain peaks, the thunder and rocks and trees. In the animal kingdom such creatures as the eagle, raven, owl, wolf, and grizzly bear were venerated, and young men tried to obtain them for manitous or guardian spirits.

James Teit, "Indian Tribes of the Interior," *Canada and its Provinces*, No.21, 1914, p.311.

The Vision, 1912

At fifteen years of age I stayed many moons in the mountains, undergoing my training, all alone, all alone.

I slept in the grass, one summer night, in an open space, near a patch of fireweeds. The wind rose at dawn and I heard a voice, a sweet voice, floating above, floating back and forth with the white cotton tufts from the fireweeds. "Dear son, listen to me, listen to my song!"

Opening my eyes, I looked around, but could see no one. Only the wind went on, singing its song, a dream song—a **sekwalah**.

Slowly I woke up and again I heard the voice of the wind; it grew louder and clearer to my ears. It was a voice with many tones, as if people afar had been singing together, singing very softly at dawn, in a dream.

Now I understood the words of my old grandfather: "When you wake up in the mountains at daybreak, you shall hear the voice of nature. Listen to it, son, for it holds treasures for you."

I listened to the voice of the wind, the voice from the valleys below growing louder with the light of dawn. Its song brushed the grass, the fireweeds, the

bushes; it swept the treetops, the trees large and small, the trees with leaves and the evergreens with needles. It was the song of the morning wind that makes Nature sing. The rivers, the canyons, the mountain gorges, the forests, the wild fruit patches at timber line, and the peaks glittering with snow, they were all singing in the wind. And I joined in the song of dawn, the song that was sweet, dreamlike, endless—and mighty.

The wind of dawn woke me, the wind blowing up the mountain slopes. And the grass, the fireweeds, the trees, the rivers, and the canyons were all singing together a sweet song, a mighty song. I learned their song and began to hum it myself. Then I picked up my hat and used it as a drum. It was impossible to sit still, for the song floated on the air, and everyone must dance when the grass, the brush, and the treetops dance in the wind.

What did I see gliding out of the gates of sunrise? Two young women—the Twin Sisters. They were not walking; their feet only swept the weeds as they drifted in the wind. They sang the song of Nature as they slowly approached, picking flowers, blades of grass, and leaves wet with dew. One of them picked up an

aspen twig and passed it on to her sister, who threw it away. The other picked up another aspen twig and handed it on to her sister, who threw it away. And they went on picking up aspen twigs and throwing them away, singing all the while until they were quite near.

Now they stood close to me like a dream of night, yet they were a vision of daylight. The elder sister had vermilion stars painted on her cheeks and the younger red moons on her breasts. The stars and the moons were like flowers

raised above the surface, yet they were the scars of healed wounds.

Never had I seen the likes of the Twin Sisters, the sisters of dawn. I fell prostrate to the ground before them. They both stooped over me and brushed my head and my shoulders with their soft leaf-like hands. Under their breath as they still sang, I passed from childhood to the rising power of a man.

Chief Tetlenitsa in Ottawa, 1912, in Marius Barbeau and Grace Melvin, *The Indian Speaks*, Toronto: Macmillan, 1943, pp.59-62.

Chief John Tetlenitsa and his wife, KwEtEmákst, in Native dress, in 1914. (Photograph courtesy of National Museums of Canada, Ottawa)

encounter, the initiate was able to make both a physical and psychological break from childhood.

The power from one's nature-helper was integral to one's total being. Because it has no counterpart in Western culture, it has often been misconstrued. But $\underline{x}$a7$\underline{x}$á7—understood as an immaterial force or energy—is not a concept unique to the Nlaka'pamux. Similar concepts are found throughout Native North America and the world. "The idea of a magic power," wrote Franz Boas, "is one of the fundamental concepts that occur among all Indian tribes . . . the fundamental notion of all of them is that of a power inherent in the objects of nature which is more potent than the natural powers of men."[4] Westerners do not easily comprehend the character of this dynamic, almost mystical concept. For one thing, says anthropologist Jay Miller, it "is poorly described by nouns [like power] because it involves verbs almost entirely."[5]

Pictographs And Painted Dreams

Traces of these traditional puberty experiences survive today in the memories of living elders, and in rock paintings. These paintings are found throughout the Interior and are densely distributed on numerous rock panels along the lower 32-kilometre (20-mile) corridor of the Stein River. Others are reported to exist but have not yet been located by archaeologists.

Many rock paintings of the southern Interior are living records of spiritual offerings and ceremonies, dreams, and visions of all ages, including boys and girls during their puberty training. Grizzly bears, owls, mountain goats, fir branches, lakes, sun and thunder all appear in red ochre on the rocks.[6] Places with natural power such as secluded lakes, streams, waterfalls, high ledges, natural amphitheatres and caves were especially favoured.

Many of the paintings were themselves considered powerful. Those associated with guardian spirits were often painted to ward off evil or possible disaster along trails. Some were painted on rocks that were thought to represent semi-animal or God-like characters from mythological tales, and "by painting on them, power in some degree . . . might be obtained from them or their spirits."[7] Other rock paintings were believed not to be the work of humans, but were "pictures made and shown by the mysteries, or powers, or spirits of the places where they are to be seen."[8]

Today everyone is curious about these mysterious rock paintings. How were they painted? How did they make paint which lasts for centuries without fading away? Why red? What do the paintings depict? How old are they? Who were the artists?

These are difficult questions to answer. Even during the period of intense creative activity, mystery surrounded the meanings of some paintings and the identity of the artists. Individuals usually painted in secret and alone. The images came from dreams and visions. As Teit explained, "one person did not know exactly the meaning of the figure painted by another, because he did not know the other person's dreams, experiences."[9] The Indians have been painting rocks with their mixture of red ochre and animal fat for longer than memory. Red was significant as it symbolized positive energy, life, goodness, and good luck. Some of the well-protected paintings,

---

The Feet Of The Shamans

Certain spots and localities are pointed out by the older Indians as the places where certain celebrated shamans underwent their fasts and training to gain their powers. There were several such spots on the banks of Stein Creek, a mountain stream that runs into the Fraser River about five miles above Lytton. Worn and hollowed places are pointed out here and there, and these are said to have been made by the feet of the aspirants after shamanistic powers in the performance of their exercises. We find several groups of rock paintings along this creek which are believed by the present Indians to have been made in the past by noted shamans.

Charles Hill-Tout, "Notes on the N'tlakapamuq of British Columbia," In *The Salish People*, Vol. 1 Vancouver: Talonbooks, (1899) 1978 ed., p.48.

Stryen Creek Pictograph Panel

Numerous interpretations have been given for this site. James Teit was told that the circles joined by lines were "lakes connected by a river." Harlan Smith was told by a local Native that "the line from the head of the lower figure at the right which extends up about ten feet . . . represented a trail over the hill on which the animal goes."

C.J. Hallisey, former magistrate of Lytton in the 1920s, travelled upriver sketching pictographs for Harlan Smith. In his retirement, he wrote:

"Some years ago A.W. Anthony, G.R. Anthony, and myself decided to make an inventory of what paintings we could locate up the Styne Valley northwest from Lytton. Starting upstream early one morning we located the first indications at the junction of the Last Chance and Styne. Here a short map was found high on the cliffs . . . The painters not only mapped every valley, but noted what kind of game was to be found, also what dangers to be met with . . . Most of their characters were in the form of kinds of game and [indications of their] locality . . ."

C.J. Hallisey, unpublished manuscript (1950s) in the possession of Jim Hallisey, Kelowna, British Columbia.

such as those in caves, may be very old. Others, which are exposed to the air and elements, may be younger, perhaps 150 to 200 years old.

The Stein Valley was a favourite place for such paintings. A travel route, a hunting area, it is above all a watershed filled with power spots. The whole valley is ideal for spirit training, secluded from the open areas around Kumsheen, its intimate environment protected by a long, high, narrow canyon gorge. Its very name, which means "hidden place," attests to this character.

The first painted panel one encounters upriver is near Stryen Creek. The panel as a whole gives the impression of being a map, perhaps of the whole valley. Jimmie, a Thompson Indian from Lytton, guided the archaeologist Harlan Smith to this spot and told him that "this was where boys and girls came to wash with fir boughs during their puberty

ceremonials." There was, he also noted, a shallow painted cave nearby where boys and girls went to fast. The creek is referred to locally as Last Chance Creek, and its Native name, **nzíkzakxn**, means "to fall a log across."[10] (Ironically, these paintings, which may have been an ancient map to the valley, and these two names identify the very place where a logging road for the Stein Valley would begin.)

Another four kilometres upriver, below the steep talus slope known as Devil's Staircase, are two panels of paintings at the bases of two cliffs. The upstream panel is one of the largest rock painting sites in British Columbia. The name for the location underscores its significance—**ts'ets'ék̲w'**, translated as "markings."[11] The looming cliff, the many paintings, and the acoustic environment created by the river echoing from the cliff make **ts'ets'ék̲w'** a place of power in the fullest sense of the phrase.

With the long lines indicating trails, the ridge marking, the strange human-like figure and encampment markings on the right, the panel could be interpreted as a map of the valley leading to the Lillooet people. Although hypothetical, such an interpretation is intriguing.

Images from the
Ts'ets'é<u>k</u>w' site at Devil's
Staircase. The Native
name for this site means
"markings."

Caves were favourite places for painting, although only a few painted caves have been found in the Interior, perhaps because many are hidden in high cliffs. At least three painted caves have been reported in the Stein. One is located 900 metres above the trail on a steep cliffside, about two kilometres from the cable crossing. It would have been impossible to identify from the trail below. A more well-known cave is found just past the Devil's Staircase site on the south side of the river. The cave is only large enough to hold two persons at a time. About 20 figures are painted on the inside.

A third cave is known to at least three Lytton elders, but remains otherwise undiscovered. It is the most intriguing power spot in the Stein today. Perhaps it is no accident that this mysterious cave remains hidden, not yet classified as one more dead artifact. And it could well remain so for some time as it is also reputed to be high in the cliffs above the river.

More sites could exist almost anywhere in the valley. They

Art Absolutely Astounding

The Stein River valley contains a world-class collection of ancient pictograph art, says an archaeologist and pictograph specialist who recently completed a survey of the disputed valley about 160 kilometres northeast of Vancouver.

"There are sites in the valley that are absolutely astounding," said Brain Molyneaux, a field associate at the Royal Ontario Museum currently conducting research for the University of Southampton in Great Britain.

"In the 15 to 20 years that I've spent studying rock art, when I say this site is world-class, I'm not kidding," he said Thursday.

"Stein Pictograph Art Absolutely Astounding," Times-Colonist, Victoria, B.C. 30 July, 1988, p. A3.

Mystery Cave

Again, I have heard a somewhat fantastic tale as follows. A few years ago some Indians on the west side of the Fraser River, north of Lytton, were hunting goats near the lake where they annually go in the late autumn to catch fish through the ice. A wounded goat disappeared in a crack on the face of some cliffs above the lake, and when the Indians followed it they found it had taken refuge in a cave. When they entered the cave, and before dispatching the goat, one of them lit a candle and to their amazement discovered that the walls of this cave were ornamented from top to bottom with paintings, of whose origin none of the tribe had any knowledge. This story I heard from Mr. Ewen McLeod, now Indian Agent at Williams Lake or Quesnel, and he obtained it from the chief of the tribe, who is apparently loth to tell a white man exactly where the spot is.

Letter from T.L. Thacker, Little Mountain near Hope, British Columbia, to Harlan Smith, March 24, 1923. In Harlan Smith, unpublished notes, Archaeological Survey of Canada, Canadian Museum of Civilization, Ottawa.

NOTE: The river above the cable crossing is so wide and calm it is often referred to as "like a lake."

Winter in the alpine meadows at the upper end of Ponderosa Creek. (Photo: Leo deGroot)

could be on remote mountain peaks which were known to be inhabited by spiritual mysteries or beings. Teit noted that the "mountain Kazik, near Lytton, was believed to possess supernatural power."[12] This is probably **k'ek'ázik'**, the local Native name for Mount Roach, which Lytton elder Louis Phillips describes as a place where young people used to go to train for guardian spirit power. "This was the best mountain for getting your power."[13]

The concentration of many such power spots is one of the greatest attractions of the Stein: ". . . the lakes and creeks in the high mountains to the west and south of Lytton are noted for being frequented by these mysteries. People passing within sight of these places always turn their faces away from them lest they might see these apparitions and die."[14] Refuges for power-seekers over the millennia, these mysterious peaks, lakes and rock bluffs in the Stein remain unaltered today, their painted dreams still patiently presiding over the valley.

Cycles Of The Seasons

Descriptions of the Native community at Kumsheen tell us of a healthy, long-lived people. This impression comes from archaeologists, from first-hand historical observations and from contemporary reminiscences by the people themselves. Teit was repeatedly told that the people were once healthy and rarely subject to disease. Simon Fraser attested to this in his journal.

This healthy picture of daily life contradicts the textbook portrayal of hunter-gatherers as living in chronic destitution, sentenced to a life of hard labour, surviving hand-to-mouth in an endless search for meagre and unreliable natural resources. We have inherited this view from the famous seventeenth century English philosopher, Thomas Hobbes, who asserted that in "a state of nature," life was "nasty, brutish and short."

There are very few photographs of the last of the pithouses in British Columbia. This pithouse in the Nicola Valley is unique, as the support posts and some of the sod roofing remain intact. (Photograph courtesy of National Museums of Canada, Ottawa)

But reassessments of old information and more careful study of contemporary hunting and gathering societies are shattering this ideological stereotype. Marshall Sahlins, in his now-classic **Stone Age Economics** (1972), even shows that hunters do not work hard—an average of three to five hours per day in food production. Even then, their work is highly intermittent, providing the people with much leisure time.[15] These people had minimal material needs, personal satisfaction coming from social and physical activities rather than from the accumulation of material goods.

Both the Nlaka'pamux and Lillooet peoples divided their year into five seasons, with further divisions into lunar units. The Lytton people began counting the moons when the marmots (high country groundhogs) entered their winter dens. The second, third, and fourth moons, corresponding roughly with our December, January and February, were winter. The four remaining seasons were grouped according to particular food-gathering activities. Spring (March and April) was the time when the first edible shoots began to appear. Summer (May to July) was the berry and root season. Early Fall (August and September) was salmon time. Late Fall, the fifth season (October and November), was the time for hunting. Clearly, the Nlaka'pamux spent most of the year away from their permanent winter homes. In fact, winter meant leaving the outdoors. It was appropriately called **N'ū́lxtin**—"going-in time"[16]: a settled season spent in story-telling, games, tool-work, and clothing or basket making.

Winter

Winter villages consisted of clusters of semi-subterranean houses on lower river terraces, usually on one side of the river only. In the same way that modern earth-shelter houses are dug into hillsides for energy conservation, the early pithouses were dug into the ground for protection and warmth. As Archibald McDonald, a Hudson's Bay Company employee, wrote in 1827 about the "salmon tribes": "in winter, they burrey themselves in circular pits underground."[17] The north bank of the Stein at the mouth was an ideal winter village site because there was adequate protection from winter winds; the soil there drained well; and water, fuel, and construction materials were abundant.[18]

With the combined efforts of approximately 20 or 30 people, a kekule house (as they were called in the Chinook jargon of the Hudson Bay traders) could be constructed in a single day.[19] These houses were built only when needed, and were used year after year. There were rarely more than three or four at one place, and often there was but a single house.[20] From 15 to 30 persons occupied a house, and larger houses were common. Hill-Tout described one winter house by the Stein which measured "59 feet from the post hole on one side to the corresponding hole on the other . . . In the very large ones sixty or eighty souls would often pass the winter together."[21] Inside it was warm enough that only light attire was needed.[22]

The close proximity of the Stein winter village to upriver winter hunting and fishing was also ideal. Rainbow trout,

Winter Homes

These were circular pits, five or six feet deep and varied in diameter according to the number of families using them. They were roofed very skillfully with an open square at the top, through which a notched and hewn piece of timber was let down to the centre of the pit. The outer part of this rose several feet above the roof on which the inhabitants hung their moccasins and other belongings...

These underground dwellings for winter occupation were delightful places to enter on days when the wind was blowing fiercely from the north, sending the thermometer at times to twenty below zero . . . [Those inside] would be enjoying a mild temperature whilst the wind and cold without would pierce the thickest clothing . . .

During what we may term our revivals, when we used to crowd these places or dens with hearers as thick as bees in a hive, then the heat would grow insufferable . . . I would come out from these protracted services utterly exhausted and everything wet on me as though I had been dipped in a bath, whilst I would not get rid of the keek-wolley [kekule] smell for days to come.

Reverend John B. Good, Missionary in Lytton, 1870s, "The Utmost Bounds," unpublished manuscript, Archives of the Anglican Provincial Synod of B.C., Vancouver.

Winter Food

An Interior Salish family's winter store might include 90 kilograms (200 pounds) of yellow avalanche lily corms or dried bitter-roots, 45 kilograms (100 pounds) or more of dried Saskatoons, as well as dried cakes of soapberries, blueberries, raspberries, "red willow" berries, black hawthorne berries, and others, a large supply of black tree lichen loaves, and many strings of dried mushrooms, not to mention several sacks of balsamroot seeds and white-bark pine nuts.

Nancy Turner, *Food Plants of British Columbia Indians, Part 2, Interior Peoples,* Victoria: British Columbia Provincial Museum, 1978, p.33.

Nlaka'pamux elder, Louis Phillips, in Botanie Valley, a traditional root-digging area. He is holding edible plants, Indian celery and chocolate lily. (Photo: Nancy Turner)

Dolly Varden char, and Rocky Mountain whitefish abound in the river from the mouth almost to the headwaters at Stein Lake. From above Earl Creek to Nesbitt Creek, the river widens and meanders through long flats, pools and side channels which provide excellent fishing. In a letter to Harlan Smith in 1923, a Hope resident remarked that there was a place, probably in the Stein, where "the Indians from the westside of the Fraser, north of Lytton, went annually in the late autumn to . . . icefish."[23] Wearing snowshoes in the heavy winter snows, men also hunted there for goat and deer.

The old people today talk of a shallow fishing pool which lies just above the location of the modern cable crossing, about 12 kilometres (8 miles) upriver. The Nlaka'pamux name of the place, **stl'imín** (pronounced approximately Klemeen), means "to ford the river."[24] This place would have been an easy half-day trip even in the winter. One place near Devil's Staircase,

sk'ázix, is believed to refer to the place where people used to spear steelhead in winter.[25]

In general, however, the Nlaka'pamux in winter lived on stored foods such as dried salmon, berries, roots, and mushrooms. Many of these foods were stored in pits dug into the ground, so-called cache pits. Ten clusters of cache pits have been recorded at the mouth of the Stein, appearing today as small round depressions in the ground. Studies of some of the preserved foods used by the Fraser River peoples show that their drying and cooking processes were healthy, providing an excellent diet even in winter.[26] Their winter foods were rich in nutrients like unusually high quantities of iron and copper in dried saskatoons, and vitamins A and D in dried salmon.[27]

Spring

In spring, the people began to use fresh foods once again. Dolly Varden char, steelhead and rainbow trout were caught in the Stein throughout April and May. At one place, several kilometres above the cable crossing, the river widens out to such an extent that it has a local name, "place of still waters." "It's like a lake," said Raymond Dunstan, "It freezes in winter." People who travelled through the Stein in the early 1900s recall two dugout cottonwood canoes that were left permanently at this spot for fishing and travel upriver. Some refer to the place as Canoe Landing.[28]

Summer

The season from May to July was busy. In early summer, many prime roots were ready to harvest. Roots were a staple food, and the women made special trips to gather balsamroot, nodding onion, mariposa lily and bitterroot. They also gathered yellow avalanche lily corms as the snow melted in the upland regions from late May until the end of summer.[29] In the Lytton area, Botanie Mountain, east of the Fraser and opposite the mouth of the Stein, was the primary berry-picking and root-digging area, and Nlaka'pamux, Lillooet and Shuswap came long distances to harvest its plants every spring.[30] The Stein was also used by the Nlaka'pamux for this

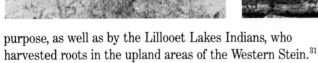

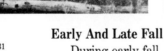

purpose, as well as by the Lillooet Lakes Indians, who harvested roots in the upland areas of the Western Stein.[31]

The ninth month, July, was the time "the sun returns" and "all the berries ripen." During this time the Nlaka'pamux picked berries by hand or raked them in bunches with long-toothed combs. Wild strawberries, squaw currants, and saskatoons were the first to appear, followed by red huckleberries, soapberries, wild blackberries, wild gooseberries, and raspberries. Additional types of berries, hazelnuts, balsamroot seeds and Douglas-fir sugar are also harvested during the summer.[32] Most of these are found along the lower and middle Stein. Mountain huckleberries and mountain blueberries are picked on Akasik Mountain and Mount Roach.[33]

Early And Late Fall

During early fall, August and September, the people focussed on the salmon runs along the Fraser, setting up special camps on the river banks for catching, cutting and drying fish. Anyone who has visited the Stein River at this time of year can also find a great variety of mushrooms. There are four edibles in the area. A favourite, the pine mushroom, is gathered on the banks of Stryen Creek and all along the Stein to Earl Creek.[34] Mary Williams, who lived near the Stein, gathered mushrooms above the cable crossing. Her husband "used to carry home sacks of mushrooms that he picked at a sandy spot way up past the bridge".[35] Willy Justice noted lots of the oyster mushroom (which grow in layers on the trunk of the dead cottonwood tree) near the cable

Traditional root-digging stick used by Native women. Note the cedar basket and tumpline method of carrying goods on the back. (Photograph courtesy of the American Museum of Natural History, New York)

Cedar root and bark soaking prior to basket-making. (Photo: Leo deGroot)

crossing.[36]

Later in the fall, the community concentrated on cedar root gathering at many spots along the river. As cedar is rare in the dry Interior plateau country, the scattered stands in the Stein provided an unusual opportunity to gather both roots and bark. Many trees from Teaspoon Creek (11 kilometres or 7 miles upriver) to Nesbitt Creek (38 kilometres or 24 miles upriver) have had large strips of bark removed.

The occasion for gathering cedar root was described by Willy Justice, who grew up at the mouth of the Stein, and travelled upriver every year on horseback with his mother and other families for this purpose. They made camp at the place called **stl'imín** "very late in the fall, about October," Willy explained. "Water's low then." The last time he was there, with a root-digging party, they killed a deer for fresh meat, and stayed until it snowed.[37]

Adam Klein, who trapped in the valley between the years 1925 and 1937, observed women gathering cedar root for basket-making about seven kilometres past what he described as Last Chance Creek (Stryen Creek).[38] This is probably Teaspoon Creek, where another stand of cedars is located. According to Louis Phillips, the women "went way up, pretty near to Cottonwood, to get cedar-root."[39]

Cedar bark was obtained by stripping it off the tree in long sheets. These could be used as roofing and siding for temporary shelters and sweathouses, as flooring for houses and canoes, and as lining for underground food caches. The most valuable part of the bark was the fibrous inner portion. This was split into strips for baskets, bags, sleeping mats, capes, blankets, and other items. It was also twisted into string to make belts, fishing lines, ropes, animal snares and nets. Finely shredded, it was made into brooms, bandaging, diapers and other items.[40] Some of the stripped bark of the

Stein cedars was used for the roofs of trappers' cabins and lean-to's in the post-1900 period.[41]

Louis Phillips, on his trip into the upper Stein Valley in 1936 with his brother Simon, travelled "past Cottonwood Creek and Battle Creek to a big bluff, red in colour" possibly near Nesbitt Creek. Here they collected gunnysacks full of "swamp tea," which he said was popular among the old people at that time.[42] Also known as Labrador tea, Hudson's Bay tea, muskeg tea, Indian tea, and trappers' tea, the leaves could be picked anytime from August to April. A popular drink, it has many medicinal attributes. It is used as a heart medicine, to relieve indigestion, and to ease the pain and induce relaxation for women after childbirth.[43]

Late Fall, roughly October and November, was the hunting season. For this, almost all the people moved to higher elevations. Those few who remained behind continued the task of processing salmon. With root-digging and hunting activities, "a large portion of the tribe lived in the mountains during the greater portion of the year."[44]

Deer was the most important animal hunted by the Nlaka'pamux, and the Stein is still recognized as a prime deer-hunting area: "Go up Stein to make a living," commented Louis Phillips. "It's an easy-going valley to get in to. For big living, that's where they used to go, like deer, goat and bear."[45] The middle valley was a particularly well utilized hunting area. Andrew Johnny claimed that the old Indians used to hunt "way up to Cottonwood Creek."[46] Albert Hance, another Native from the Stein village at the mouth of the river, also mentioned Cottonwood Creek as a good hunting and fishing area.[47] Ron Purvis of Lillooet was also told by the local Indians of an old Indian trail which forked upwards toward the high valley about a half mile past Devil's Staircase where "the Indian people of long ago spend a month or more every year

This place, known to the Indians as stl'imin, and also "horse-crossing," is the first fording place upstream from the mouth of the Stein. It is located just above the cable crossing. The cedar trees at this place were used annually for root gathering. (Photo: Dennis Darragh)

The people of the Lytton area have long made use of the steady sunshine and strong winds to dry their salmon after it has been cleaned and cut. Salmon-drying racks can be seen near the homes of many families today. (Photograph courtesy of the Vancouver Public Library, Vancouver)

A Strong People

I met a day or two ago a party of Indians—a family they seemed. I felt the weight of each [pack]. The woman's load must have been at least 80 lb. A little girl was carrying 40 lb. Today I was in the store of a shopkeeper, Mr. Griffin, and saw packs made up for Indians to go off with in the morning. They weighed 100 lb., 120 lb., and 130 lb. each . . .

We met many Indians today laden with packs weighing from 60 to 130 lbs. They go the 75 miles from Yale to Lytton for 8.50 dollars per 100 lbs. Some take only 3 days. One Indian we met I was informed had 149 lbs. and would perform the 75 miles in 2.5 days. A girl of about 12 was carrying a load of at least 50 lbs.

Bishop George Hills, unpublished diaries (1860, 1861). Archives of the Anglican Provincial Synod of B.C., Vancouver.

Rose Skuki and her mother, Mary Roberts, with cedar baskets, 1923. Lytton Natives have traditionally gathered roots for making baskets at cedar groves upriver along the Stein to the middle valley. (Photograph courtesy of the Village of Lytton, British Columbia)

before the heavy snowfalls to collect their winter supply of deer meat."[48]

Studies of wildlife in the Stein confirm Native accounts. In winter, mule deer are found along the south-facing slopes of the hills from Earl Creek to Nesbitt Creek.[49] Mountain goats live throughout the valley at higher elevations. A particularly good population is found in the higher elevations of Nesbitt and Cottonwood Creeks in summer, and along the south-facing slopes of the Stein and Cottonwood in winter. Goat hunting in the Stein was almost as common as deer hunting.[50] Natives also hunted marmot, black and grizzly bear, beaver, porcupine, hare or rabbit, squirrel, grouse, duck, goose, and occasionally lynx and coyote.

Fresh-killed meat was dried or smoked in the high country for transport back to the winter village. As most of the temporary camps were in the mountains, travel back and forth was done on foot. Packing goods was a way of life and everyone, including the women and children, could carry remarkably heavy packs. They walked either barefoot or in deerskin moccasins laced round the foot with a strip of deerskin, stopping every half hour for a five-minute rest: "They generally squat down near a ledge of rock, on which they can rest their burdens without removing them."[51]

Beginning Again

By December, the seasonal rounds completed, it was again "going-in time" for the cold winter months. There was some trading of goods with neighbouring groups but, in general, the local environment served the Nɬaka'pamux well, providing them with a healthy and varied diet year round. Throughout thousands of years, throughout the cycles of life and the seasons, "from time immemorial," the Natives' intensive use of the environment depleted neither the plants nor the animals.

15-Minute Moccasins

I have known occasions when an elk has been killed by me, and within a quarter of an hour after its death all the meat has been slung at their backs and its skin been laced upon their feet.

Richard C. Mayne, *Four Years in British Columbia and Vancouver Island*, London: J. Murray, 1862, pp.99-100.

Cherry Pip Pass, a common high-country route for hikers entering the Stein Valley from the west. (Photo: Neil Baker)

This maritime image is painted on a rock face near Earl Creek.

As he travelled through the "wilderness," Simon Fraser was a stranger to the people who lived there. But his hosts along the river were surprisingly friendly, greeting him royally, and even celebrating his arrival with a pipe ceremony, speeches and gifts. Though he was the first White man to travel the river, Simon Fraser's arrival was not unanticipated, and it began a process that was to alter every aspect of Native life. The process continues to this day, providing the inescapable context for the present struggle over the Stein Valley.

Contact Before Contact: Goods, Guns And Grisly Tales

Although the first actual contact of the Nlaka'pamux with the White man occurred with Fraser's arrival in 1808, the influences of indirect contact were already well established. The evidence was seen by Fraser himself, who noted the presence of "several European articles" which he was led to believe had come from "beyond the Mountains." On the coast, Europeans had first dropped anchor in 1774, with active trading beginning a decade later. Cloth, jewelry, kettles, tobacco, molasses, biscuits, as well as alcohol, guns and ammunition, were becoming available to the Natives.[1]

The impact of these new goods preceded Fraser. There was a report of a fight between the Nlaka'pamux and Lillooet Indians involving the use of a gun as long as 20 years before Fraser's journey. Strange diseases, too, arrived before Fraser. Smallpox was reported on the coast as early as the 1770s, although the major smallpox epidemic occured in the 1860s. In the lower Fraser Canyon, probably near Yale, the disease was

present in 1800,[2] and even earlier in other interior areas, notably in Washington, among the Spokane Indians.[3] In addition to smallpox, Natives were vulnerable to other, previously unknown diseases such as measles, influenza and tuberculosis, which perhaps explains Fraser's eerie account of the poor health of the Nlaka'pamux children when he returned to their village on his homeward journey one month later.

With trade goods and new diseases came strange stories of these powerful visitors. Fraser encountered Chilcotin and Lillooet men who had been to the coast and seen well-dressed White men who lived "in a modern enclosure upon an island"[4] (deep-sea ships). Those creatures and their vessels must have been as terrifying and as awe-inspiring to them as extra-terrestrials and their spaceships would be to us today. Stories about the Whites travelled fast, assaulting the local imagination with images of almost unbelievable beings who had descended to make great changes to the landscape and its people.

The Nlaka'pamux had among them certain prophets or dreamers noted for their ability to foretell the future. Recounting their dreams and visions in song, they led ceremonies in which great numbers of people joined the dreamer, singing, dancing, and swaying their hands and bodies in an ecstatic group-homage to the impending transformation. Some of these songs were still circulating at the beginning of this century.

Firearms, diseases, stories of strangers, prophetic rituals—these pervasive changes did not bode well for the old ways. At this time, grisly battles took place between the

Simon Fraser At Kumsheen, 1808

At 8 A.M. set out, divided as yesterday. A mile below, the natives ferried us over a large rapid river [the Stein River]. I obtained, for an awl, a passage to the next village, a distance of three miles through strong rapids. The others who went by land met some of the Indians on the way who were happy to see them. This was the village of the Chief who had left us in the morning. We were told here that the road ahead was very bad, and consequently we should meet with much difficulty for most or part of the way.

The Indians of this village may be about four hundred souls and some of them appear very old; they live among mountains, and enjoy pure air, seem cleanly inclined, and make use of wholesome food. We observed several European articles among them, viz. a copper Tea Kettle, a brass camp kettle, a strip of common blanket, and cloathing such as the Cree women wear. These things, we supposed, were brought from our settlements beyond the Mountains.

Indeed the Indians made us understand as much.

After having remained some time in this village, the principal chief invited us over the river. We crossed, and He received us at the water side, where, assisted by several others, he took me by the arms and conducted me in a moment up the hill to the camp where his people were sitting in rows, to the number of twelve hundred; and I had to shake hands with all of them. Then the Great Chief made a long harangue, in course of which he pointed to the sun, to the four quarters of the world and then to us, and then he introduced his father, who was old and blind, and was carried by another man, who also made a harangue of some length. The old [blind] man was placed near us, and with some emotion often stretched out both his hands in order to feel ours.

We had every reason to be thankful for our reception at this place; the Indians shewed us every possible attention and

"We had to pass where no human beings should venture; yet in those places there is a regular footpath impressed, or rather indented upon the very rocks by frequent travelling . . ." From The Letters and Journals of

Simon Fraser, 1806-1808. (Painting by John Innes, Courtesy of the Archives of Simon Fraser University)

supplied our wants as much as they could. We had salmon, berries, oil and roots in abundance, and our men had six dogs. Our tent was pitched near the camp, and we enjoyed peace and security during our stay.

Thursday [Monday], June 20. The Indians sang and danced all night. Some of our men, who went to see them, were much amused. With some difficulty we obtained two wooden canoes; the Indians, however, made no price, but accepted of our offers.

The Letters and Journals of Simon Fraser,
1806-1808, Toronto: Macmillan, 1960, pp.86-87.

Simon Fraser Returns

Friday, July 14, 1808. At 2 P.M. arrived at the confluence or forks of Thompson's River. Two of our men who were behind came up with us accompanied by some Natives. Having been invited we visited a camp which was on elevated ground . . .

Most of the children were really afflicted with some serious disorder which reduced them to skeletons. The women of this tribe had the neatest dress of any we have seen in this quarter. . .

Still we could perceive something unpleasant in their demeanour . . . [There was a] disagreeable gloom which attracted our notice.

The Letters and Journals of Simon Fraser,
1806-1808, pp.118-119.

A Native Account

Story told by SEmali'tsa, a Nlaka'pamux woman from Styne Creek:

My grandmother told me that when she was a young girl she was playing one day in the summer-time (about the time the service-berries get ripe) near the river-beach at the village of Strain, when she saw two canoes, with red flags hoisted, come downstream. She ran and told her mother, and the people gathered to see the strange sight. Seeing so many people gathered, the canoes put ashore and

several men came ashore. Each canoe carried a number of men (perhaps six or seven in each), and many of them wore strange dresses, and everything about them was strange. Some of the men looked like Indians, and others looked like what we now call white men. Among them was a Shuswap chief who acted as interpreter.

Our people were not afraid of the strangers, nor were they hostile to them. The strangers produced a large pipe, and

had a ceremonial smoke with some of our men. After distributing a few presents, they boarded their canoes and went on to Lytton. They remained one or two days at Lytton, where they were presented with food of various kinds, and gave in exchange tobacco, beads, and knives.

James Teit, "Mythology of the Thompson Indians," *Memoir of the American Museum of Natural History*, 1912, pp.414-415.

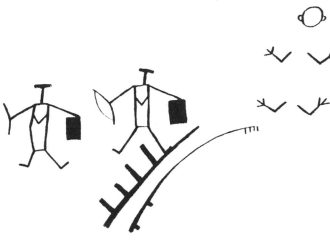

Warfare And European Contact

An increase in warfare in the latest prehistoric and early historic periods in the Interior may reflect residual pressures of the Athapaskan expansion, as well as competition for trade goods and resources stimulated by the overland approach of European fur-traders. Many indirect influences from the expanding European presence in eastern North America were probably felt in the British Columbia interior, as well as on the Coast, long before the first white men appeared on the scene. Occasional discrepancies between historical descriptions of Plateau lifeways and the picture revealed by archaeology may therefore be a result of rapid unrecorded cultural changes that took place very early in the contact process.

Knut R. Fladmark, *British Columbia Prehistory*, National Museums of Canada, Ottawa, 1986, p. 140.

Nlaka'pamux and Lillooet, the most notable clash occurring deep in the Stein, along the trail toward the territory of the Mt. Currie people. Stories about these battles have led to the popular image of the Lytton and Mt. Currie peoples as long-term enemies and warriors, and of the Stein as a battle route.

The accuracy of this image will likely never be known. But it bears close scrutiny in the light of our ideological disdain for life before "civilization." In a famous phrase of the English philosopher, Thomas Hobbes, we automatically characterize this life in "a state of nature," as "a war of all against all." A careful reading of the early ethnographies indicates that the period of warfare which culminated in the great fight at Battle Creek (present-day Scudamore Creek) began with an incident in the 1770s. At a potlatch near what is now Hope, several Nlaka'pamux murdered a Lillooet man, beginning a feud which saw the man's son take revenge on several Nlaka'pamux hunters three years later. In turn, this provoked a party of Nlaka'pamux to travel up the Stein for a raid in Lillooet territory, setting off a series of exchanges over many years. These feuds were, wrote Teit, "carried on during the last and early part of the present [ie. 19th] century,"[5] the very time of first contact with White society. The last battle at Battle Creek, in which a returning party of Nlaka'pamux was surprised by the Lillooet and soundly beaten, probably occurred around 1830. Chief Cixpē'ntlam made peace in 1850, re-establishing what he described as the traditionally peaceful relations between his people and the Lillooets.

Contact And Change

Actual contact transformed the scattered rumblings of change into an earthquake. On his journey, Fraser laid claim for his employer, the North West Company of Montreal, to the rich fur-bearing territories of New Caledonia (as mainland British Columbia was called until 1858). At the time, the Nor'Westers were battling the Hudson's Bay Company for control of the colonial fur trade. This was the final frontier in the westward push that had laid down a broad network of traplines and outposts, trade routes and markets. From the Ottawa Valley to Fort Garry and Rocky Mountain House, a new empire had been created, now extending from Fort Kamloops upstream from Kumsheen to Fort Langley downstream near the coast. For over 300 years, across an entire continent, White expansion powered by the export of primary resources—fish, furs, and timber—created a deadly dynamic for the Natives and their environment.

In the past, the Natives used local resources only when needed, and then primarily for their own use. With the arrival of the European traders, Natives participated in an entirely new market-driven process of production for distant consumers. Their resources were now needed to satisfy the fishmonger in London and the furrier in Paris, people who were oceans away from understanding the local impacts of their purchases.

In 1812, a mere four years after Fraser's exploratory trip, a fur-trading post was established near Kamloops and 2,000

Indians came there to trade. Archibald MacDonald was in charge of the outpost and, in his report in 1827, he listed the goods that the Indians traded: 12,086 dried salmon, 739 fresh salmon, 1,268 pounds of venison, 1,171 quarts of berries, 97 partidges, 48 gallons of roots, 25 bears, and 5 gallons of nuts.[6] This was enough food to provide for many people throughout the winter. In exchange, the Indians received a blanket, shoes, beads, tobacco, and a few pounds of gunpowder and shot, items which could not feed anyone. The trade was clearly unequal, and it was of a rather predatory kind—huge quantities of food gathered with great effort in exchange for irresistible consumer items and more powerful tools for the hunt.

Commercial hunting constituted not just an economic vocation, but a cultural transformation. Before contact, the bond of the hunter with the hunted was often so close that "the animal he hunted [was] almost part of himself."[7] As a Shuswap elder from the Neskainlith Reserve close to Kamloops, Aimee August, tells us today, "They're begging the bear for food as they skin it . . . They wouldn't just skin it and cut it to pieces and eat it. They got to sing this song for the respect of their food that's all out there in nature. Ancestors done it."[8] Wide-scale trapping for trade was not compatible with maintaining the respect for the environment and its creatures, something which is inherent in the subsistence hunt.

With the denigration of nature's sacred character, the social controls which had long enforced a balance with nature fell apart under the influence of the market. Traders from Kamloops made four or five trips to "Fraser's River" every fall and winter, putting great pressure on the area's resources. The change was dramatic. By 1827, only 15 years after the establishment of the Kamloops post, the fur-bearing animals in the vicinity were gone.

Dreams Of The Prophets

Before the first white people came to the country . . . [Kwālós] had a series of dreams or visions which impressed him very much. He told his dreams to the people and gathered them together to sing and dance. He told how his spirit left his body and passed rapidly to the shores of a great lake in the far east where the clouds always hung low along the edge of the water. Here his spirit left the land and rolled along on the clouds until it came to a land on the other side of the great lake. Here there were many strange people who spoke a language very different in sound from Indian languages. (He imitated the speaking of these people and what he said sounded very much like French.) These people were very different from Indians and had many beautiful and wonderful things the Indians knew nothing of. They had light skins and different colors of hair and eyes and many kinds of fine clothes and ornaments. Both the men and women dressed differently from Indians and their clothes were of peculiar patterns and materials. The women especially had very striking and beautiful dresses. These people were very numerous and did very strange things. They lived in many high houses made of stone. They had fires inside of stones (probably stoves) and much smoke could be seen coming out of the stones (probably chimneys). Their houses had mouths and eyes . . . and around them were many open grassy lands and plots where there were many kinds of beautiful flowers and plants and grasses some of which they used as food . . .

In the dances Kwālós prayed that the people he had seen would come over and enlighten the Indians and make them powerful, wise, rich, and happy like themselves. He further stated that he believed these people would come to the Indians some time soon and then great changes would take place among the Indians . . .

James Teit, unpublished notes on a song by Chief John Tetlenitsa, 1918. Canadian Ethnology Service, Canadian Museum of Civilization, Ottawa.

In 1927, a cairn was erected in downtown Lytton and dedicated to the memory of Chief Cixpéntlam, a famous Nlaka'pamux chief who made peace with the Lillooet, and, later, with the White colonists. (Photograph courtesy of the Village of Lytton, British Columbia)

A Rod Of Iron

I have made it my study to examine the nature and character of Indians and however repugnant it may be to our feelings, I am convinced they must be ruled with a Rod of Iron to bring and keep them in a proper state of subordination, and the most certain way to effect this is by letting them feel their dependence upon us . . .

Letter from Fort Garry, 1822, in Harold Innis, *The Fur Trade in Canada*, Toronto: University of Toronto Press, (1930) 1956 ed., p.287.

On The Verge Of Extermination

The Beaver is I believe the most common animal in the district, and alas he is but rare enough considering the extent of the country—A person can walk for days together without seeing the smallest quadruped, the little brown squirrel excepted . . .

For this sudden falling off, there is no other pheasable way of accounting, than the Beaver run is on the verge of extermination, which the natives themselves observe, and not only deprecate this loss, but the rapid disappearance of the wood animals also.

Archibald McDonald, "Thompson's River District Report" (1927) in *Simpson's 1828 Journey to the Columbia*, London: The Hudson's Bay Record Society, 1947, pp.226, 230.

Some contemporary scholars, such as historian Robin Fisher of Simon Fraser University, argue that the fur trade brought only minimal cultural change to the Natives because it was a trade which the Natives could control. "In reality," writes Fisher, "the Indians accepted the existence of the trading posts out of self-interest rather than fear and, therefore, they can hardly be described as a conquered people during the fur-trading period."[9] Others, such as Calvin Martin, argue that in wide areas of North America, the fur trade caused a breakdown in the Native belief and subsistence systems, and resulted in an abandonment by the Indian of his conservationist principles.[10]

The Natives of Kumsheen did not choose their fate as they did not invite the White man in, but had to react to his arrival and his alluring new forms of wealth. In response, the dreamer's messages took a decidedly apocalyptic turn. These prophets now travelled about foretelling of the approaching destruction of the world, at which time the present suffering would end. Although by 1830 Christian missionaries had not yet directly contacted the Natives of the area, the Nlaka'pamux were holding ceremonies weekly, on Saturdays, blessing themselves by making the sign of the cross, and reciting the phrase, "In the name of the Father, Son and Good Spirit."[11] It is not surprising, therefore, that the Native inhabitants welcomed the first missionaries in the 1860s as they had welcomed Simon Fraser—with the dreamer's foreknowledge of their arrival and of the demise which it implied.

Forging A New Economy

The depletion of the fur-bearing wildlife in the 1840s and 1850s transformed Native life. Ironically, it also depleted the means of financing colonial expansion into the interior of New Caledonia. By 1854 there were only 450 settlers in the whole territory and less than 500 acres had been colonized. However, a new fuel for expansion was soon found, and it continued the process of laying the foundation for the resource extractive economy which persists to this day.

Gold was discovered quite by accident in 1856. As Governor Douglas recounted in his diary, an Indian was taking a drink out of the Thompson River about a quarter of a mile below Nicomin, and "having no vessel, he was quaffing from the stream when he perceived a shining pebble which he picked up, and it proved to be gold. The whole tribe forthwith began to collect the glittering metal."[12]

By the fall of that year, gold had become one of the most prized trading items in Kamloops[13]. The search for it was actively fostered by the Hudson's Bay Company "which was equipping them with shovels, picks and pans [so that] the Indians were finding more and more gold in the area around the confluence of the Fraser and Thompson Rivers."[14] This close arrangement was a well-kept secret, even with the unwelcome arrival of a few American miners in 1857. But in February 1858, Governor Douglas made a mistake which blew the story wide open—he shipped 800 ounces of the precious metal to the San Francisco mint. That summer, 25,000 White gold miners, many from California, descended on Kumsheen and other Fraser River settlements in search of their fortune.

25,000 alien men loose without law in villages that did not know the world beyond the mountains. Toting revolvers and boasting a wild west bravado, the miners drove the Natives from the gold-bearing sandbars. Women and young girls were pulled from their dwellings, sold as prostitutes, and murdered. Winter stores of food were pillaged. In a matter of weeks, a whole culture was besieged. The Natives reacted in desperation, and the ensuing battles with the miners were gruesome.

Stories Of Things To Come

Some Indians prophesied by means of visions. They foretold the coming of the whites, the advent of epidemics, the final extinction of the Indians, the introduction of whiskey, stoves, dishes, flour, sugar, etc. One instance related is that of a Lower Thompson chief, called Pê'lak, who travelled through the tribe forty years or more ago, and foretold the coming of the white settlers and the great changes that would take place, even going into minute details. He also told the Indians that they would "die out like fire" on the appearance of the whites; in other words, that they were doomed to extinction. It seems that he obtained his information from employees of the Hudson Bay Company whom he had met. Pê'lak was also a worker of miracles, for near Thompson Siding he put some fish-bones into the river, and turned them into salmon. Great crowds of Upper Thompsons went to Thompson Siding to see him and to hear him speak.

James Teit, *The Thompson Indians of British Columbia*, pp.365-366.

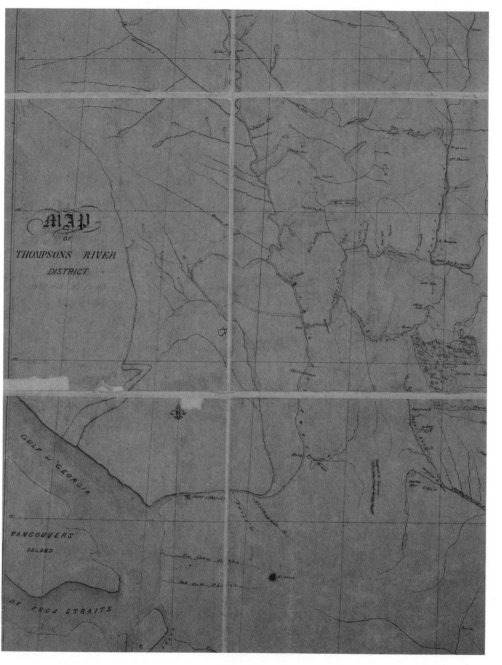

This undated and unsigned map appears to have been derived from a map of 1835 made by Hudson's Bay Chief Trader and later Chief Factor, Samuel Black, who was based at the Thompson's River Post in Kamloops from 1831 to 1841. The Royal Engineers used this same map as a basis for their mapping of the area in 1861. However, neither the Black map nor the Royal Engineers map shows the trail through the Stein. Although there are markings on this undated and unsigned map which were not in existence until 1848-49, such as "Hope," "Campement du Cherrevil" and "Campement des Femmes," at the same time, there are features which clearly come from an earlier period: there is no mention of gold; the Nicola River is named Chewhack, Quilchena Creek is named "Governor's River", the Hudson's Bay Company trails of 1848-49 from the Fraser River are not shown; and the Coast is poorly depicted. The exact date of this map is, therefore, not certain. (Map courtesy of Surveyor General Branch, Ministry of Forests and Lands, Victoria)

In a hasty trip to the area Governor Douglas restored order with the assistance of Chief Cixpē´ntlam, but the cultural transformation was conclusive and irreversible. Gold was the colony's new economic staple, and Lytton was its new boom town. Saloons, hotels, houses, blacksmith shops sprouted on the barren hillside above the river. The **British Colonist** described the new village of Lytton as "a lively little camp . . . with 22 cabins . . . style California primitive, with a weekly average of one fight to every house."[15] So far, the paper noted, there "are no places of worship here—except for temples dedicated to Bacchus. There are many quantities of spirituous liquors here . . . bars well-stocked and warehouses well filled."[16]

Once again, the Native economy adapted, but often in tragic ways. Indians found employment building the Cariboo Highway and the Harrison Lake trail, and packing huge loads along them. But the new commercial ventures, the theft of their stored food, and the disruption of their families and seasonal cycle led them into a dangerous neglect of traditional subsistence activities. In 1858 many were without food, and starved.

At the height of this chaotic commercial boom, the Indians were decimated by the worst smallpox epidemic in recorded Canadian history. An infected sailor from California landing in Victoria on Vancouver Island in 1862 probably introduced the disease, which spread quickly through Victoria's Native population of about 2000. Banished from the city, they fled inland, carrying the disease with them. By the end of that year, the toll was reported at 20,000 dead, one-third of the province's estimated Native population. A vaccine was available, but frequently went unused. As the **Colonist** expressed it, "were it likely that the disease would only spread among the Indians, there might be those among us like

The Miners' War Reported In The London Times

Lytton, 1870s. (Photograph courtesy of the Village of Lytton, British Columbia)

I never saw so many sinister countenances collected in one place—ill-bred curs, as cruel as they are dishonest. Here is the nest whence issues the wretch who will shoot an Indian in the back when he finds one alone and unarmed, and who is the first to run, even out of a crowd, when he sights a body of Indians, armed or unarmed; and here is the Alsatia to which the coward flees for shelter . . .

After the endurance of much indignity, the Indians retaliated, caught the Frenchman, and cut his head off and sent his body down the river as an example, perhaps, to all poachers on other men's manors. Altogether four headless trunks came down from the upper waters, and were picked up by miners between Fort Yale and Fort Hope. The sight naturally roused the inhabitants to action, and a fellow named Graham, a Californian, burning to distinguish himself, raised a company of volunteers to fight the Indians.

His plan was very simple. He was to commence killing the Indians at the nearest village, just beyond Fort Yale, and keep killing as he went up the river as far as the Forks, 90 miles. No investigation, no discretion, no segregation of the guilty from the innocent. It was to be an exterminating raid. This fellow was not only a beast but a vain fool. One tribe of these Indians would have sent him and his party of raggamuffins after the lecherous Frenchman.

The London Times, London, England, 25 December, 1858, p.7.

Indians at Lytton, 1868.
(Photograph courtesy of
the Royal British
Columbia Museum,
Victoria)

our authorities who would rest undisturbed, content that smallpox will rid this community of a moral ulcer that has festered at our doors through the last four years."[17]

The Emerging Structure Of Boom And Bust

If the pain of forging this new economy was great, the profit was fleeting. When the gold bars were played out in the late 1860s, the economy, driven by the reckless spending habits of the gold-miners, plummeted into depression. On the coast at this time, abundant salmon supplies led to a growing canning industry at several outport towns. But in the interior, the small towns turned inward for their survival.

After the Gold Rush, James Douglas opened land for sale by public auction, fixing the basic (or "upset") price at 10 shillings per acre, and requiring payment of only half the purchase price at the time of the sale and the remainder two years later. In January of 1860, British subjects and aliens who took an oath of allegiance were allowed to claim unilaterally ("pre-empt") 160 acres of land at no more than the upset price.

In this scramble for wealth, the new White residents looked around for the best land, and took it. Gold Commissioner Henry Ball saw some particularly nice benchland on the west side of the Fraser River, as did the independent (or "free") miner, Thomas Earl, and they established their farms there. Their lands were the precursor of one of the province's most magnificent farming estates, Earlscourt Farm, extending from the Fraser over hundreds of acres to the banks of the Stein River.

With the pre-emptions near the river's mouth proceeding quickly, White attention was soon directed to the Stein. Although a map possibly dating to the 1830s or 1840s already indicated a trail in the Stein, the first official survey of the

Stein valley was undertaken in 1860 in search of a mule trail to Pemberton and the coast, and to check for gold.[18]

In the process of cultivating the land, a different kind of gold was discovered, for the wide benchlands overlooking the Fraser and Thompson canyons turned out to be some of the finest farmland in British Columbia. In 1863, the **British Colonist** reported that "a good deal of farming is carried on in the vicinity of Lillooet and with complete success . . . the crops which have been grown are equal to any produced in the richest soil in Canada."[19]

As the Gold Rush moved northward, the Chinese miners stayed behind to clear the rocks and work the sandy bars along the river. These rock mounds are an imposing monument to their labours. (Photo: Gary Fiegehen/ Robert Semeniuk)

Starvation

The Indians all over the country suffered fearfully from want of food last winter, a great many dying of starvation. It was owing in great measure to their improvidence, most of them leaving off the fishing, hunting, etc., last summer in the general mania for gold-digging, and making no provision for the winter.

Lieut. Richard Mayne, "Report on a Journey in British Columbia in the Districts Bordering on the Thompson, Fraser, and Harrison Rivers," *Journal of the Royal Geographical Society* 31 (1861), p.216.

As to . . . all other descriptions of theft, they have almost invariably been of articles of food: committed too, before the arrival of the salmon, and under the pressure often, of actual starvation.

Letter, Judge Matthew B. Begbie to Governor James Douglas, 7 November 1859, Provincial Archives of British Columbia, Victoria.

After The Gold Rush

Pemberton: Here too everything was desolate. It seemed as though death and emptiness, twin monsters, had taken up their dwelling here to the exclusion of all besides. Our solitary waggon with its attendant mules stood like a spirit from the vast deep as if conjured up by some magic power to render the mockery of life but real . . .

Port Seaton: The same melancholy emptiness saddened the heart. Deserted houses, silent taverns, idle wharves! How changed from the busy bustle of former days! I slowly rode off to Lillooet with an old Indian . . . He lamented the changed character of the times. His own people were few in number and the few were scattered up and down the river fishing. The white man, he said, had abandoned the place.

Lillooet: Lillooet, though possessing more life than any hamlet I had yet reached on this abandoned route, was nevertheless a melancholy relic of its former self . . . Lillooet, I fear, has seen its best days unless some mighty change takes place in the situation of the mines.

Rev. A.C. Garrett, unpublished manuscript (1865), Archives of the Anglican Provincial Synod of B.C., Vancouver.

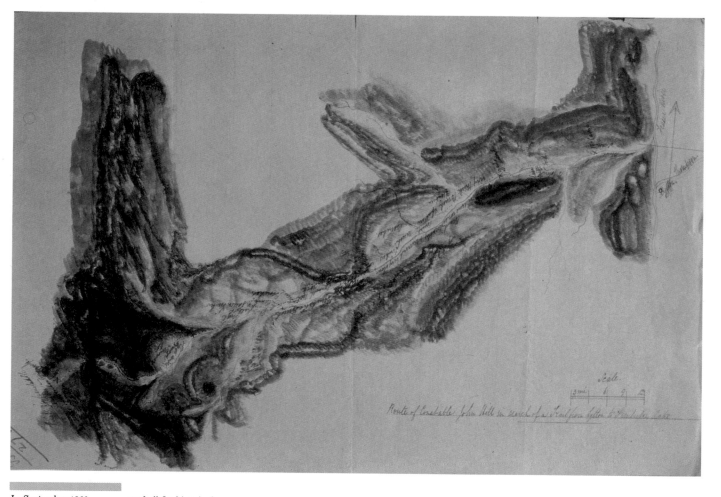

In September 1860, Constable John Hill surveyed the "Last Chance Creek" (the Stein) in search for both gold and a mule trail to "Pemberton Lake." Just over the divide towards Lizzie Lake, Hill turned back concluding that "a practicable mule trail would in many places be utterly impossible to make." On his trip, he made this sketch for Governor James Douglas. (Sketch courtesy of the Provincial Archives of British Columbia, Victoria)

The quick shift from a hunting/gathering economy to a settled agricultural economy also saw Native people forcibly corralled onto a small land reserve. Initially Governor Douglas compensated Indians for the surrender of their land and attempted to select reserve areas for the Indians which were comparable to the land given over to White settlers. Yet funds were short, and so too were White sympathies for the local Native population. After 1859, compensation was suspended and limited reserves were laid out, without treaties ever being signed to extinguish Native title to the land. In the next decade, under the sharp eye of the Chief Commissioner of Lands and Works, Joseph Trutch, Native pre-emption of land was prohibited, while White pre-emption was made ever easier. Any White man could pre-empt 160 acres and purchase another 480. In contrast, from 1866 to 1875, only one Native pre-emption was allowed, and Native families were expected to farm on just ten acres each.[20]

In July, 1870, Trutch laid out the Stryen Reserve (located at the mouth of the Stein River), to the disapproval of the local Native population. But, once done, the Native residents showed great industry as they "dug irrigation ditches, cleared the land of rocks, and planted crops of potatoes, hay and beans, even though continual shortages of water hampered their production."[21] In 1873, Quohipkan, grandfather of present-day Lytton Native, Willie Justice, helped build the first church on the Stryen reserve.

By 1873, economic activity of a very different kind from the earlier gold exporting boom was taking off. The growth of agriculture stimulated locally-generated industry. Lytton soon boasted five flour mills, two sawmills, a wheat mill, a school, two butchers, two hotels, two livery stables, three general stores, four bakers, a blacksmith and shoemaker. At the farm by the Stein, large crops of barley, turnip, and beets were produced.

St. David's Church, as it looks today, on the Stryen Reserve at the mouth of the Stein. Missionary records indicate that a church was built here in 1873. Services continued until the mid-1960s. (Photo: Gary Fiegehen/ Robert Semeniuk)

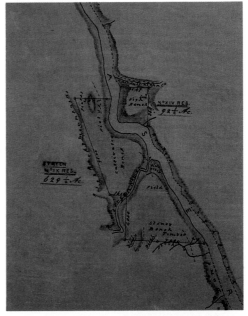

Map drawn by W. S. Jemmet, on June 24, 1887, based on his survey of the "Stryen" reserve in 1885. The original is held by the Surveyor General Branch, Ministry of Forests and Lands, Victoria.

Self-generated, based on the renewable use of the local land and water, community-based—this was a promising local economy. Just as it was taking hold after the collapse of the Gold Rush, however, distant changes were underway. British Columbia had entered Confederation in 1871 with the promise of a transcontinental railroad. The possibility of a link through the mountains seemed to offer prosperity for all—for landowners whose land values would rise; for farmers who sought access to a wider market and cheaper freight rates; for politicians who wanted to enhance east-west trade to offset the worrying flow of commercial activity south to the American territories along the natural watercourses of the Kootenay, Columbia and Okanagan rivers running into the United States. Before the railroad united the Pacific frontier

Would-Be Monopolists

At present the railway work in the vicinity is not of a character to render any great benefit to the place, for wherever there may be found workmen employed, the Company have supply stores stretched along the line, ever ready to grasp the outlay of the employees; and having facilities for buying in Oregon and California as handling freight in bulk it is difficult for private enterprise to compete with the would-be-monopolists. It is known that those not of the railway employ are inclined to buy in the company stores, where it is thought a few cents or dollars can be saved, and this lessens the natural trade of Lytton, etc. There are those that fear when the Railway Co. have more of their line in working order . . . that advantage of freight will make it difficult for private parties to hold their own with Messrs. Onderdonk & Co. and in this event for a time the progress of inland towns may be checked.

Inland Sentinel, Yale, British Columbia, 30 November 1882, p.2.

---

with the rest of Canada in 1886, Americans had talked freely of annexing large areas of the Dominion that lay "empty" before them. The completion of the railroad brought new settlers into Canada's west and, from then on, the land was secured for the national interest. Just as towns had grown up by the trading posts, the new centres of Vancouver, Calgary, Regina and others were largely the creations of the Canadian Pacific Railway.

In the Fraser Canyon, the construction of the railway brought another remote-controlled economic boom. From the blacksmith shop to the bar-room, railroad construction created demands for labour, goods and services, demands that could not be met locally. Chinese and American workers flooded in, barely 20 years after the first onslaught of California prospectors. In 1882, Andrew Onderdonk, the American engineer in charge of construction through the sheer-sided Fraser canyon, brough in 6,000 Chinese "coolies" from Hong Kong.

The completion of the CPR marked the emergence of a truly radical new economic infrastructure for the Nlaka'pamux and the Stein region. The railroad opened up hitherto remote areas by dramatically lowering the costs and increasing the speed of transport. This created better access to British Columbia's far-flung resources for a receptive international market. The enthusiasm was palpable. The **Inland Sentinel** (a newspaper published first in Yale at the southern end of the Fraser Canyon, later moving to Kamloops) prophesied: "Lytton bears the honored name of a once popular colonial secretary, and evidently has a bright future . . . With the progress of a little time, Lytton will become a thriving inland place."[22]

But the new railway changed the rules in unexpected ways yet again, and did so irrevocably. The local economies, depressed by the construction exodus, found themselves even more vulnerable because of competition from large, distant producers.

Hints of this change were evident even during the flurry of railroad construction. The CPR was so large that it was often called the "government on wheels," and it endeavoured to capture for itself much of the commercial activity generated by the construction. Certainly with the demand for 40 million board feet of lumber for cribbing, trestles, bridges and ties in the canyon section, there was much need for local sawmilling. As well, during these years, fresh fish, game, livestock, and farm produce found ready markets in Lytton.

But the CPR maintained supply stores along the route, even stipulating in its employment contracts that supplies were to be purchased in company shops. The **Inland Sentinel** went so far as to complain that the construction was "not of a character to render any great benefit to the place." The CPR was already "buying in Oregon and California, handling freight in bulk. It is difficult for private enterprise to compete with the would-be monopolists."[23]

The new railway infrastructure actually reduced the viability of many local businesses. Towns along the Cariboo trail had always provided important stop-over points for overland travellers. Local farmers and businesses prospered by servicing their needs, from pack horses to fresh food. The advent of the railway rendered many of these businesses redundant. Services became centralized in places like Vancouver (the "Terminal City") and Kamloops where size and location provided commercial advantages.

Food from California now arrived through Vancouver on the railroad, while surcharges were assessed to handle the smaller volumes of the local producers. When volumes fell below levels profitable to the railroad, sidings were closed.

Repeated calls were made upon the government to "enforce a tariff of charges" upon the CPR and to ensure that the local rail sidings be kept open, "at least those that are adjacent to important settlements."[24] In a soon-to-be-familiar process, the new transportation infrastructure furthered the needs of a larger, more distant economy, while the local communities bore the cost.

With the transportation infrastructure in place, the economies of new towns like Lytton and Lillooet had to choose a new economic path. Only one option was realistically open to them—specialized production for a market beyond their control. In 1862, when Bishop Hills visited Commissioner Ball's farm, it produced an array of crops for local consumption, including barley, potatoes, turnips, beets, hay, as well as meat and dairy products. By 1884, the farm (now owned by Thomas Earl), had become a **specialty** producer of apples for export. The production here, though of high quality, was relatively small compared to the foreign competition, so that the railway siding at Winch's spur (on the rail line near Earlscourt Farm) was closed many years later. Until that happened, Earlscourt and its exports were the pride of Lytton.

Once again, the Nlaka'pamux were plunged into a new economy. Only seven decades after the first shake of the White man's hand, everything had changed. A river of steel was now in place to export local resources. Every riverbed and mountain valley was now a fair target, and eventually all would be mined, trapped, roaded and logged. All except the Stein Valley.

CPR engine British Columbia. (Photograph courtesy of Vancouver Public Library, Vancouver)

PORTRAIT OF A WATERSHED

Grizzly bear. (Photo: Tim Fitzharris)

Alpine meadow and pond. (Painting: Stephen Fick)

T

The thick bark of the Ponderosa pine protects mature trees from the grass fires which periodically sweep through the dry underbrush. (Photo: Gary Fiegehen/Robert Semeniuk)

he Stein River Valley is a unique watershed that straddles two climatic regions—the cool, wet Coast and the hot, dry Interior. The headwaters of the Stein River begin in the west in the rock, tundra and glaciers of the cloud-covered crest of the Coast Mountains; the river's mouth is in Interior Plateau country, its water spilling into the Fraser River amid sage and pine-clad benchland.

Lying between the Lillooet River on the west, and the Fraser Valley on the east, the Stein Valley is surrounded by a ring of summits and ridges 195 kilometres (120 miles) long that enclose 1060 square kilometres (430 square miles) of land. A dozen peaks exceed 2500 metres, including Mt. Skihist which, with a height of 2944 metres (9660 feet), is the highest mountain in southwestern British Columbia. Within the confines of that protective ridge are remnant icefields and arid benches, cedar glades and pine forests, motionless swamps and rushing rapids.

This special character of the Stein as a transition zone is extremely rare. Writes forest ecologist, Jim Pojar, in the hikers' guidebook to the Stein, "Few rivers in British Columbia traverse such a wide range of landform, climate and vegetation in such a short distance. Certainly no park in southern B.C. comes near to matching the diversity of the Stein drainage."[1]

From a reconstruction of its deep geological history, to an understanding of the habitats still hidden in the cottonwood groves by the river, the natural history of the valley is rich.

Shaping The Land

The Stein Valley is a young landscape, the main valley having been moulded during the last glaciation period. Granitic rocks, formed over 50 million years ago, underlie most of the area. Streams, following weaknesses in the bedrock, carved the main creeks and valley during the creation of the Coast Range. But many of the Stein's natural features have been shaped by glaciers during the past 30,000 years—a short time in geological terms.

The most recent glacial period ended about 10,000 years ago. For about 16,000 years before that, the main valley was dominated by a large glacier with smaller arms feeding new ice down into it from the higher side-valleys. If more ice was added during the winter than melted in the summer, the glacier advanced down the valley; if not, the glacier retreated. In either case, the glacier was constantly moving back and forth along the valley floor, grinding the rocks beneath it along its way. The glaciers left deposits in the valleys as they slowly retreated back toward their source high in the mountains. This glacial till consists of a compacted mixture of rocks of all shapes and sizes, including some ground down to fine rock flour. The glacier's eventual withdrawal carved the characteristic U-shaped valley trough with its steep sides and wide, flat floor.

As the ice receded, the side-valleys were left hanging above the much deeper floor of the central valley. While their grades are steep near the main river, the hanging valleys have

The mouth of the Stein at the Fraser River. (Photo: Martin Roland)

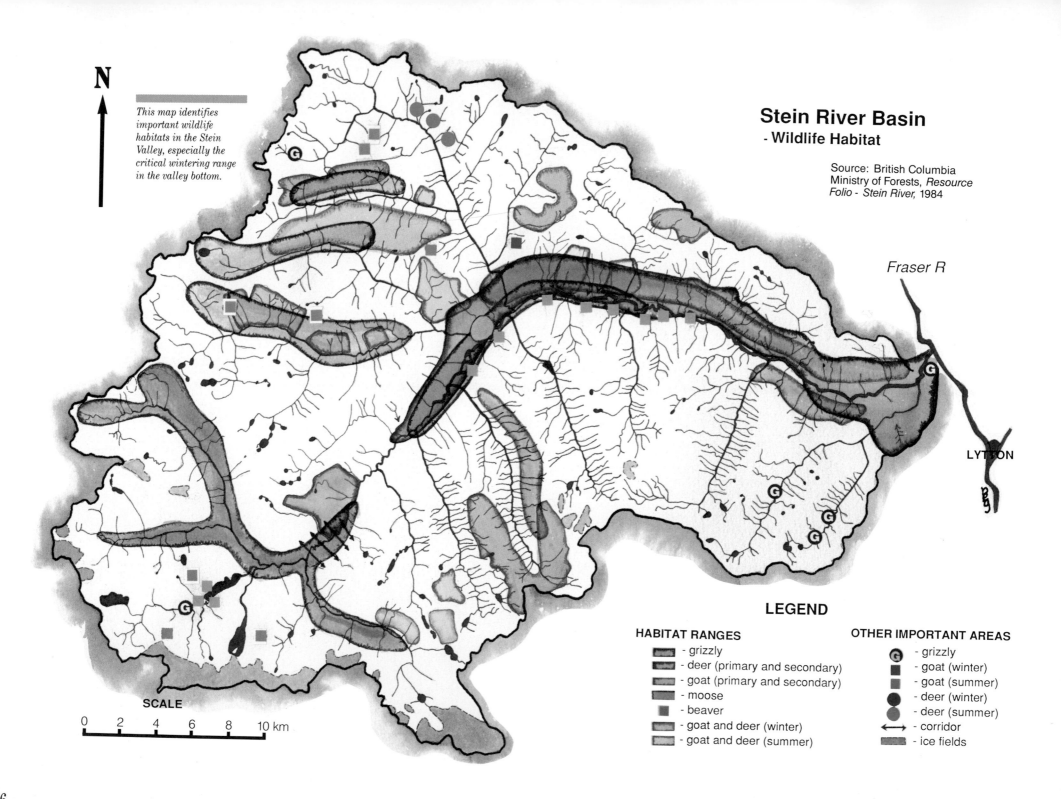

N

This map identifies important wildlife habitats in the Stein Valley, especially the critical wintering range in the valley bottom.

Stein River Basin
- Wildlife Habitat

Source: British Columbia Ministry of Forests, *Resource Folio - Stein River,* 1984

Fraser R

LYTTON

LEGEND

HABITAT RANGES

- grizzly
- deer (primary and secondary)
- goat (primary and secondary)
- moose
- beaver
- goat and deer (winter)
- goat and deer (summer)

OTHER IMPORTANT AREAS

- G - grizzly
- goat (winter)
- goat (summer)
- deer (winter)
- deer (summer)
- corridor
- ice fields

SCALE

0   2   4   6   8   10 km

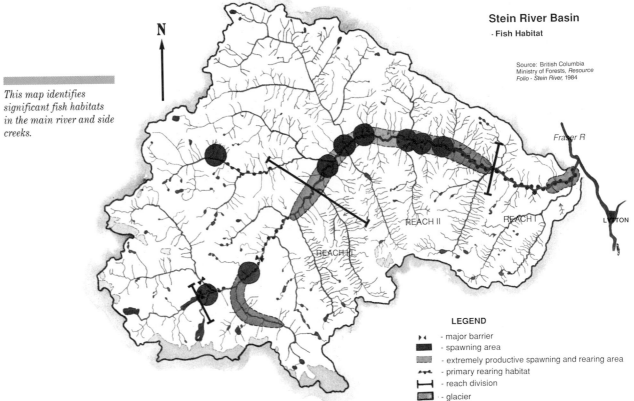

Stein River Basin
- Fish Habitat

Source: British Columbia
Ministry of Forests, *Resource
Folio - Stein River*, 1984

*This map identifies
significant fish habitats
in the main river and side
creeks.*

Fraser R

REACH II

REACH I

REACH III

LYTTON

LEGEND

- major barrier
- spawning area
- extremely productive spawning and rearing area
- primary rearing habitat
- reach division
- glacier

---

*Though it is claimed that
logging is planned for
only nine per cent of the
valley's land base, this
map illustrates how
seriously roadbuilding
and logging would affect
both the critical fisheries
and wildlife habitats
along the entire length of
the river, as well as
virtually all the
commercial timber.*

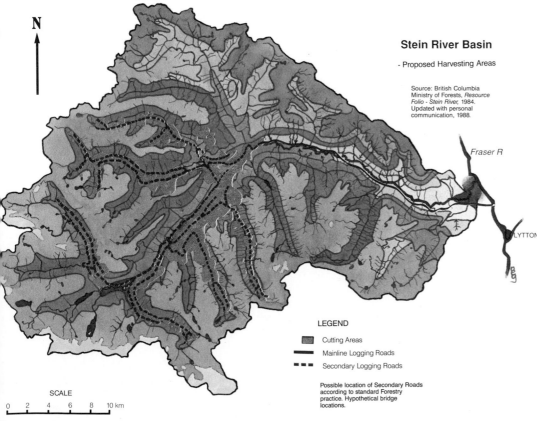

N

Stein River Basin
- Proposed Harvesting Areas

Source: British Columbia
Ministry of Forests, *Resource
Folio - Stein River*, 1984.
Updated with personal
communication, 1988.

Fraser R

LYTTON

LEGEND

- Cutting Areas
- Mainline Logging Roads
- Secondary Logging Roads

Possible location of Secondary Roads
according to standard Forestry
practice. Hypothetical bridge
locations.

SCALE

0   2   4   6   8   10 km

Values Of Utmost Importance

Maps for both fisheries and wildlife values indicate the importance of the drainage . . . Grizzly bears inhabit the area and [the drainage] contains relatively large numbers of mountain goats. Black bears and mule deer . . . are present in good numbers especially within the central portion of the main river. Some moose activity was noted in the swamps near Scudamore Creek. Beavers are very numerous within the main system.

We feel that fisheries values are of the utmost importance and that from Mile 10 to approximately Mile 20, the main river and the lower sections of its tributaries with the attendant backwaters is particularly vulnerable to any disturbance . . . Whether the disturbance is a result of either road building or actual logging operations is immaterial . . . It is vitally important to maintain water quality throughout the entire system, including the quality of the tributary streams both within this section and upstream of it . . . Water quality deterioration will markedly reduce the spawning and rearing capability of the central section of the system and this, in turn, will reduce the food available for both black and grizzly bears. Logging anywhere within the central section will likely reduce wintering capabilities for deer . . .

G.A. West, Regional Director, Fish and Wildlife Branch, Kamloops, British Columbia, *Memorandum*, November 16, 1973.

77

Glaciers have shaped much of the Stein Valley. Grinding glacial ice has carved the steep U-shape of the upper and middle valleys.

relatively gradual grades for most of their earlier course in the high country away from the river. Near the Stein, the streams running down the side-valleys carved steep canyons or fell in long cascades as they made their way down to the river. Some streams have created alluvial fans as they spill debris and sediments carried from their headwaters down into the central valley.

The river has also put its imprint on the valley. At the eastern end of the valley, erosion by the main river since the end of glaciation cut into the meta-sedimentary rocks and produced the familiar V-shaped gorge (steep walls, narrow valley bottom) where the river gradient steepens en route to the Fraser. The floodplain along the valley floor shifts back and forth in the upper and middle valley. The side creeks still wash down fine materials eroded from glacial till and volcanic rocks, and occasionally let loose a new slide of rock, mud, and forest debris. In contrast, waterborne deposits in stream beds are predominantly smoothed or rounded rocks, sorted by flowing water into many layers of nearly uniform rock sizes.

In the upper two-thirds of the valley, the river channel is underlain by small rocks, sand and gravel—ideal fish-spawning habitat. Rich backwater swamps and bogs of the wide floodplain lie in gentle contrast to the wooded and rocky terrain along the valley slopes. Larger rocks and boulders dominate the eastern third of the river channel, the result of debris slides, landslides and avalanches from the steep slopes above. This canyon area is hotter and drier, and the river's current is far more rapid than in the flatter central valley.

The soils of the valley are the product of this history. Because the glaciers have recently scraped away any pre-existing soil, the soils in the Stein have had a relatively short time in which to develop. This limited time for development, the valley's steep slopes and its granite rock base combine to produce poor, shallow soils. Only a small proportion—four percent—of the forested area is classified as being on good quality, or nutrient rich, sites. The shallow soils and rigorous climate of much of the valley limits tree growth—only 40,246 hectares (100,000 acres), or 38 percent of the valley excluding

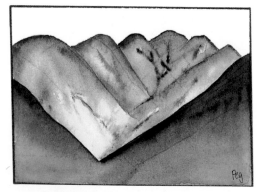

V-SHAPED MOUNTAIN VALLEY

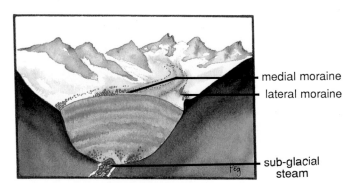

medial moraine
lateral moraine

sub-glacial steam

GLACIATION

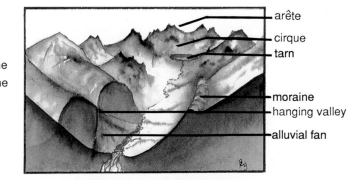

arête
cirque
tarn

moraine
hanging valley
alluvial fan

U-SHAPED POST-GLACIAL MOUNTAIN VALLEY

A TRAPPER'S JOURNAL

The story of the Stein watershed can best be told through the eyes of those who have known and loved the valley. One such person is Adam Klein, one of a small group of Stein trappers who worked the valley during the winters of the early decades of this century. Born in 1907, Klein spent his childhood as a farmboy in southern Saskatchewan. Tending horses and livestock, Klein got his schooling largely through the books he borrowed from the local library in Plessis, books like the western novels of Zane Grey. At the age of 17, Klein was so infuriated by a dispute with his brother and his father that he took a load of wheat to town, sold it, and with the proceeds, bought a train ticket to Vancouver.

The runaway's journey led him ultimately to Lytton's Globe Hotel and, from there, into the Stein Valley. Klein's writings provide one of our few remaining links to a very different way of life in the wilderness. It took a special kind of person to thrive in the woods in those days—a physical stamina which most of us can hardly imagine, and a woodsman's lore and skill that even the most ardent outdoors traveller simply doesn't need in our era of synthetic sleeping bags, Gore-Tex jackets and lightweight stoves.

The following is an account of Klein's first trip to the Stein Valley in 1925 with Young Easter Hicks, son of Cixpéntlam's half-sister. It was written as a letter by Klein to the authors several years ago.

Arriving in Vancouver I spent some three weeks time in the city. I needed work. I saw a man unloading wood from a truck, and asked if I could get a job helping with the wood. The man said that he was from Lytton, and felt sure I could get a job as a janitor with the Globe Hotel, operated by Alphonse Hautier. Arriving in Lytton, I got the job, and worked long and hard, splitting wood, and doing many types of chores.

The last week in January a man came into the hotel, with a bundle of marten pelts over his shoulders. I was beside myself with desire to go on a real trap line, went to the man's room, knocked on the door, and said, "Good day sir, I know that you are Mr. Young Easter Hicks and trap in the Stein Valley. I want to learn to be a trapper, and want you to take me with you."

Hicks eyed me, and asked "How old are you?" I answered, "I will be 18 years old tomorrow, I was born 29 January, 1907." Hicks said, "Have you ever trapped before?" I answered, "Yes, I trapped ermine, muskrats, and shot four coyotes." This seemed to amuse Hicks. Hicks asked, "Have you ever slept on the snow, without any blankets or sleeping bag?" I answered, "Well if you can, I am sure that I also can." I added, "I don't want any money. I only want to learn how to be a successful trapper."

Hicks said, "Come back tomorrow. I will give this considerable thought." The next day Hicks said, "I will have to go to Vancouver to sell my furs, and when I get back we will consider you coming along."

Hicks returned with two dozen No.(0) traps and a pack board, and told me that we would leave for the trap line. Hicks went to a rancher and bought a piece of cowhide, about 18 inches square. This was to be used to make snowshoe laces.

Hicks was told that an Indian trapper by the name of Jack Thompson went on a trap line in November and was now more than a month overdue. This caused considerable concern with the Lytton Indian Band. Hicks told them that he had seen no trace of anyone being in the valley, but then he did not go where Jack Thompson's line was located. He told them that we were going in the valley the next day, and that we would be on the lookout for any signs of life.

We started our trek with two heavy backpacks. Being only 18 years old, and in good physical condition from the hard work on the farm, I had no difficulty keeping pace with the 56-year-old seasoned trapper.

The slow plodding steps of Hicks under the heavy pack slowly ate up the distance. I almost got impatient with the stunted alpine wooded areas, is actually forested at all.[2]

The mining potential of the valley is low relative to other areas throughout B.C.'s southern Interior. Knowledge of lead, zinc, silver, gold, molybdenum, antimony, and deposits of semi-precious gemstones (vesuvianite) has existed for years, but there have been no major mining operations because of low quantities and high extraction costs. Recent exploration has

The metamorphic rock face at the head of Nesbitt Creek on the south flank of the watershed. (Photo: June Ryder)

not uncovered any major deposits, and new discoveries or vastly different economic conditions would be required before large-scale mining operations could be considered.[3]

Watersheds And Ecosystems

The end result of glacial action and river erosion has been to carve the large watershed that we now know as the Stein. To those with an interest in ecology, one of the most attractive features of the Stein is that it is a single watershed unit. Ecology is a new science that looks not at animals or plants in isolation, but at relationships—the interaction of organisms with each other, and of living things with their physical environment. An ecosystem is the sum of these relationships that connect organisms to their place in the landscape: the cycling of nutrients, the decay of dead plants and animals, the growth and change of the forest cover, the local patterns of weather and water.

A watershed ecosystem such as the Stein is defined as a land area that drains into a central stream or river. On a small, intimate scale, we find a watershed in every little hollow feeding a seasonal creek in the spring. On a grand scale, much of central British Columbia is part of the Fraser drainage basin, just as much of the central United States is encompassed within the Mississippi watershed. A large watershed ties together countless smaller ones in a network of infinite complexity. Brimful Lake in the alpine meadows flows into a side creek, which flows into Cottonwood Creek; Cottonwood flows into the Stein River; and the Stein flows into the Fraser.

Water links life at a micro-level too. It passes through a forest canopy as mist, rain or snow, and as it does, it is changed. Leaves and lichen remove nutrients from the water and change its acidity. On the forest floor, leaf litter, humus,

The headlong rush of the Stein River as it falls steeply through the lower canyon on its way to the Fraser. (Photo: Robert Semeniuk/Gary Fiegehen)

slow gait. Then as the sun went down, Earl's Cabin came into view. Hicks shed his pack and so did I. Looking about, Hicks got his axe and started to make firewood for the night. This done, a cheery fire was going, and I packed the wood in and neatly stacked it against the wall.

It was twilight when Hicks asked me, "Lad will you fetch a bucket of water?" I eagerly accepted the chore, and as I neared the river to dip out a bucketful of water, Hicks yelled, "Look out, a cougar!" I screamed in terror, dropped the bucket and rushed into the safety of the cabin door. Hicks whooped and rolled over with laughter.

After awhile, the fire going briskly, supper had to to be made. Hicks said, "I don't suppose you want to fetch the water?" I shook my head. Hicks got the water, and made tea. Supper ended. Hicks, in the best of spirits, sat down on one bunk, and said, "Lad, you asked me to teach you the way of trapping. Well first of all, there are no cougars around a beaten trail where people walk. All the bears are now in hibernation and there is nothing in the woods to harm you."

"See this axe? This axe is your bed, your home, and your shelter. There are two very important things in the woods to learn—one how to use your axe, and the other to be sure to carry matches in waterproof containers. Have one container in your pack, the other in your

Soapberries, or
soopolallie, as they are
sometimes called, are still
a popular Native food.
(Photo: Ken
Lertzman/Dana Lepofsky)

The mist-enshrouded
forest of the central Stein
Valley. (Photo: Leo
deGroot)

and minerals each leave their imprints in the chemistry of the water, some adding and some taking away materials. The water carries nutrients through the soil where they can be taken up by plant roots and used to produce new growth.

The food chain of a stream depends on material from the land. Leaves falling from a streamside cottonwood into the water are decomposed by bacteria, providing food for tiny invertebrates. In turn, these invertebrates provide food for fish. Small logjams and other accumulated debris provide physical structure for the stream's ecosystem, holding decaying vegetation and offering habitat for predators and prey. In these ways, big and small, water flowing through a watershed weaves a web of relationships that literally ties it all together.

Watersheds disturbed by logging, road building, or mining lose many of the mechanisms through which this recycling is accomplished. Clear streams turn brown as the soil is washed away from the surrounding slopes; fish and game disappear as their habitat is lost. Few places remain where these complex ecological processes persist as they have over the ages.

A variety of unaltered ecosystems woven into a single landform by a still living, still wild, river—this is the essence of the Stein. It is a rich classroom where natural relationships are still whole. Such a place retains entire communities of natural animal and plant life, communities which are disrupted or even lost forever once the wilderness is roaded and logged. The Stein is an oasis of ecological integrity in an increasingly degraded landscape, an "island in a sea of stumps."

The Path Of The River

The Stein River has five sections. It begins in the glaciers and headwater lakes, falls steeply in the upper canyon, slows in the more gradual and open middle valley, races down the

Earl's Cabin at Earl Creek photographed in 1921, was built by Fred Earl, a trapper and prospector probably related to the Thomas Earl family of Earlscourt Farm. It is said that Fred took out $12,000 in granulated gold from *Earl Creek. After his death overseas during World War I, numerous unsuccessful attempts were made to locate his cache of gold near his cabin. (Photograph courtesy of Jim Hallisey, Kelowna, British Columbia)*

vest pocket, and carry a smooth small pebble with your match container. There will be times when the deep snows will prevent you even starting a match, so you use the small flat stone to do the work for you."

The next day it snowed about four inches. The trek from Earl's Cabin to Cottonwood cabin took ten hours. Here again the same chores were done. I got the water from the Cottonwood Creek and stacked wood against the wall. After supper we were both now ready for an early sleep. There were no blankets or sleeping bags. The fire in the fireplace was kept going. The inside of the cabin was almost too warm. We both slept in our clothes.

Early in the morning I woke up, pulled on my rubber boots, and ventured outside. A light snow was falling. I stood in awe, gazing up the majestic mountain

83

towering over the flat valley below. This was so different from the barren prairie lands.

Hicks made breakfast. The aroma of fresh coffee wafted over the pure crisp air. After breakfast, Hicks pulled out the piece of cowhide, singed the hair of the hide, then made a wooden gauge for his pocket knife, and cut the hide into 1/3-inch ribbons of rawhide. These were placed into a five-gallon tin can which was filled with warm water. Hicks said, "We have to make our snowshoes, so we will have a three day stay in the cabin."

Mike Brown, a Nlaka'pamux hunter, at a cairn in the high alpine. (Photograph courtesy of Rita Haugen, Lytton, British Columbia)

There were two deer carcasses hanging on a crossbeam, away from the cabin. Hicks had hunted them before he left for Lytton, and they were the meat for winter.

I had helped with the butchering of the farm animals. It amazed Hicks how expert a job I did removing the meat from the hide. This done, Hicks said, "Take the frying pan. Cut two rashers of bacon. Then cut venison steaks. Fry them until they are done. Then set the steaks aside to cool. These we will pack into a five pound lard pail, and carry them in our packs. We will only eat two meals a day — breakfast and supper. If we do get hungry we can eat a bunch of warmed up venison steak and bannock, (a type of bread made of flour with baking powder and a little salt added) and a quick pot of tea."

The next day Hicks took the rawhide ribbons out of the water, took them outside and fastened one end to a smooth birch tree. He pulled on the ribbon. It stretched nearly twice as long. He cut the string into several pieces. He tied one end on to a small tree and with a stone fastened on a fish line, threw the stone over a tall branch of a cottonwood tree. He then cut heavy pieces of green cottonwood log and suspended them from both ends of the rawhide rope. This was done so that when the snowshoes were strung, the webbing would not stretch in the soft snow.

lower canyon, and finally fans out where it meets the Fraser River. Each of these sections is a special aquatic ecosystem with its own particular combination of habitats and inhabitants.

The streams that feed the Stein originate in the glaciers and seasonal snowpacks at the western height of land in the Coast Mountains. These meltwater streams feed into several alpine lakes, such as the renowned Elton Lake. Turquoise blue in colour, this lake lies high in the alpine tundra amongst snowy peaks, its colour produced by the silt and clay which lie suspended in it, ground out by the glaciers as powdered rock. The river proper begins as the outflow from Stein Lake, 1020 metres (3350 feet) above sea level.

The headwater lakes are icy cold and low in the organic nutrients needed for building complex aquatic ecosystems. The crystalline clarity of many of these lakes is visible evidence of the very low density of phytoplankton, the algae which form the basis of the aquatic food chain. Many of these lakes are ice-free for only two or three months each year, and do not support fish populations at all. Instead, the alpine lakes harbour intriguing communities of small invertebrates adapted to cold, rigorous conditions.

From Stein Lake, the river surges through an upper canyon, with pounding rapids and waterfalls so fast and precipitous that they block the movement of fish upstream to the lake. The high volumes of water rushing over the coarse rock bottom limit life in the river to a few resident rainbow trout, and to invertebrates which live in the protected layer on the bottom and glean their food from the water flowing by.

Below the upper canyon, the valley broadens and the river slows, meandering through side channels and pools with occasional breaks through small rapids and riffles. This central valley is the most fertile land, hosting rich stands of cottonwood, fir and spruce, as well as being the most productive fish habitat. This is extremely productive spawning and rearing habitat for Dolly Varden char, chinook and coho salmon.[4] Steelhead, rainbow trout and rocky mountain whitefish also inhabit these waters and some of the major side-creeks.

For the last 12 kilometres (7 miles) of its course, the river is once again constrained by steep-sided canyon walls, rushing down a long incline before it meets the Fraser. Unlike the upper canyon, however, this section is replete with eddies, pools, and occasional side channels that allow migrating fish to move upstream. This part of the river would be particularly sensitive to road construction on the steep slopes above. Rocks and earth falling into the channel would easily narrow it, blocking upstream migration.

A couple of kilometres upstream from the river's mouth, the valley opens out into the rolling benches and terraces that border the Fraser River. Pink salmon spawn here, being found only in this part of the Stein as it flows along a rocky course through dry Ponderosa pine woodland to the small delta it creates at the Fraser. Here the clear glacial waters are quickly swallowed by the muddy brown, swirling currents of the much larger Fraser River.

Habitats And Inhabitants

With its concern for the inter-relationships between plant and animal, wood and water, hot and cold, the science of ecology is greatly enriched by places like the Stein. Varied in vegetation, transitional in character, stretching from low valley river to high mountain glacier, the Stein is diverse in habitat, and in the mammal and bird life which still thrives there. In the Stein, the diversity of habitats required by wild animals (such as the grizzly bear which needs large unbroken tracts of

Alpine heather meadows near Elton Lake. (Photo: Kevin Oke)

85

Steep waterfall from a
"hanging" valley. (Photo:
Robert Semeniuk/Gary
Fiegehen)

Aerial view of marshy
floodplain. (Photo: Gary
Fiegehen/Robert
Semeniuk)

old growth forests) is preserved.

The mosaic of old-growth Douglas-fir and floodplain forests of the middle valley provides the core habitats for many of the Stein's wildlife species. Key winter homes are located here, and the area provides access corridors for animals moving from forested to sub-alpine areas in mid-summer, or crossing from one side of the valley to the other. The middle valley and the North Stein—prime grizzly habitat—would be slated for the heaviest logging, and this would inevitably spell the demise of the grizzly bear in this, his last local refuge. The combination of coniferous and deciduous vegetation along the streams of the mid-valley adds diversity to food and shelter available to deer, moose, bear, marten, mink, beaver and many other mammals as well as for numerous bird species such as water pipits, horned larks, warblers, sparrows and juncos.

Many other important wildlife areas exist in the valley. The Cottonwood Creek drainage is the best summer range for mule deer, and mountain goats use both the Cottonwood and Scudamore side valleys to raise their young. Beavers thrive in the waters around Stein Lake. Bear, moose and deer graze on the meadows of the headwater lakes area, and grizzlies search for food among the varied vegetation of the valley's many avalanche tracks.

A forest or meadow's usefulness for wildlife changes with the seasons. As snow melts from the alpine meadows in mid-summer, bears and mountain goats move higher in the valley to feed on the lush vegetation. The subalpine of the North Stein is the valley's best-known summer goat range. The berries ripening in the meadows offer food for bears preparing for winter.

In the high country, marmots, living in colonies, keep watch over an active landscape. Their piercing whistles warn other members of approaching hikers or predators. Birds of

Hicks went in search of snowshoe frames. He came back with an armful of hazel trees. These were trimmed, measured in lengths, cut, and then heated over the hot coals of the wood fire. As the hazel frames sizzled and steamed, the frames were bent into shape over a round block of wood. The two frames were securely tied together near the middle of the frames, and a short piece of wood was forced into the front of the frames. This made a four-inch rise and a bow. When the snowshoe was pulled on, the very front of the shoe had a four-inch clearance. As the foot was lifted to walk, the rear end of the shoe would remain on the snow at all times, the front end would rise about 12 inches above the snow, and a forward thrust made a new step a safe and secure method of walking over any depth of snow.

The next day was an idle one for both of us; the hazel frames had to become perfectly seasoned and dried before the webbing could be strung. I was anxious to explore the surroundings. When I asked if I could walk down the river a ways, Hicks said, "Sure, but be sure a cougar don't eat you."

I walked down the river. Coming to a deep pool, I stopped short. There in the clear waters, were three large rainbow trout well over three feet in length. They were beautiful to behold. While gazing at the trout, a small animal came swimming up around the bend. It was a sleek dark-

coloured mink.

Returning to the cabin, I related the beautiful scene that I witnessed and said, "Is there no way we can trap the mink, and catch the fish?" Hicks replied, "We have to trap marten now till the season is over. Then, when we get back from the marten line we will trap beaver. And then we will have all the time in the world. There are all kinds of beaver signs below and above the cabin. I will make a fish spear. Then you can catch all the fish you want."

As a pair of trappers, one 56 years of age with over 40 years of outdoor experience, the other 18 years old, with less than a week's experience, we became fast friends. We started next morning for the upper regions of the Stein Valley. The Cottonwood had a small tree felled across it acting as a bridge. Then, after an hour's walk, we came upon another creek called Battle Creek by the Natives of Lytton. The name stemmed from a war that once was fought by the Pemberton and Lytton Bands. This creek also had a tree felled as a bridge. We were heavily laden with backpacks. Thus the slow plodding with the snowshoes seemed to make the distances far greater than they were.

About noon, coming to a small stream, Hicks said, "We will have a lunch." He kindled a fire up against a large fir tree. In very little time the venison and the tea were heated up.

It was cloudy and a light snow fell all day long. When it started to become dark, we came upon a clearing in the timber. This was caused by a forest fire many years ago. There was a massive fir stump, about five feet in diameter, leaning downwards and about 30 feet high. Hicks made for it. He took off his pack and said, "Welcome to the Waldorf Hotel lad. Do you think we can sleep on the snow? Well now, take your frying pan and clear away the snow." Taking his axe, Hicks

went to a clump of second growth fir, cut two poles about three inches in diameter and trimmed them to about 16 feet in length. He also got two small poles about six feet in length.

Taking one pole, he told me, "Take the other one and we will pry the bark from the fir stump." With a little effort, pushing and prying, a slab of bark about 20 feet long and about six feet wide fell with a plop into the snow. Hicks measured the slab to about a six-foot length and cut it

away from the slab. As we were going to carry the shorter slab to the back of the stump it broke in two. This made two pieces about three feet wide each for a cradle-like base for our beds.

This done, Hicks said, "Come here lad, and see how to start a fire." Cutting a deep hole into the rotten stump, there were seams of solid dry wood in the centre. Cutting a piece of the dry seam, this was split into two inch wide pieces. Then taking out his pocket knife, he started to slice the pieces of the solid wood making them look like a bird's wing. Taking out his waterproof matchbox he took out a match, and with his small stone ignited the match. Holding it under one of the wooden wings, the fire rapidly engulfed the whole wing. Laying it in the hole, the other wings were placed on the top of one another. In less than ten minutes the entire stump was ablaze with a heat that extended well beyond the two pieces of bark slats.

While the fire was starting to burn, all the other bark was cut up into smaller pieces and piled behind the fire. These served as chairs, a table and then as firewood, when the stump would be burnt down to the ground. The two pieces of bark that were acting as a bed, were now steaming with the heat. They dried and warmed up.

After supper we slept like logs. Hicks said, "What do you think of sleeping out on the snow, in the open, without any

Beaver and other fur-bearing animals bore the brunt of the arrival of the White colonists. (Photo: Kevin Oke)

Moose forage on the lush vegetation of the central Stein valley. (Photo: Derek and Jane Abson)

Mountain goats provided a significant food resource in the Stein and were depicted in many rock paintings. (Photo: R.W. Laurilla)

Cougars. The abundant mule deer population of the lower Stein draws cougars into the valley. (Photo: Richard Wright)

Marmots. Marmots live in colonies among the Stein's alpine meadows and ridges. Nicknamed "the whistler," they use a sentry system to protect themselves from grizzly bears and wolverines. (Photo: Gunter Marx)

Pileated Woodpecker. The sounds of woodpeckers are familiar to hikers following the wooded valley trail. (Photo: Terry Willis)

many kinds are abundant, and pikas (small rabbit-like animals) scurry around the rocks and crevasses of talus slopes. Pikas can be seen with small stacks of drying vegetation that they store near their houses for their winter life beneath the snow.

Our knowledge of the wildlife of the Stein reveals to us a complex tapestry of natural life. Beyond this limited understanding, however, much is still tentative, drawn as much from trappers' accounts and hikers' anecdotes as from the incomplete inventories compiled by government experts. The provincial government's 1984 Stein Folio, compiled as a guide to manage logging in the valley, lists as "unknown" the wildlife uses in at least 25 percent of the management units. The number of grizzly bears, or even the presence of the endangered spotted owl, is unknown. There may yet be large populations of fur-bearers in the central valley—lynx, marten, wolverine, weasel and mink—but the trappers of the early part of the century knew much more about their abundance and distribution than we do now.

blankets or sleeping bags?" I answered, "Zane Grey described just that kind of a campsite, before the cabins could be built."

Hicks said, "There is one thing that you should be aware of. Never, ever build a fire under the leaning side of the tree and sleep under it. Several campers have been known to perish doing just that." This was common sense, and good advice.

We made the trip to Hicks' lean-to in good time. Being away for nearly three weeks, the fireplace was full of snow. While I cleared away the snow, Hicks cut the firewood. A fire was started, and the whole shelter warmed up. There can be no words that can describe the satisfaction of being at the end of the trek or trapline, enjoying the comforts of a warm woodfire.

Next day Hicks divided the food supplies and packed them into a five-gallon square tin box. Placing the cover over the box, he said, "Tomorrow we will bail my line, which should take us two days, and then we will go into the lake area which will also take two days. Then we will set out a 15-mile long line on the south forks of the Stein. When that is done, we will go back to Lytton and bring in a supply of grub. There are several large beaver dams above the lake and a beaver lodge. On our return trip, the marten season will be over. We will spend a week trapping beaver at the lake. This done, we will travel on down to the Cottonwood

cabin. I will make you a fish spear there while I trap beaver at both ends of the river from the Cottonwood cabin. You can while away your time until the trapping season is over."

The next day, having a much lighter load, we followed the blazed trapline. On the third trap setting, a marten was hanging. The traps that Hicks set were such that, as the animal got his foot caught, it would struggle to get free. This caused the trap to turn upside-down, and the animal was then suspended by one leg, down and away from the tree, with the furious struggle to free itself. Tiring, the marten laid his head to the side and, within less than an hour, would be dead. The steel leg-hold trap took much longer if it wasn't upside down, and was indeed a cruel device for capturing the fur bearers, with the exception of beaver trapping. The beaver trap would hold and drown the beaver.

Hicks was a kind man and did not wish to see the animals suffer. For this reason he would never set traps for mink. If a mink trap was set so that the animal would drown, it would be in the water too long, the fur would slip, making the pelt useless. And if the set was made on land, the mink would not struggle too long. It would simply sit beside the trap for days until it starved. And it would be anywhere from 10 days to 14 days before a trap line could be tended to in a round trip.

(continued . . .)

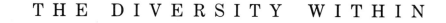

In the heart of the Stein watershed is a diverse, untouched old growth forest. That phrase rings in the mind with images—of ancient cedar, spruce and Douglas-fir reaching high into the heavens; of fallen timbers decaying on the forest floor; of grizzlies pawing for salmon in rushing streams; of new growth struggling to reach the sun through the canopy of the surrounding giants.

Old Growth

Trees on North America's west coast reach incredible ages—500 years, 1000 years, and more. However, old age alone does not old growth make. A stand of trees achieves the mantle of old growth not by age, but by developing to a particular stage of maturity, with its characteristic mix of species, sizes and ages. In the drier, more fire-prone parts of the Stein, much of the old growth is 200 to 300 years old, but in both wetter and alpine areas trees may be much older.

After a major natural disturbance like a fire or insect attack that kills off a forest's dominant trees, a process of ecological succession begins. Young trees grow up, forming a new canopy that shades the forest floor. Competition for light and space becomes more intense, and many trees die off, continuously thinning out the developing young stand. Eventually, the surviving trees, which are often of a species different from the first new trees, emerge to dominate the forest canopy. When the early successional trees are old enough so that some of them begin to die, the canopy opens enough to let another successional stage establish itself.

This continuous process of succession leads to a mature forest. With time, a mature forest develops into an old growth forest, which can be by far the longest stage of a forest's life-cycle. The death of canopy trees is critically important to the character of old growth, providing the snags, stumps, and logs that are habitat for many of the forest's wildlife species. Ironically, the very characteristics that cause some foresters to shake their heads at "the decadent, overmature forest" are those that give it its diversity of species and richness of structure. This is the climax forest—old and stately, dying yet intricately alive.

In the Stein, the old growth is diverse. Ecologists have described 12 distinct ecological groups—or biogeoclimatic zones—within the province. Areas within each zone share a common climate which influences the soils, vegetation, and wildlife. With the exception of the alpine tundra zone, the various biogeoclimatic zones are named for the climax species that dominate the ecosystem. Fully six of these twelve zones are represented in the Stein watershed, a diversity resulting from many factors, especially the great differences in the amount of rainfall. The valley lies in the rain shadow of the Coast Mountains and received far less precipitation than do the forests west of the divide. Over 200 centimetres (80 inches) of rain and snow fall in the headwater lakes area each year, while only 45 centimetres (18 inches) fall at the mouth of the river. In a traverse of the valley, the traveller passes through a range of environments, from open to dense forest, from wooded valley to grassy meadow.

This is perhaps the most familiar view of the Stein River. (Photo: Richard Chester)

A hiker on the Douglas-fir-lined trail at Teaspoon Creek. (Photo: Jeff Gibbs)

The entire marten line that Hicks had set out netted him seven marten. The marten were frozen solid. These were taken out of the traps, placed in a white cotton sack, and packed to the main camp. The next day was spent in skinning and stretching the pelts. The skinning of a marten was much the same as that of the prairie ermine, so both of us prepared the pelts.

The next day I had to do the backpacking, as well as carry the rifle. This gave Hicks a free hand to cut, blaze and prepare branches where the traps were to be set. Hicks used the entrails of goats and a piece of red flannel cloth about two inches square. These were tied under the spring of the steel trap and acted as bait. He also had a pint jar of rotted salmon eggs. These gave off a powerful smell. Any marten within 1000 feet would catch the scent, run up the tree, and investigate the piece of red flannel and the stench of the rotted eggs.

It was this line that was being set out that made Hicks consent to take me, an 18-year-old as a partner. Aside from being a companion, it eased and expedited the setting of the new trapline. The high-powered rifle was taken along. This was mountain goat country, and a goat would have to be shot to supply meat as well as bait.

The first day we set out 18 traps. The traps were spaced about three to the mile, so the distance was judged to be about six miles.

The next day when the traps were being set, and Hicks being about a quarter of a mile in advance, I heard a plopping sound made on the hillside. Looking over, I saw three mountain goats, a large one and two smaller, and whiter-looking ones. Taking the rifle, I shot one of the smaller ones. The other two vanished into the heavy timber. Hicks heard the shot and came back in time to see me dragging the goat down the mountain. Hicks lifted the goat and said, "Well, well, a yearling kid. Lad, you sure did my day for me. You can hang the goat and rifle at this setting."

When the last trap was set, a suitable campsite was chosen at the end of the line. Hicks said, "We will leave the tea can here, and in this way we don't have to pack one in. And it will also show us that it is the end of the line."

The next day on the return trip Hicks packed the goat and carried the rifle. The trek took all day to accomplish. The day's work being done, the goat was skinned and the meat prepared and hung outside on a bar that was set between two trees. The skin was dressed to a two-foot by three-foot piece of pelt, stretched and dried. This made a warm base for the bunk.

The next day a return trip to Lytton was started. Hicks said, "Jack Thompson died somewhere on his line. Instead of following down where we came up, we will go down on the south side, and find out where his head camp was located."

It was midday when we came upon a camp. It was a large fir tree with several poles standing against it. An axe handle was leaning against it sticking out of the snow several inches. Leaning up against the tree, Hicks took in the scene and said,

Urban Hicks and Albert Hance, two Stein trappers and prospectors of the early to mid 1900s at a camp in the Stein. (Photograph courtesy of Anita Nixon, Lytton, British Columbia)

"Let's move on lad. I think we are standing right on top of him."

Walking down the south side of the Stein River, we came to a creek, named Rogers Creek. This creek had deposited sand for centuries into the Stein, making it a shallow place to ford. Crossing over to the north-side, we arrived at the Cottonwood cabin well after sundown. From Cottonwood cabin, hiking up to the Hicks main lean-to camp required two days hike, with a full backpack. Coming back by stretching the daylight hours, the trip could be made in a single day.

The next day while travelling to Lytton we met a search party coming up the Stein Valley, well past the Canoe Landing. They had a horse with harness on. There were seven men in the group. Hicks was asked if he had seen any signs of Jack Thompson. The reply was that there were no signs of life anywhere, but that there was a campsite below the second canyon, with an axe handle sticking out of the snow, leaning up against the tree. The troop of Indians, who were all strangers to Hicks and myself, remarked that Jack Thompson was under the snow, for Jack Thompson never let the axe get out of his hands except in camp.

Four days later, we met the search party coming home, below the Cottonwood cabin. They had Jack Thompson's body wrapped up in a

Ponderosa Pine

The effect of the rain shadow is felt most strongly at the eastern end of the valley near the river's mouth. There, on flat dry benches, open forests are dominated by Ponderosa pine with its deeply cut, reddish-yellow, jigsaw-puzzle bark. The widely spaced trees each have an extensive root system to collect precious water. In places, the ground cover between the trees is still the original bunchgrass, a vegetation type that has been lost throughout much of its original range in the Interior due to extensive cattle-grazing. It has been replaced with weeds like cheatgrass and knapweed. This is the Ponderosa Pine-Bunchgrass (PPBG) zone, the driest and hottest zone in the province.

Throughout the Stein's lower canyon, Ponderosa pine dominates the sunny dry benches and steep rocky slopes, especially on south-facing hillsides on the north side of the river. Douglas-fir dominates the north-facing slopes on the south side of the canyon, and other moist and more shaded areas. Ponderosa pine recurs in dry sites well up into the middle valley, relic stands that represent one of the most westward occurrences of this species in British Columbia.

Throughout this zone many traditional food plants grow, such as Saskatoon berry, balsamroot and soapberry. The latter is whipped by the Nlaka'pamux into a delicious, bitter froth known as "Indian ice cream." The variety of tree and shrub species, and low snowpack in winter, are the reasons the lower canyon is the most valuable winter and spring range for mule deer, mountain goats, black and grizzly bear. The mature Douglas-fir and Ponderosa pine also provides habitat for a large variety of birds, such as blue grouse, Clarks nutcrackers, woodpeckers, nuthatches and chickadees.

Mule deer in Ponderosa pine forest. (Photo: Richard Wright)

Douglas-Fir

In the heart of the central valley and up the main reaches of the side valleys, Douglas-fir dominates the forest, mixed occasionally with Engelmann spruce and lodgepole pine. This is the Interior Douglas-fir (IDF) zone. Here the forest varies greatly, spruce and fir being interspersed with deciduous trees (such as aspen and birch) and Western yew, whose distinctive foliage and berries grow slowly under the Douglas-fir canopy.

The character of the Douglas-fir forest changes, too, as one moves westward up the Stein, and precipitation increases. There, the forest includes more coastal trees, such as amabilis fir and western hemlock, and the forest canopy becomes more closed. This type of forest is found in the North Stein, up Rutledge Creek, and near Stein Lake. In the drier forests to the east, grasses are a dominant groundcover, but in more moist sites farther west, grasses diminish and mosses become more common, and there is an enormous variety of mushrooms. Many of the berry-producing shrubs are

Stellar's jay, the official bird of British Columbia. (Photo: R.W. Laurilla)

cowhide. The horse was pulling it like a toboggan. Hicks said, "I see where you found him. As one trapper to another I offer my condolences. I wish to introduce myself and my partner."

The spokesman, who introduced himself as Jules Adams, said, "Yes we found poor Jack. He must have died before the first snowfall, as he was well under four feet of packed snow." They asked Hicks if he would consider shutting down Thompson's trap line, and if there were any marten, he could keep them as his own for his efforts.

The next day we camped near Jack Thompson's camp. The following day Hicks said, "You stay in camp, keep the home fires burning, Klein, and I will spring the traps."

It was nearly dark when Hicks came down the trapline, remarking "What an ungodly way to set a trapline — over steep hills and down into thick bush. I only found 17 traps. Thompson used salmon heads cut into small pieces as bait. I believe this is what killed Jack Thompson. The salmon heads cut with an axe were very sharp. They cut holes in his pack, and it is my guess that somehow or other he lost his matches. Losing ones' matches would prove fatal. If Jack came down to the camp unable to kindle a fire, he would have laid down, and falling asleep from sheer exhaustion, never awakened."

traditional foods of the Nlaka'pamux, several having medicinal uses.

These mixed forests of Spruce-Pine-Fir sweeping up the valley bottoms offer important winter habitat and travel corridors for wildlife. This is also the prime timber sought by the forest industry. The loss of such lowland forests is a common concern to ecologists and outdoorsmen alike. Along much of the boundary of Garibaldi Provincial Park, for instance, the park begins at the point where logging stops— Douglas-fir gives way to the sub-alpine landscape. The Douglas-fir forest prefers a more moderate environment, avoiding the deeper snowpacks and colder winter temperatures of the higher elevations. Yet, despite the great ecological importance of low-lying valleys, most parks in

The brilliant red leaves of Canadian bunchberry. Ash from these leaves was used for medicinal purposes on cuts and sores by the Nlaka'pamux. (Photo: Scott Rowed)

British Columbia are banished to these higher, less economically valuable areas. Even there, they are blanketed with mining claims. As a result, this Douglas-fir biogeoclimatic type is greatly under-represented in the province's park system.[1]

Cedar Hollows

The variation in forest cover begins even in the extreme easterly portions of the valley. The hiker who leaves the scorchingly hot benches of the Fraser River en route up the Stein immediately descends into a moist, cool cedar hollow astride Stryen Creek. Several such cedar groves line the creeks that feed the lower Stein, such as Teaspoon and Earl Creeks. Rare in the dry lands east of the Coast divide, western red cedar abounds along these creek beds, becoming more abundant as one moves farther west in the watershed. They give the valley pockets of the rainforest feeling, and add to the valley's ability to support a great diversity of wildlife. In the western end of the valley, a full-fledged Coastal Western Hemlock (CWH) zone emerges from the Interior Douglas-fir zone. There, mixed stands of hemlock, cedar, spruce and fir provide a real coastal forest.

Floodplains

Special ecological communities develop on the sandbars and valley bottoms that are regularly flooded during the spring runoff. Not limited to any zone, these deciduous clusters are distinct from their coniferous surroundings; exuberant oases beside a clear running mountain river, a celebration of moisture and dense variety in a generally dry landscape.

The floodplain forests are dominated by the stately black cottonwood, mixed with aspen, birch, and coniferous western

Flooded cedar trees below
Stein Lake. (Photo: Leo
deGroot)

Central valley floodplain.
(Photo: Gary Fiegehen/
Robert Semeniuk)

97

Heather meadows of the
alpine area near Elton
Lake. (Photo: Kevin Oke)

Indian Paintbrush.
(Photo: Gunter Marx)

red cedar. Mountain alder is also common, and further west in the valley, Engelmann spruce may be found. In somewhat higher terraces that are less frequently flooded, the forest is a mix of the floodplain community and the surrounding coniferous forest.

The shrubs which form the understory of the floodplain community are tall and difficult to pass through, the willows and alder sometimes forming almost impenetrable thickets. Their luxuriant growth though becomes valuable habitat for grizzly bears, deer and moose in late spring and summer, as well as home to numerous bird species.

The Subalpine Mosaic

The subalpine zone is another kind of transition zone, but, unlike the transition zone for the Stein as a whole, it is one of higher elevation rather than greater distance from the coast. At higher elevations, one leaves the forest blanket in the valley, climbing through more sparsely wooded hillsides, and emerging finally onto the subalpine parkland where islands of stunted trees scatter across a meadowy landscape. In the subalpine, one is on the cusp between the forest below and the open alpine above.

Engelmann spruce and subalpine fir are dominant throughout much of the middle and higher elevations of the valley, such as in the upper reaches of Cottonwood and Scudamore creeks. This is the Montane Spruce (MS) and Engelmann Spruce-Subalpine Fir (ESSF) zones. Where fires are more frequent, such as on south-facing slopes, lodgepole pine abounds. In the drier, higher subalpine areas to the north and east, Engelmann spruce and small, gnarled whitebark pine are common. In the western Stein, coastal trees like amabilis fir, and hemlock are found.

Snow plays an important role in the sub-alpine. Small

Next morning we set out with the heavy backpacks. Arriving in the lean-to shelter well after sundown, Hicks complained that he had a stiff neck, arising from the hard trek over Jack Thompson's line. The next day Hicks would at times scream with pain. His neck muscles would knot up in bunches. I was at a loss for any aid I could offer, so I spent the whole day cutting firewood, and stacking it against the trees.

Early next morning I awakened. Hicks was now sleeping soundly. I packed a lunch, filled the bait bag, pulled on my snowshoes, and with axe in hand, started out to bail out the 15-mile-long south fork line.

The snowshoes twanged like banjo strings on the frozen trail, without making any marks in the snow. Taking off the snowshoes I learned that the previous packline was now solid and could be travelled on without the need of snowshoes. Now without the snowshoes to slow my gait, I dog-trotted from one trap to the next. The first two traps were not touched. The third one had a large dark marten. Taking the marten out of the trap, I placed it into the white sack, reset the trap, and re-baited it. There were 42 traps on this line. Some were untouched; others had two weasels, three flying squirrels, and three Jack Daws—a white type of crow. Resetting

and re-baiting the traps, the line had seven martens, five large and two small ones. It was still about two hours before nightfall. I had made the end of the line in about eight hours, and nearly half of this time spent in the resetting.

Taking the tin tea can along as proof that I was indeed at the end of the line, I started down the valley at a brisk jogging pace. As the daylight started to wane, Mount Roary came into view. About 20 minutes later I came upon my snowshoes, gathered them up, and within the next five minutes was in camp. Hicks was

Winter on the Cottonwood Creek divide at Texas Creek. (Photo: Leo deGroot)

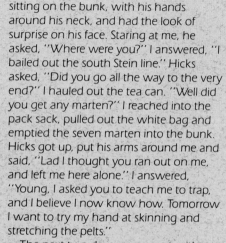

sitting on the bunk, with his hands around his neck, and had the look of surprise on his face. Staring at me, he asked, "Where were you?" I answered, "I bailed out the south Stein line." Hicks asked, "Did you go all the way to the very end?" I hauled out the tea can. "Well did you get any marten?" I reached into the pack sack, pulled out the white bag and emptied the seven marten into the bunk. Hicks got up, put his arms around me and said, "Lad I thought you ran out on me, and left me here alone." I answered, "Young, I asked you to teach me to trap, and I believe I now know how. Tomorrow I want to try my hand at skinning and stretching the pelts."

The next two days were spent with preparing the pelts. Hicks had recovered and now could trust me, as a partner, to manage the lines. He said, "Lad, we will take most of the grub up to the lake. I will pack it there and you run the line to the end and be sure you camp there. There is still some goat meat hanging. Bring it back on the return line, and then meet me at the head of the lake. We will bail out the marten line. The next two weeks, you can do that and I will trap beavers."

The next two weeks passed very quickly. Trapping is not a monotonous or humdrum task. When bailing out the traps, the eagerness to see if there is a marten in the next trap spurred us on, oblivious to time, and when the end of the line is reached, there may be

disappointment or delight of having scored a good catch or, as was often the case, nothing at all.

The last days of trapping marten were a delight. No baiting was necessary. If a marten was caught, he was bailed out and the trap was left, unset. When an empty set was passed a quick rap with a stick sprung the trap.

Hicks had little success at catching beaver at the head of the lake. The beavers had a large supply of wood stored and were reluctant to venture out of their lodges.

Hicks said, "We will stay another two days and if nothing is doing, we will go down to the Cottonwood." The next day a beaver got caught. This pleased Hicks. Now the entire day would be spent waiting for the next one to be caught. We walked through tall stately timber stands.

"If people would know about Mount Roary," Hicks said, "it is my firm belief that there is not another mountain like it anywhere else in the world. This mountain on a heavy snowfall will produce as many as 3 avalanches in 24 hours. These slides could be viewed, from the safety of well-built cabins. It can be an attraction as is the Yellowstone geyser, Old Faithful."

While walking to the upper beaver dam, a trail of small footprints was seen coming out of the small creek and headed back and forth to the side of the mountain. Following these tracks they led

changes in slope angle, elevation, and orientation to the sun make for large differences in the character of the vegetation. With increasing elevation, the forest thins as trees become restricted to areas of early snowmelt and better drainage. The trees tend to occur in clumps trailing along small ridges or on other raised areas. The dark trunks of the trees heat up faster than the snow surface, helping to produce the little craters around their base so often noticed by backcountry skiers. The shrubs generally cluster around the periphery of the tree islands, while the meadows between the tree clumps are dominated by heath in the west, and herbs in the east. This is a parkland setting, a striking mosaic of tree, shrub and flower.

Life At The Alpine Edge

Although lush in the summer when alpine flowers bloom in an extravaganza of crimson, yellow and blue, the alpine meadows are a harsh, snowy-white environment for all but two or three months of the year. The active stages of life—from spring shoot to summer wildflower to autumn seed—are packed into one short season between the snows. Even more than in subalpine areas, small changes in topography cause large changes in the character of the alpine communities which line the upper rim of the Stein watershed.

Few trees can live above 1800 metres (5900 feet) in this Alpine Tundra (AT) zone. Those that do are stunted and wind-sculpted, shaped more like prostrate shrubs than upright trees. They are low-lying, their protruding branches killed quickly from exposure to winter frost and wind. They occur in clusters called **krummholz** (German for "bent wood"), formed by subalpine fir, Engelmann spruce and whitebark pine. They are at the upper limit of tree growth. Above "treeline," only smaller plants tucked close to the ground can survive.

Heather meadows, or heaths, also sprawl across the alpine

Alpine tundra with krummholz in the foreground. (Photo: Robin Draper)

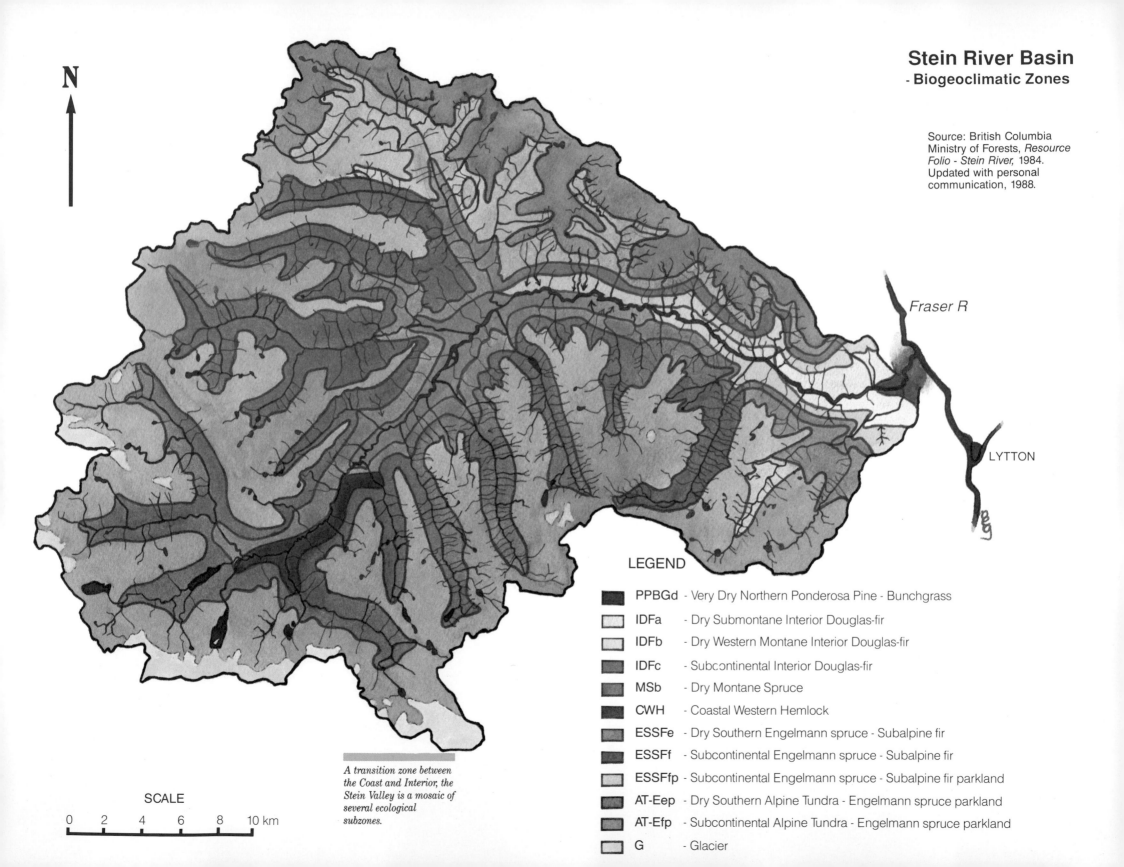

Stein River Basin
- Biogeoclimatic Zones

N

Source: British Columbia
Ministry of Forests, *Resource
Folio - Stein River,* 1984.
Updated with personal
communication, 1988.

Fraser R

LYTTON

*A transition zone between
the Coast and Interior, the
Stein Valley is a mosaic of
several ecological
subzones.*

SCALE

0   2   4   6   8   10 km

LEGEND

PPBGd - Very Dry Northern Ponderosa Pine - Bunchgrass

IDFa - Dry Submontane Interior Douglas-fir

IDFb - Dry Western Montane Interior Douglas-fir

IDFc - Subcontinental Interior Douglas-fir

MSb - Dry Montane Spruce

CWH - Coastal Western Hemlock

ESSFe - Dry Southern Engelmann spruce - Subalpine fir

ESSFf - Subcontinental Engelmann spruce - Subalpine fir

ESSFfp - Subcontinental Engelmann spruce - Subalpine fir parkland

AT-Eep - Dry Southern Alpine Tundra - Engelmann spruce parkland

AT-Efp - Subcontinental Alpine Tundra - Engelmann spruce parkland

G - Glacier

to a small goat carcass that had slipped in the loose snow and fallen down upon the rocks below. Two traps were set.

The next day each trap had a mink in it, and Hicks caught another beaver. The next day there were no more mink, and no more beaver. We packed up and headed down the valley and made camp about two miles below Jack Thompson's. The campfire was burning, the evening meal was finished. The Stein was below the campfire. The waters were very quiet and flowed smoothly.

Around a bend a mink came swimming upstream. Hicks grabbed his rifle, pumped a shell into the barrel. From only about 20 feet, Hicks fired. The bullet splat into the water two inches in front and an inch below the mink. The mink made a quick dive, and Hicks said, "A clean miss. I only wanted to hit him on the nose. I could have blown him to bits." The mink surfaced and began to swim around in a circle, then kicked furiously, stopped and the lifeless body floated downstream. I ran down the river's bank, jumped waist deep into the river and caught the mink as it floated by. Looking the mink over, there were no signs of any injury made by the rifle shot. But when the animal was skinned, it revealed a very tiny fragment of the nickel jacket bullet which had struck the mink in the side of the neck. It was imbedded about half an inch and had cut open the jugular vein. The mink simply bled to death. This lucky shot

compensated for the loss of a marten, which a wolverine stole, trap and all, on the upper end of the trapline.

The next two weeks were the most pleasant ones ever experienced by anyone that ever travelled in the Stein Valley. A mile beyond Walter Isaac's camp, a lay of land facing the sun was warmed earlier than any other parts of the valley. There are about a thousand acres of rich orchard land. Hicks remarked, "What a beautiful peach orchard this would make." The hooting of the mating blue grouse, the drumming of partridge, squirrels chattering — these sounds were all around us. Hicks said, "All my life I never killed anything for sport. God has created these creatures for man's needs, but not for pleasures or greeds." Being the son of a Methodist minister, Hicks led a saintly life in the wilds.

While Hicks was trapping beavers, I would be contented to spear white fish and trout, always being pleased to catch from two to four fair-sized fish.

Another week went by. Hicks said, "If I don't catch another beaver, we will leave for home." The traps were empty, and true to his word, the next day Hicks hung up all the cooking utensils, his snowshoes and axe. Taking along his rifle with a large but light pack, walking down the Stein Valley without the need of snowshoes made travel a pleasure.

Words could never describe the emotional feelings that I had, as a young

18 year old, looking back at the Cottonwood cabin that was home to me. I now had learned a trade. I only knew how to farm on the prairies. But I believed I had burned the bridges behind me. Having run away, I was reluctant to return home to my parents, and was now determined to earn my own living. Hicks was a much older man than my father, being 38 years my senior, or old enough to be my grandfather. I was thankful that Hicks had provided for me, and had passed on 40 years of outdoor life experience.

On the way down to Lytton, Hicks pointed out the Indian paintings, telling me that he believed they were about 200 years old. Hicks said, "It can easily be determined. One drawing showed a two masted ship. So, all one had to do was look back into history, and find out when such kind of ships sailed past the land." Another picture showed a man with a dip net. But at no time was a drawing of a gun made.

We stopped at the Hotel, washing our clothes and getting hair cuts. Hicks left me at the hotel, while he went to

Vancouver to sell his catch of furs. On his return, he told me "Look lad, here is $50.00. You said you did not expect anything. But you proved your worth to me, more than you will ever know. When you went over the south fork of the Stein line, I thought that you had run out on me, and me with a sore neck and all. I want to give you sound advice. Go back to your home. You are too valuable to leave a paying farm such as your parents have. I am sure your father has regretted his rash judgment of you."

Hicks said, "I won't be trapping the Stein next year. Trapping an area is like any other livestock farming. You must let the animals increase, and this can only be done by giving them at least a rest." We shook hands. Hicks said, "You were the best companion I ever have had—and that includes both of my younger brothers."

We parted company. I never saw Young Easter Hicks again. Hicks lost his life in 1948 in the big flood that struck the Fraser Valley. It caught Hicks while asleep.

Well-known Stein trapper, Walter Isaac, with packhorses on Stein ridge. (Photograph courtesy of Rita Stewart, Lytton, British Columbia)

landscape, especially in the wetter, high snowfall areas of the western Stein. More spectacular than the subtle colours of the heather flowers (but less resilient to the impacts of backcountry travellers) are those herb meadows that blossom in a riot of colours from mid-July to mid-August, especially on the northern drainages of the Stein: Scudamore, Cottonwood and Ponderosa creeks. From yellow glacier lilies, anemones, and buttercups in mid-July, to Indian paintbrush, lupine, cinquefoil in August, to sunflowers, daisies, ragwort, arnicas and alpine sage at the end of the season, the moist, flat slopes of the high alpine meadow are a kaleidoscope of colours and hues.

Pushing still further out to the ecological edge is the true alpine tundra of even higher and more exposed sites. Lacking in soil, windswept and dry, this area hosts special plants like moss campion and alpine pussytoes which have adopted a flat cushion to reduce moisture and heat loss. This fragile vegetation is striking not for its colour or lushness, but for its very ability to persist in the face of such extreme conditions. One should visit this powerful landscape, but treat it gently.

A Modern Intrusion?

Through the ages of traditional Native use, and even after decades of trapping in this century, the Stein has survived, its ecology and wildlife intact. The valley now stands on the threshold of a more intensive usage than it has ever seen, and its survival is in jeopardy. Road-building and logging would transform the valley irrevocably. Inappropriate recreational uses would also have serious impacts.

Opponents of the industrial development of the Stein are probably just as concerned over the effects of the proposed road-building as they are about the logging to follow. Road construction can trigger catastrophic slides of huge volumes of soil and rock. Just one such slide could deposit many times the amount normally deposited in the river over many years. One study of two Oregon watersheds found that roads triggered 41 times the number of debris torrents in one, and 130 times the number in the other when compared to those occurring in the natural state.[2] Once this material is deposited, it accumulates in slow-moving pools and covers the porous gravels where fish spawn.

In the first 30 kilometres (19 miles) of the mainline logging road planned for the Stein, there are three major rock slide areas, 14 snow avalanche sites, and 20 debris slide areas.[3] In at least 12 locations, less than 50 metres (165 feet) stands between the river bank and the side of the V-shaped valley

Truck on logging haulroad. A logging road planned for the Stein Valley would traverse the river's entire length, having an impact as serious as the logging that would follow. (Photo: Jeff Gibbs)

Hundreds of large boulders strewn throughout the lower canyon offer a source of amazement to hikers, but pose a nagging obstacle to road engineers. (Photo: Dennis Darragh)

The steep walls of the lower canyon make road-building in the valley an environmentally hazardous task. (Photo: Robert Semeniuk/Gary Fiegehen)

Cut and burned slash is all that remains of a creek bed in a valley just north of the Stein near Duffey Lake. (Photo: Clinton Webb)

wall for the road to be placed. Moreover, "blasting is required for much of the construction through steep slopes."[4]

Roads change the flow of water even where slides don't occur. Ditches and culverts channel water into new gullies. Fill placed in the river changes the shape of the channel, usually speeding the flow, hastening riverbank erosion, and making it more difficult for fish to move upstream. The road itself can act as a dam, obstructing natural flows and creating a whole series of barriers throughout the valley bottom. The road proposed for the Stein must pass through three major swamp areas. The compacted surfaces of the roads would also be significant sources of sediment in the rivers, through runoff and even from the dust caused by passing traffic. The very presence of the road increases dramatically both the likelihood

of fires caused by visitors, and the over-exploitation of the fish and wildlife.

As experience elsewhere has shown, an access road would lead to the defacing of many pictograph sites even if the sites are not directly affected by construction. By breaching the integrity of the natural valley, the spiritual context of the pictographs would be irreversibly damaged, rather as if a cathedral were converted to a bowling alley, with the individual icons left standing at the side.

Logging adds another level of disruption. When the slopes are forested, the trees and layers of plant litter diffuse the impact of the falling rain. Remove the trees, and the rainwater which previously filtered down into the soil now flows over it, eroding the surface and flowing into the streams where the sediment it carries clogs fish-spawning channels. Both the speed and volume of the runoff increases after clear-cutting, causing river levels to peak more quickly, literally flushing out juvenile and spawning fish from hitherto quiet side channels. With less moisture retained in the soil, and with logging slash accumulated on the hillside, the vulnerability to fire increases as well. With less moisture retained, the vegetation changes, decimating wild plants such as the pine and cottonwood mushrooms so prized by the Nlaka'pamux.

A Harmonious Intrusion?

The Stein Valley's isolation and preserved state, its majestic scenery, moderate climate, low elevation river, and varied forest cover make it attractive for many recreational activities. The warm season in the river valley is unusually long—March through October—making it one of the only sizable hiking locations in southern British Columbia available during several months of the year. The gradual trail makes it suitable for the young and old, novice and experienced

106

A Measure Of Growth

It is growth that coils at the heart of this deep green world. It has been as many as a thousand years since some of the oldest trees in the forests of the Pacific Northwest first sprouted—many of them from the rich and rotting trunks of other thousand-year-old tees that had fallen, death servicing the needs of life.

There are plenty of fallen trees in the present forests, too, and many of these are also very old. It can take half a millennium for a great dead tree to fully decompose, and along the way it gives sustenance not only to seedlings, but to crowded generations of other living things—trillions of bacteria; billions of mosses, ferns, and fungi; millions of worms and insects; thousands of salamanders and voles. While it lasts, each dead and fallen tree is a kind of island where the rhythms of growth are ceaselessly repeated. That is the way of forests: from the slime mold on the bottom of a rock to the tangled canopy of treetops that splits the sun into fingers of light, these enclaves are living demonstrations of all that growth can accomplish.

It is the way of humankind, however, to cut them down more often than not. We have been cutting them down in the Pacific Northwest ever since the nineteenth century, when two-man whipsaw teams felled the great trees with superhuman labour: when ox-teams skidded the bucked logs out of the forests and down to the rivers or the railroads for transport to the mills; when sawn boards filled the holds and piled the decks of the sleek lumber schooners . . .

The cutting does not take place in the dead of night; it is planned and programmatic, endorsed by the highest authorities, and a lot more of it is scheduled for the future. Conservationists call the cut and threatened stands "old growth forests," and protest their disappearance; timber people call them "decadent forests" and celebrate the straight grained lumber they produce. So far, it is the timber people who prevail. In another generation or so, there will be precious little to argue about: most of the ancient forests, and the wildlife populations in them, will be gone.

We will have lost the growth of centuries, an irreplaceable storehouse of diversity and genetic richness whose importance we have not yet even learned to measure. That is worth mourning. So is another loss, in its own way one quite as important to our species. In making the decision to destroy these last forests in spite of what we know, in consciously repeating the careless traditions that have brought these remnants of biological time to the edge of extinction, we will have lost the opportunity for another kind of growth: our own.

T.H. Watkins,"A Measure of Growth," *Wilderness*, Spring 1988, p.17.

Cut, Slash And Burn

[Forests] influence temperature, rainfall, humidity and wind . . . The forest canopy breaks the force of heavy rains, allowing water to drop gently to the forest floor, where it is absorbed by spongy soil and stored . . .

Fibrous, interwoven roots of trees and shrubs bind soil to the earth's rocky skeleton, maintaining the vital soil base that has taken centuries to accumulate.

Bare soil, as is found after clear-cutting, will absorb as little as 5,500 gallons of rain per hour per acre. The rate for soil covered by grass or shrubby vegetation may surpass 25,500 gallons per acre, and soil covered by forests will readily absorb four to five inches of rain, more than 100,000 gallons per acre.

During a gentle rainfall of about 0.4 inches (1 centimetre) of rain per hour, up to 17 inches of water, or more than 400,000 gallons per acre may be retained in the ground . . .

We have profligate waste that leaves gutted landscapes, bared, torn up soil and massive piles of slash for burning. Resulting slash fires often produce so much heat that soil organic matter is effectively destroyed. What makes such fires unusually severe is that the fuel is directly over the soil, whereas in forest fires, much of the fire is in the crowns of the trees and often leaves large-diameter trunks standing and sometimes alive . . . This increased fuel sometimes produces hot burns that may reach 800 to 1,000 degrees Celsius, destroying soil matter and resulting in the critical loss of nitrogen . . . Studies have disclosed that it would take free-living, nitrogen-fixing bacteria up to 800 years to replace the nitrogen loss in a single slash burn.

Robert F. Harrington. "Cut, slash and burn," *The Globe and Mail*, Toronto, 4 June, 1988, p. 7.

Teaspoon Creek. (Photo: Gary Fiegehen/Robert Semeniuk)

backpacker alike. With access from the mouth or over the ridge from the logging roads in adjacent valleys, the area offers low and high elevation travel, of lengths varying from day-trips to two-week wilderness treks. Many of the high ridges provide easy and highly scenic hiking above untouched forested landscapes below. The combination of pristine environment, healthy fish and wildlife, and unaltered Native heritage sites is virtually unknown for such a southern latitude in Canada.

The headwater lakes area offers a "wide variety of outstanding features related to alpine meadows, lakes, waterfalls and geologic occurrences. All of these features are of an extremely high scenic quality."[5] However, this area cannot be viewed in isolation from the upper main valley and side valleys (especially the North Stein) which are seen from these headwater alpine areas. These natural views would be destroyed by roads and logging scars. In addition, the attractiveness of the area is enhanced by its connection with the rest of the river valley. The week-long traverse (a journey through the valley from one end to the other) is fast becoming one of the valley's most popular attractions, similar to that of the now over-used West Coast Trail. Such continuous journeys—especially where one passes through an entire sequence of vegetation zones without leaving a wild setting— are a rare experience in our heavily-developed modern landscape.

The middle and lower reaches of the valley also offer

unique features. The variety and lushness of the habitats in the middle Stein make it an excellent area for wildlife observation. At several spots, the slow-moving, lake-like river is ideal for family camping and relaxation. Throughout this area, excellent fishing still exists. Above all, the lower canyon—with almost flat trail, steep canyon walls, whitewater rapids, open pine benchlands, side creeks and cool cedar hollows, as well as numerous archaeological sites—provides a stunning wilderness and cultural experience. Yet it does this in an hospitable climate and safe terrain that suits the novice well. And it is all within easy walking distance of the road at the river's mouth. Three hours from Vancouver, this is one of the very best accessible wilderness camping opportunities available in southern British Columbia.

Minor improvements in facilities could support recreational use while still maintaining the watershed's wilderness character. Campgrounds, trails, a hut-to-hut system of shelters in some areas, even a lodge and interpretation centre on the valley's periphery, would be popular with tourists and local outdoors people, both Native and non-Native. This system would have a long snow-free season, while also being attractive for cross-country skiers on clear trails in winter.

There is, though, a fine line between encouraging use, and ruining the very wilderness people are attracted to. Recreational use poses hazards, though proper management of the area can minimize these problems. One factor above all others poses the greatest environmental threat—road access. Limiting access to those willing to go on foot (or, possibly, with packhorses) serves as a well-proven device to screen out the ecologically less-sensitive visitor. Rifles and beer cans do not ride well in the heavy pack of the hiker; vandalism is a product of roadside convenience. Moreover, roadside recreationists already have abundant opportunities in the region, whereas only a single opportunity remains for those wishing a more natural experience. If the environmental and cultural history of this last large wilderness watershed is to survive into the future, one thing will make the difference: making the valley accessible in the way which it has always been, on foot.

Horse-packing expeditions in the Stein have been common throughout the valley's recent history. Here a group of tourists is led into the valley. (Photo: Adrian Dorst)

PART

III

THE JOURNEY TO HERE

Boulders beside the trail in the lower Stein Valley. (Painting: Stephen Fick)

Two Nlaka'pamux sisters, Hilda Austin (foreground) and Millie Michell. (Photo: Thom Henley)

Exported worldwide under this historic label, the quality of apples from Earlscourt near the Stein attests to the great agricultural capabilities of well-managed benchlands along the Fraser and Thompson Rivers. (Label courtesy of Victor Spencer, Vancouver)

The deep mountain gorge of the Stein River is visible from any street corner in Lytton. Over the last century, this panorama has stood as a silent backdrop to the booms and busts of the farms and settlements along the Fraser and Thompson Rivers. Against this setting, the people of Kumsheen have struggled for a hundred years, so far without success, to create a stable new community on the hillside. Today, that great cut in the mountains may hold the answer to the stability that has been elusive for so long.

After The Railroad

With the CPR rails in place by 1886, Kumsheen was irrevocably tied into the new world of international trade and commerce. But how it was going to fit into that new world was still very much an open question. With its productive agricultural benchland, rich mineral deposits, and stupendous mountain scenery, prospects appeared good. In those days, the town had much to draw on. And it would soon need these resources since the very railroad which brought the world economy to Lytton cut off, then replaced, the old Cariboo road from Vancouver which had connected Lytton to the coast since shortly after the Gold Rush. From 1886 to 1927, Lytton depended completely on traffic by rail for its contact with the outside world.

Agriculture quickly became the area's primary industry, with reports year after year of huge harvests of fruit, vegetables and seeds. Ma Murray, the famous editor of the **Bridge River-Lillooet News**, wrote that Lytton in that period was "the cradle of the interior orchard industry."[1] The first commercial apple orchard was on the benchland by the Stein at Earlscourt, and its owner, Thomas Earl, was the Interior's first fruit inspector. With the many gardeners, labourers, pickers and packers it employed, Earlscourt was the economic and social hub of a prosperous local industry. The superb quality of its apples was known as far away as London, England. Twenty-five railcar loads of apples were exported from that one farm in 1905, while Kumsheen's Native population exported 10 to 12 carloads of beans and potatoes from the local reserves. This was a strong farming community.

Mining, on a smaller scale and at a slower pace, was still an employer for decades after the Gold Rush. On Van Winkle flats adjacent to the Stein, the Van Winkle Bar Hydraulic Co. of Vancouver made significant investments in the 1890s, and gold dredging was active on the Fraser in the early 1900s.

A second railroad boom, however, took over Lytton with the construction of the Canadian National Railway from 1911 to 1914. The town's population rose, counting some 5,000 people for a time. Eleven sawmills operated in the far-flung Lillooet district, serving both the CNR and the new Pacific Great Eastern railway being constructed through Lillooet. With little memory of the consequences of the CPR boom 30 years earlier, optimism reigned. But as before, with the completion of construction, payrolls dried up and businesses pulled out, throwing the town back on its own resources, especially its farms.

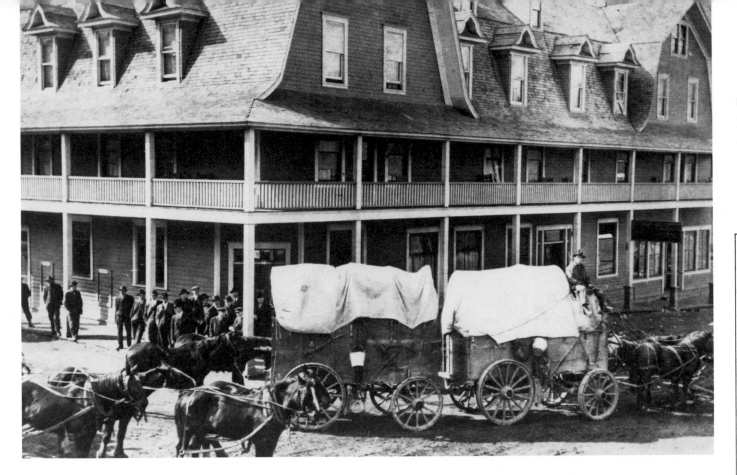

Freight wagons ran regularly between Lytton and Lillooet. This wagon is pictured in front of the Globe Hotel as it rounds the corner on Main Street, Lytton. (Photograph courtesy of the Village of Lytton, British Columbia)

Everyone Busy At Lytton

J.H. Anthony's store is now nearly completed and he will shortly move into his new quarters, where he will be able to accommodate his trade in a much more efficient manner . . . Lytton now boasts of four pool rooms and each are [sic] apparently doing a good business. The butcher shop is still in full swing under the management of C. Meinel, and is now doing a good business both in town and in the camps . . . The new general store built on the Mckay block has started under the supervision of Mr. Robinson . . . The new hotel being erected by Alphonse Hautier, is now nearing completion . . .

The Prospector, Lillooet, British Columbia, 11 December 1911.

Neglecting The Natives

Despite their active participation in farming, life in the new cash economy was not easy for the Natives of Kumsheen. Working largely as migrant labour for the railroads, in distant canneries, and on local White farms, Natives moved frequently from job to job, often abandoning their homes in large numbers during the farming season. They were a "much needed class of labour,"[2] pulled into the wage economy at its lowest levels, becoming increasingly dependent on it at the expense of their traditional subsistence activities. Making their own farms productive was a constant struggle as well, particularly as they were often cut off from water for irrigation. This was particularly true for the Stryen reserve where many complaints of discriminatory treatment were heard during the 1914 Royal Commission on Indian Affairs—

The Fraser Sees Another Boom

Exactly fifty-six years from the first rush of '58 in the month of April, I sat on the banks of the Fraser at Yale and pointed across the rapids in a flat-bottomed boat and swirled in and out among the eddies of the famous bars. A Siwash family lived there by fishing with clumsy wicker baskets. Higher up could be seen some Chinamen, but whether they were fishing or washing, we could not tell. Two transcontinental railroads skirted the canyon, one on each side, and the tents of a thousand construction workers stood where once were the camps of the gold-seekers banded together for protection . . .

Agnes Laut, *The Cariboo Trail,* Toronto: Glasgow, Brook & Co., 1916, p.14.

Indians panned for gold along the banks of the Fraser and Thompson Rivers through the 1800s and early 1900s. (Photograph courtesy of the Royal British Columbia Museum, Victoria)

Sides Fighting For Land

I am only a young man, and was put in as chief here, but I have been asked to come forward and speak to you folks and tell you how poor we are on my Reserve. We have a very large Reserve marked out for us, but there is very little of that land that is fit for cultivation. The rest is very stony. Besides that, we haven't any water. There is a good creek, with plenty of water in it, but it is so deep. I mean the hillside, that we cannot raise the water up to our Reserve, and it is so rocky that we cannot do anything with it. And I would be very pleased if you would help us to get water up on our Reserve . . . The two acres that I cultivate is on the Government land, and the Reserve land is stony and hilly, and I can't cultivate any of it.

Chief Jimmy Justice addresses members of the the Royal Commission on Indian Affairs for the Province of British Columbia, in Lytton, Friday, 13 November 1914.

poor land, absence of water, a dangerous road to their reserve because of a dilapidated bridge across the Stein River, even the loss of access to their own Stein trail because White farmers had fenced it off.

Some of these problems were rectified; access into the Stein was assured. In the development of the region, however, the solutions to the "Indian problem" often made matters worse. The most notorious instance of this was the opening of the Anglican Indian residential school, St. George's, on the eastern banks of the Fraser River.

This school taught some very valuable skills for life as a farmer or rancher. But the lessons came at great cost. For several generations, Native youth have been intentionally cut off from their own people and their ways by White educational authorities. For decades after the school opened in 1901, Native reserves were devoid of children for some 49 weeks a year. Use of the Native language was also forbidden at school, on pain of punishment by whipping. Through compulsory

attendance at this school, it was illegal for children to spend that time with the elders, in the mountains and by the river, that has kept Native culture whole.

The Boom During The Depression Years

In 1927, the opening of the Alexandra Bridge reactivated the Cariboo Road and introduced a boom along the Fraser River stretching right up to Barkerville. The resulting "progress and development," Ma Murray wrote 40 years later, "was unbelievable. Resorts for tourists sprang up all along the line."[3] With the road link to Vancouver re-established, the area around the Stein became a closer component of the regional economy based in the Lower Mainland. This was the first time that the Lytton economy became truly diversified, supplying a variety of goods for local, regional and international consumption. While the outside world staggered through the Depression and Second World War, the new economy at Kumsheen worked well.

The Cariboo Road in 1930. (Photograph courtesy of the Diocese of Cariboo Archives, Kamloops, British Columbia)

Cariboo Highway B.C. 18 Miles east of Yale

No 1.

Lytton townfathers overseeing road construction on Jackass Mountain, 1927. (Photograph courtesy of the National Museums of Canada, Ottawa)

Main Street, Lytton, 1920s. The fire of 1931 destroyed 23 buildings. (Photograph courtesy of the Vancouver Public Library, Vancouver)

Native girls in the dormitory of St. George's School, a stark and lonely transition from life at home, circa 1950. (Photograph courtesy of Ron Purvis, Lillooet, British Columbia)

Branding cattle at the old Stein Village, circa 1900. (Photograph courtesy of   *Rita Haugen, Lytton, British Columbia)*

Where Have All The Children Gone?

All the children that are of school age have been sent to St. George's and the girls have been sent to All Halla [Old Hallow's School at Yale] . . . I reckon that the children of that age [between six and fourteen] are all at school . . . [T]he Indians are not satisfied at that school [St. George's]. They see their children running away all the time and they cannot find out the reason why . . . The children run up on the hills—they don't go home. One of the reasons I am sorry for is I think some of the children might freeze to death when they run up on the mountains . . .

Head Chief Paul Klawaskut addresses the members of the Royal Commission on Indian Affairs for the Province of British Columbia, in Lytton, Friday, 13 November 1914.

The Hance family circa 1910-20, at their farm at "16-Mile" (16 miles upriver from Lytton along the west side of the   *Fraser). They have traditionally run their cattle up Siwhe Creek and into Cattle Valley at the top end of Cottonwood*   *Creek. (Photograph courtesy of Graham Everett, Lytton, British Columbia)*

Agriculture was still the primary industry. Earlscourt Farm was a hive of activity, producing its renowned apples, winery grapes and, increasingly, alfalfa seeds for export. A packing house was built on the property, and the goods were loaded into boxcars at Winch's Spur alongside the CNR main line. In 1920, Colonel Victor Spencer obtained the farm when he married Gertrude Winch, the only daughter of Mr. Earl's successor at Earlscourt, R.V. Winch. From the 1920s to the 1950s, Earlscourt supplied the large Spencer store in Vancouver as well as the overseas market. Almost all of the Stein people worked on this magnificent farm, and were proud of it.

Throughout this period, mining remained Lytton's second industry, and prospectors worked the Stein. In 1926, a westside native, Jimmie Johnson, discovered gold in Stryen Creek and staked out a mine which produced some ore in the 1930s. Between 1927 and 1930, Urban Easter Hicks staked the Silver Queen mine high in the alpine meadows of Cottonwood Creek. Serviced by the trail up the Stein, the first bridge at the site of the present cable crossing was built to gain access to this mine in the 1930s. After it was washed out by high water in 1937, a second bridge was built in 1942 by Urban Easter Hicks, Jimmie Johnson, and Walter Isaac. In 1948, it too was washed out. Despite this activity in the Stein, the mainstay of mining for Lytton was still the Fraser with its dredges and placer operations.

The 1920s and 1930s were also years of renewed commercial fur-trading, when renowned local names like Adam Klein, Young and Urban Easter Hicks, Jimmie and Joseph Justice, Albert and Henry Hance, Walter Isaac, Jack Thompson, Raymond Dunstan, as well as Charlie Mack and Baptiste Ritchie of Mt. Currie trapped in the Stein. This trapping provided many families with a consistent livelihood until the market for furs crashed in 1938.

The most significant change in the local economy was brought about by the new road which carried an influx of tourists eager to explore the ranchland and the wild spaces of the province's Interior. In 1934, at the depth of the Depression, the **Bridge River-Lillooet News** reported that "tourist traffic is steadily increasing and it looks as though a busy summer lay ahead of Lytton."[4] As it had been in the Gold Rush, Lytton again became an essential stopover point at the head of the Fraser Canyon on the only route into the Interior. Everything went through it. Yet tourists did not just stop out of necessity, but were very much attracted to "this town with a future" because of its "magnificent gardens and fruit orchards" and its location beside one of the most dramatic river junctions in the world.[5] Despite a major fire in 1931 that destroyed some of the town's finest buildings, the economy was strong. In February 1937, the local newspaper reported that only 12 people were unemployed in Lytton.

The "Depression" Of The Boom Years

Soon after the end of the war, after 25 years of prosperity, the economy began to falter. While agriculture remained the area's primary industry, its character changed. The old products, such as apples, beans, and winery grapes, were labour intensive (providing income for many local families) but were, therefore, costly to produce compared with the new agribusiness farms in California. Despite attempts to encourage the grape industry (it being well suited to the soil and climate of the area), fruits and vegetables were gradually

A Stein Homesteading Fiasco

Ricky started to farm at the mouth of Scudamore Creek in 1912. He cleared about 8 acres and built a cabin and a small barn. In the spring of 1913 he went out to Lytton for supplies. He left his wife and two small children at his homestead. He got a wood tick in his head by his spine and went paralysed. The Indians took him to the Lytton Hospital and then shipped him to Vancouver. He died there, his speech paralysed. His wife stayed at his cabin. Two Indians, Molly and Billy Cisco, went hunting in the fall and found this wild woman. They hauled the three of them out to Lytton by canoe halfway and then backpacked the kids from Canoe Landing to Lytton.

"History of the Stein River" by Jimmie Johnson, unpublished manuscript, courtesy of Eileen McWilliams, Lytton, British Columbia.

A Sportsman's Paradise

Not many years ago Lillooet was a sportsman's paradise. We had 20 guides making a good living. They could take their parties out [from here to what is known as Duffey Lake, at the head of Cayoosh Creek; from there to Harrison Lake, north from there to Lytton and back to Lillooet] and see hundreds of goats in herds of 100 or more each; several hundred deer, hundreds of sheep, and other game, all in a day's trip.

A.W. Phair, *Bridge River-Lillooet News*, March 1950.

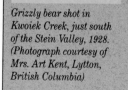

Grizzly bear shot in Kwoiek Creek, just south of the Stein Valley, 1928. (Photograph courtesy of Mrs. Art Kent, Lytton, British Columbia)

Harry Thom (Kanu), from Spapium, on the west side, preparing to guide hunters into the Stein. (Photograph courtesy of Howard Thom, Lillooet, British Columbia)

phased out. Farming gave way to ranching, and fields of alfalfa replaced acres of orchard trees. These new endeavours employed fewer people, and were not profitable for the small family acreages held by most Native and non-Native farmers.

Even with these changes, however, Earlscourt prospered under Colonel Spencer's astute management. Recognizing the need to maintain a quality stock of breed cattle, Spencer imported purebred Herefords from England via supply ships returning during the war. He built up a large herd, and from his Earlscourt base supplied his other ranches: the Pavilion Ranch near Lillooet, the 350,000-acre Circle S ranch at Dog Creek, and the 650,000-acre Douglas Lake Ranch in the Nicola Valley (later sold to the Woodward family). In a rapidly changing agricultural marketplace dominated by centralized producers from Washington and California, Colonel Spencer adapted well. Some years before his death in 1960, Spencer sold his Vancouver business to the T. Eaton Company. Earlscourt was sold to an American missionary, Raymond Mundall. This spelled an end to the century-long economic mainstay of Kumsheen.

Another cornerpost had been knocked out from the town's economic foundations, in 1950, with the opening of a second southerly route to the Interior—the Hope-Princeton highway. This highway offered a more direct route to the Okanagan valley, which was quickly becoming the province's premier inland tourist destination. By 1964, the Fraser Canyon highway was upgraded, eliminating Lytton as a necessary stopping point. Tourism began to die, the new highway higher up on the hillside now bypassing the town. Some stalwarts fought the trend, most notably Adam Klein, who opened a tourist manor, and spent several years attempting to improve the trails in the Stein with a view to starting a tourist

The mansion at Earlscourt Farm, built by R.V. Winch in about 1910. (Photograph courtesy of Barbara Bruce, Kelowna, British Columbia)

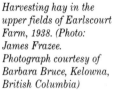

Harvesting hay in the upper fields of Earlscourt Farm, 1938. (Photo: James Frazee. Photograph courtesy of Barbara Bruce, Kelowna, British Columbia)

Better Than California

Year after year from the little town of Lytton, 160 miles by motor from Vancouver, some 300 carloads of farmstuffs have been shipped. Apples, potatoes, alfalfa, onions, beans and roots—these are the commodities which make up the freight consignments . . .

Mangolds, fifty tons to the acre; potatoes, twenty tons to the acre—these are commonplace crops at Lytton . . . "Better than California!" was what father used to say, stated Mr. Adolph Hautier, veteran hotel man of Lytton, in referring to farm prospects thereabouts. "Father was here before the Cariboo rush of the sixties was underway," continued Mr. Hautier. "He had been south and north and everywhere and he had never found a finer place than Lytton. The land will grow anything if you can get water on it . . ."

George Murray, *The Province*, 8 July 1933, p.4.

Earlscourt Sold

All of them farms through there [the West Side of the Fraser], I don't know what happened. They all dried up. Ever since Earlscourt sold out, looks like everybody sold out. We used to go across the river on this side. Go up to Lillooet way. Used to see places here green right up to Lillooet.

Willy Justice, Nlaka'pamux elder, August 1985.

The Governor General of Canada, Viscount Alexander of Tunis, being greeted by Colonel J. Victor Spencer at the CNR whistle stop, "Winch's Spur," on a visit to Earlscourt Farm in 1946. (Photograph courtesy of Barbara Bruce, Kelowna, British Columbia)

The Governor General inspecting one of Colonel Spencer's prize Hereford bulls during his stay at Earlscourt farm, 1946. (Photograph courtesy of Barbara Bruce, Kelowna, British Columbia)

business there for wealthy Americans. But Klein's vision was ahead of his time.

The 1950s and 1960s were hard on small rural communities. These were the decades of "bigger is best"— faster cars and super highways, sprawling cities and higher buildings, multinational companies and big government. This was the dawning of the age of the megaproject, boom projects that were the powerhouses of the postwar international economy. Every town hung its hopes on attracting one of these projects. The "boom that was the daddy of them all" came to Lillooet in the form of the Mission Mountain Hydro Project, and between 1949 and 1959, the construction of the dams, diversion pipes, and power facilities pumped $69 million into the Lillooet economy. [6]

This project too "left Lillooet more impoverished than it ever was." [7] The change was structural, for the local economy had become increasingly dependent on distant employers, be it the Pacific Great Eastern railway (now BC Rail), BC Electric, or the provincial Highways department. Scarcely any wealth was generated locally. Geothermal power from the Lillooet valley, coal developments at Hat Creek east of Lillooet, a heavy water plant at Lillooet, even a dam on the Fraser River were envisioned as possible megaproject saviours of the local economy, none of which materialized. Meanwhile, with tourism in decline and agriculture changing, local small business began to shrink.

There was little room for the local Native workers in this centralized new economy. Without access to a market, farm families fell into unemployment and onto welfare. There was less and less call for the seasonal labour that had once been a main source of cash for the Native economy. Electricity, sewage, and other services on the reserves were underfunded and in poor condition. In a chronic state of disrepair, the Stein bridge finally collapsed in 1946, killing Amelia Justice from the Stryen reserve. A fire in the 1960s wiped out the Stein village, leaving only the Stein church standing. With the death of the old village, the church ceased holding services about 1965.

The postwar boom passed Kumsheen right by. In 1966, the local member of the provincial legislature advised Lyttonites that it was not a disgrace to designate the district as a "distressed area." Distressed it was, not only because of the immediate problems of abandoned buildings and grinding unemployment, but because the healthy, diversified economy that had developed in the 1930s and 1940s had been lost. In the 1930s, 300 rail carloads of farmstuffs were exported from the town every year! By the 1960s, Lytton had virtually stopped producing local goods and supplies for the larger region, becoming dependent instead on large and remote organizations. With local industry moribund, whatever money came into the community went right out again to buy food and consumer items not from local farms and businesses, but from California or Japan. In 1965, the diversity of business in Lytton was a fraction of that existing 80 years earlier. This was a depressed economy, vulnerable to outside changes, with very little local control over its destiny.

The New Saviour?

One more resource waited to be exploited, however—the

Ahead Of His Time

The Cypress Manor is going full blast again after the winter lay-off. Mr. Klein is also busy with his Stein River Trail. From the sound of it, it's going to be one of the musts for sightseers around the Lytton area. If it develops as Mr. Klein plans, the 20-mile trail will carry tourists in to view the wonders of Indian writings of long ago on rock walls, as well as the breath-taking beauty of the valley itself. He has two miles completed already with more to come.

Lytton Leader, 6 May 1965.

Convinced of the potential of the Stein . . . Klein moved to Lytton and proceeded to build Cypress Manor as a resort base for tourists to explore the Stein . . . [With] 23 rooms, conservatory, swimming pool, [it was] "the dream of a prairie boy come true."

Lytton Leader, Supplement to the *Bridge River-Lillooet News*, 17 December 1964.

Klein's Cabin, near the cable crossing, built by Adam Klein and his son in 1953. (Photo: Gary Fiegehen/Robert Semeniuk)

St. David's (Stryen) Church congregation, in 1961 with Bishop Ralph Dean and Reverend Stanley Leach. (Photograph courtesy of Graham Everett, Lytton, British Columbia)

year after year. By the 1950s, companies turned their sights from the shrinking coastal forests to the largely untapped stands of the Interior Plateau.

Small lumber mills had been utilized throughout the Lytton and Lillooet area from the first colonisation in the 1850s. Many were actually located away from towns in the woods because of the difficulty of hauling uncut logs out of the steep, high mountain valleys. The loggers' market was local: lumber for houses and hotels, ties and trestles for the railroad. The pattern of several transient, owner-operator mills scattered throughout the forest, and supplying the local market continued right into the 1960s.

With the industry's shift of geographic focus, however, this pattern changed quickly. In 1961, 22 mills operated in the Lillooet area, and forestry surpassed mining as the town's major industry, with over 18 million board feet of lumber being cut and marketed. The Forest Service opened up valley after valley with new roads, making it physically and economically feasible for larger and more centralized mills to develop. New stands were opened up in Slok Creek north of town, and Duffey Lake to the west. In Lytton, the announcement of a new planer mill for the town in 1964 was the best news in years. Originally employing 25 people, Spatzum (later Lytton) Lumber quickly became the town's new economic mainstay and its hope for escaping the depression in which the town was mired.

The most productive mill was, however, the Hampton mill in Boston Bar south of Lytton. Bought in 1953 by an American from Portland, this large operation already employed over 200 people in the 1960s. After substantial rebuilding from 1971 to 1973, it produced lumber in even greater quantities so that it could take better advantage of "economies of scale." This was the key to success in the international marketplace—mass production that achieves low

forests. Forestry had been the province's most important industry since the turn of the century, and it had grown exponentially after the United States introduced restrictions on domestic timber harvesting in the early 1900s. The fuel for this growth was the rich stands of fir and cedar on the coast. Little attention was paid to the smaller trees and less accessible stands in the interior. Over the years, the rapid growth of the industry prompted concerns about provincial over-cutting, and several royal commissions recommended changes in forest management practices. Despite the introduction of a forest policy that was supposed to be premised on "sustained" yield, the province's annual cut rose

More Impoverished Than Ever

The [Mission Mountain Hydro] boom and all the wages left Lillooet more impoverished than it ever was in its long hundred and fifty years of history. So here is Lillooet with everything and yet with nothing! There isn't an industry worth the name save lumber and outside of a pittance of wages and hauling fees, the cut goes off on the rails without so much as a window or door manufactured here. Not more than a few hundred tons of produce went to market from here including fruits and vegetables.

Ma Murray, *Bridge River-Lillooet News*, 5 January 1961.

unit costs. In 1969, the American multinational, Evans Products, took over Lillooet's largest operator, Commercial Lumber, and expanded that mill. In 1975, the giant British Columbia Forest Products company bought out Hampton in Boston Bar and immediately announced an increase in output of 25 percent.

The change for the region was dramatic. Within a few years, forestry had become the major industry and employer. Multinational forest firms replaced small operators, consolidating cutting rights and increasing the rate of harvest. This was the new boom industry. With the cut increasing, some wondered whether forestry, like the industries before it, would soon "bust" and be gone. By 1970, the alarm went up as the Forest Service began to examine logging in the only large valley remaining undeveloped in the region, the valley of the Stein River.

Survival Through Neglect?

Throughout all these changes, the Native people at Lytton have retained a surprising number of their traditional ways. Virtually every household maintains its fishing station, drying and canning salmon for non-commercial family uses. Many of the wild foods, like "Indian celery," huckleberries, Saskatoon berries, and mushrooms, are still gathered and preserved. Hunting is common, one of the activities which still takes the Nlaka'pamux into the Stein valley. The language is widely spoken, although much more among the older than the younger members of the community. Many of the younger people are rediscovering their heritage, some even undergoing a form of "training" in the Stein. Above all, neglected by the dominant society, the Native community has remained, living where its forebears have always lived, still wedded to its place at Kumsheen.

Only One Left

It is a long time since British Columbians hiked through timbered valleys or paddled by tree-lined shores. So long in fact that they accept tree stumps, logging slash and drowned shorelines as standard.

There are no lakes under 2500 feet in altitude within 100 miles of Vancouver that have not been logged to the shoreline, dammed or both. **Not one.** Not Pitt, nor Alouette, Chilliwack, Bunsen, Buttle, Dickson, Sproat, Stave, Weaver, Alta, Chehalis, Horne, Nahatlatch, Alice, Norton—**none.**

There is **only one** major valley within 100 miles of Vancouver that has not been logged, flooded, or both. **Only one.** It is the valley of the Stein River. It's just that simple.

By the year 2000—just 27 years from now—there will be three million people within a 3-hour drive of the Stein basin. How can we afford **not** to preserve this area . . . ?

Roy Mason, December 4, 1973. From the first submission made to the provincial government on the future of the Stein River Valley by the Federation of Mountain Clubs of B.C.

In the 1960s, a huge roadbuilding and logging binge began in the valleys of southern British Columbia, putting at risk the natural environment of every sizable watershed in the area. A broad destructive swath was cutting across the natural landscape in a very short time, something that had not even been considered as a possibility before.

Logging the Stein had been looked at in the 1920s, but was rejected primarily because of the high cost of providing road access. In the 1960s, as larger lumber mills moved into Lillooet, Lytton, Boston Bar and other towns scattered throughout the region, every forest fell under the industry's covetous eye. This was an era of rapid economic growth, a time before environmentalism, and well before the environmental movement had seen the light of day.

Nevertheless, a few individuals could see the trends that were emerging in the forest industry: the concentration of control in a few corporations, the singular dependence which it was creating in rural British Columbia, and the increasing scale of the cut. There were jobs and profits here, but there were also great dangers. For the communities, their hard-won economic diversity and stability had recently been lost; now they were single industry towns, their economies dependent on the ever-expanding consumption of the environment around them. In the 160 years since Fraser's journey through the wilderness, the almost invisible signs of traditional use and occupation had been replaced by a highly visible, near total transformation of the landscape. The survival of even one remnant wilderness ecosystem of significant size was in danger. It was time to draw the line.

The first person to show concern was Chris Adam, the only individual to have a small homestead in the Stein. In 1968, he approached the British Columbia Wildlife Federation and, in 1972, he contacted Roy Mason of the British Columbia Mountaineering Club to ask the organization to lobby for the preservation of the valley. By 1972, logging roads had penetrated every major valley surrounding the Stein, and the Forest Service had completed a new feasibility study of logging in the Stein watershed itself. A prospector, Ken Morris, had staked a vesuvianite claim near Skihist Mountain on the Stein's southern ridge. The momentum for exploitation was building. In response to this rising environmental pressure, the regional Fish and Wildlife officer urged his head office in 1973 to seek a moratorium on development in the Stein. His request was backed up the next month when Mason submitted a similar request to the government on behalf of the Federation of Mountain Clubs of British Columbia.

A Moratorium Comes, And Goes

Responding to these requests, the newly elected New Democratic government in Victoria announced a two-year moratorium to study the options for developing or preserving the Stein. This was a government flush with its first electoral victory, and eager to begin a new era of "rational management." But it was also a time of enthusiasm for the idea of "multiple use" of resources by both industry and recreationists, and for planning by the government, not the public. The Federation of Mountain Clubs was concerned about the process from the beginning and, not trusting

Region To Headquarters: Stein Alert

This is a Regional request to Headquarters to utilize all of the influence at its disposal to effect a logging moratorium within the drainage of the Stein Basin.

The drainage is the last major system on the whole of the Fraser River which is still unlogged, and is otherwise practically free of human interference. For this reason alone, we feel the area should remain in its pristine condition if at all possible.

The wildlife values, as indicated, are incomplete and much survey work remains to be done. However, they indicate the importance of the drainage as a wildlife habitat . . .

We feel that fisheries values are of the utmost importance . . .

. . . [A]ll agencies concerned should take a long, hard look at the complexities of this drainage before a major commitment is contemplated.

G.A. West, Regional Director, Fish and Wildlife Branch, Kamloops, B.C., *Memorandum*, November 16, 1973.

This postcard-perfect picture greets the hiker arriving at Stein Lake. (Photo: Brian K. Smith)

The Official Conclusion

Undoubtedly the most significant value of the Stein, as a special recreational or preservational entity, is in its natural state as a total wilderness area. In this condition it is clearly a unique entity in such close proximity to the population centers of the Lower Mainland.

If the area were to be developed for resource extraction the Stein would lose that special value, becoming no more significant than the Kwoieck or Nahatlatch valleys on its flanks . . .

Conclusion
No final decision on the resource allocation should be made at this time. If the area is to be set aside as part of the park system there must be a marked shift in the need for wilderness areas. If and when it becomes economic to develop the Stein a study should be undertaken to investigate development pressures on all of the wilderness and large area recreation opportunities within one hundred miles of Vancouver to determine whether there has been any continuous and significant reduction in recreation opportunities in these areas.

Resource Management Concept
1.) At this time the committee is agreed that the best option for this area is that it should be operated for a mix of resource uses, as and when this option becomes economically feasible.

At that time the resource evaluation should be updated to confirm or otherwise, if this present recommendation is still the most appropriate course of action.

2.) **Pending upward changes in the economic conditions, to the point that viable harvesting would be imminent, that portion of the Botanie Allowable Cut contributed by the Stein drainage should be temporarily removed from the total A.A.C. [Annual Allowable Cut] of the whole P.S.Y.U. [Public Sustained Yield Unit].**

This will ensure that, should a future examination conclude that the area would best serve as a wilderness, the forest industry is not already totally committed to using the timber in the drainage.

Province of British Columbia, *The Stein River Basin Moratorium Study*, January 23, 1976, pp.35-37, 53.

Hiker in late summer looking over the Lower Stein, near Teaspoon Creek. (Photo: Pat Morrow)

The Unofficial Conclusion

The Stein offers a different range of experiences than other parks in the region, and can be used for hiking, backpacking, camping, and horse travel for a much longer season. It is a natural unit with natural boundaries.

The substantial-sized parks within 3-4 hours' drive of Vancouver are all either mostly alpine and subalpine with logging around their lower-level borders, or have boundaries touching rivers or lakes (usually on only one side) often above valuable timber which was excluded from the park when the boundaries were drawn. These parks already receive heavy use and their carrying capacity may well be exceeded in the near future.

In a very real sense the Stein could be an "upside-down" park for B.C. We have mountain parks, lake parks, and marine parks, but no **watershed parks** in this region . . .

WE STRONGLY URGE . . . multiple-use recreation without resource extraction.

REASONS:
- Last unlogged watershed within 100 miles of Vancouver;
- Full range of excellent recreation potential;
- Acknowledged superb features;
- Better weather and longer season than other parks in the region;
- Substantial difference in type of area from existing parks;
- Adverse effects of logging on the natural environment which is the watershed's major attraction.

Federation of Mountain Clubs of British Columbia, *Stein River Watershed: Volume 2, Options and Recommendations*, A Brief presented to the Government of British Columbia, October, 1975, pp.16-20, 24.

Victoria to take a far-sighted approach, it undertook its own study of the valley. This study, completed in 1975, concluded that no logging or mining should be allowed in such a diverse and accessible wilderness so close to Vancouver. Instead, the Federation recommended developing the area for a variety of recreational and conservation uses **only**—as the study put it, "multiple-use recreation without resource extraction."

As anticipated, the official government report was less conclusive, and not so timely. Undertaken under the joint authority of two bureaucratic adversaries, the Forest Service and the Fish and Wildlife Branch, the Moratorium study was a sit-on-the-fence compromise. It recommended that the area be removed from present supply calculations for the Botanie PSYU, something that would preserve future options for decision-makers. And it left the final decision on the valley's fate to some unspecified future date when another review could be undertaken in light of the forestry or wilderness needs then prevailing. But rational planning is only as good as the government's continuing commitment to it, and even before the study was released, the NDP government fell from power.

In retrospect, the planning process had not worked decisively—it was too slow, it failed to make a concrete recommendation, and it left the final decision to some later officials. But there was merit in the reassessment process it recommended. The study had concluded that, in 1975, logging was not economical and would not become economical without major changes in the market. Because it also chose not to designate the valley as a park, the only possible result was a reassessment at some later date. But even this conclusion was ultimately rejected.

Well before the Moratorium Study was released to the public, a new Social Credit cabinet committee announced that logging in the Stein would proceed. The valley was not removed from the area's timber harvesting calculations, and no provision was made to review the situation in light of future trends. On the contrary, for a decade after the announcement, no advisory body was even allowed to consider whether or not the valley should be logged. The only permissible question was **how** it should be logged. The Forest Service began again to plan for logging development.

Public Organizing Vs. Public Participation

The government decision was reached without public advice, and without public hearings. Frozen out of official decision-making, conservation organizations arranged their own unofficial public meetings in Vancouver and Lytton in late 1976. In January 1977, the Sierra Club held an organizational meeting out of which emerged the Save the Stein Coalition, a coalition of 17 non-governmental environmental and recreation organizations representing about 45,000 members. Newsletters began to spread word of the Stein to a widening audience.

"Stein" was by no means a household name in these early days, and the new Stein conservationists sought to change this. Of immediate concern was the need to have people visit the valley, a difficult task for an area which was almost totally without trails. A major achievement serving this purpose was the publication in 1979 of a guidebook, **Exploring the Stein River Valley**, produced by David Thompson (the co-ordinator of the Federation's 1975 study of the valley) and Roger Freeman. The guidebook was exhaustive, the product of two years of research including months of hiking through densely forested mountain hillsides. With this guidebook, and the stimulus provided by a trickle of newspaper and magazine articles, more and more people began to venture into this

The Decision

The Honourable James A. Nielsen, Chairman of the Environment and Land Use Committee, today announced the decision of the Government to allow controlled development of the Stein River drainage . . .

. . . [T]he consensus was that prevailing Crown land management policies would afford a practical and desirable basis for guiding future development . . . Carefully planned and executed logging and mining, guided for example by the folio system . . . will ensure that adequate environmental safeguards are undertaken. This will assist in achieving acceptable multiple use . . . The B.C. Forest Service will be the principal management authority.

Province of British Columbia, Ministry of Environment, News Release, May 12, 1976.

Traverse

Joe Foy traversed the whole valley, west to east, in 1980 when the area was still little known except to a handful of enthusiasts—and still without a trail. His photograph album of the traverse introduced many people to the Stein.

"I did a lot of hiking in those days, but just day stuff. Then I saw this article in the Province, 'Writing on Wall for Unlogged Stein Valley' and I wanted to go. I wanted a real adventure, real wilderness. You don't have to be a millionaire to see wilderness, with the Stein. Normal people can go there. It's so close."

Close meant Lizzie Creek, a logged out valley on the western slope of the Stein. "It didn't take long. As soon as we left the logging, we were in the meadows and right away we were on compasses.

The trees were skinnier here; they had a tougher look to them. It was a good feeling with days and days ahead of you. But we knew that we had to have our act together—this was different."

At the top of the ridge were Cherry Pip Pass and Cloudraker Mountain, "sidehilling through wildflowers on grassy slopes—avalanche lilies, anemones, lupens. You could see a long way from this ridge and it's all wild, all around you . . . You could see forever, and it was a real awakening. That day was one of the most memorable of my life.

"We were only on the ridge for a day; 10 hours of hiking. Each place we passed was a huge area, a whole side-valley, a chain of waterfalls and little lakes. From that one ridge, you could pick a lifetime of exploring."

Here, at elevations above 7000 feet, the creeks that will become the Stein begin . . . "We came down from the ridge and into the first side valley, the North Stein, which joins the main river just past Stein Lake. It was a long climb down and we were really hot and dry. We literally fell into that river. We were so tired that night we went to bed with no supper.

"When we woke up the next morning, everything had changed. Now we were in a jungle. Game trails so packed down as if a whole herd of cattle had gone through. This really is what they say—an island in a sea of stumps.

"From the air it looks like one big forest. It's not. It's a series of different habitats. For grizzly bears and wolves, for mountain goats, and moose. The valley changes constantly. One of the things you learn when you travel this valley is that the forest is all patches. All different ages of trees. Some places, a big cedar grove, then devils club and cottonwood, beaver ponds galore, then a forest like my parents' backyard in Surrey, all alders and maples.

"As you walk, you know that on both sides of you are these giant drainages— Scudamore, Cottonwood, Nesbitt Creek,

Joe Foy, relaxing beside Brimful Lake at the first Stein Voices for the Wilderness festival, Labour Day weekend, 1985. (Photo: Pat Morrow)

Ponderosa. As you walk, you know that you're missing so much. A lot of country that can support life. Alive. It just has a feeling that there's a lot going on in there."

The trip through the central portions, still without any trail, was tough: "Thrashing through the underbrush, over god-awful slide areas, wading through beaver swamps. We even shinnied over the river on a log, my heart pounding like a jackhammer. But soon we toughened up and were at home there. When you go with a friend, you protect each other. You never have that relationship any other way. We weren't nervous; it had become a sport. And every night we'd come down to the river. And every night it was different.

"It was nice to catch the first signs of the old trail. It was a luxury and we moved fast. And soon we were at Ponderosa Creek, the third-to-last big side valley on the way out. Here we came across the shelter they'd built a few years ago. Civilization again.

"There's a market for the Stein, the largest in the Province. A million-and-a-half people in the Lower Mainland. You can get a number-one experience in that valley. It's like going to Africa or to the Amazon, yet it's only a three-hour drive from Vancouver."

Joe Foy, Vancouver British Columbia, August, 1984

Looking east from the middle valley toward the narrowing at the Stein's lower canyon. (Photo: Gary Fiegehen/Robert Semeniuk)

little-known wilderness.

At the same time as they prepared the guidebook, members of the Stein Coalition juggled an equally formidable task. In the spring of 1978, after continued pressure from the Stein Coalition, the Minister of Forests, Tom Waterland, announced the creation of a Stein River Public Liaison Committee. Interested members of the Coalition were invited to participate, and many signed on. Hopes were high that the ad hoc decisions of the past would now be replaced by more open planning and decision-making.

Committee involvement demanded enormous energy—writing countless letters, travelling to meetings between Lytton and Vancouver, anxiously attempting to monitor events. Unfortunately, the committee was doomed from the start. Its terms of reference, set unilaterally by the government, were based on the premise that the Stein would be logged. The committee's function was to exchange information and gather data which would assist in later developing the logging plans. The committee had no decision-making power, which stayed with officials in the Ministry of Forests who could act when and how they pleased. With no funding or staff, the committee had to rely on the good faith of government officials to get and provide much of the necessary information. To this day, information remains sketchy, as indicated by the lack of any thorough wildlife inventory of the valley.

Although the Forest Service was formally bound by the decision to log the valley, it retained a lot of discretionary power, in particular the power to set the Annual Allowable Cut for the mills of the region, and to designate—or exclude—areas from that cut. An ideal time to exclude the Stein occurred in 1979 when the timber supply boundaries were reviewed and changed following the passage of the new Forest

Fishing along the banks of the lower Stein. (Photo: Richard Chester)

The Formula For Frustration

All of the efforts, all of the time, all of the meetings by all of the people concerned, seem now all for naught. The writing has been on the wall all along. In chronological order this is Forestry's letter-perfect formula for frustration:

I.
Listen and show concern for prostestations of the public, bearing in mind the ultimate goal—logging.

2.
Pay lip service by holding public input meetings, bearing in mind the need to log.

3.
When public pressure looks dangerous, set up a public liaison committee, bearing in mind the compulsion to log.

4.
Spend endless hours of endless meetings for six years if necessary in order to pacify, lead down forestry paths, prevaricate and provocate and in any other way negate the efforts of the public, bearing in mind the absolute end—logging.

5.
Declare suddenly that a folio for log extraction must be in place in less than a year and switch principal personnel in order to further negate the past endeavours, bearing in mind that trees must be cut.

6.
When challenged, have a senior override your promises by stating emphatically a policy that will order the trees to be cut no matter what the public thinks.

This and more, ladies and gentlemen, is what has happened to the Stein Coalition in the name of public participation. A perfect formula for frustration? Yes, but annihilation, absolutely not!

Dale Denney, Presentation to British Columbia Wildlife Federation Convention, April 1982.

Act in 1978. The 1976 Royal Commission that preceded the new legislation recommended flexibility in allocating the allowable cut to provide for the creation of parks and other reductions in the forest land base. The government disregarded this recommendation and, when the new boundaries were being set for the Lillooet TSA, the decision was made to include the Stein timber. The Forest Service forgot to notify members of the Stein Public Liaison Committee of the discussions.

Restricted in its terms of reference, powerless, and dependent on the government's goodwill, the committee's primary role from the Coalition's point of view was to get better information and provide an official vehicle for dealing with day-to-day crises. And crises abounded, especially the running battle with one developer, Ken Morris, who attempted to use his 1971 mining claim on the Stein's southern ridge as a basis for building a 35-kilometre access road through the valley, cutting timber along the way. Court injunctions followed Cabinet appeals in an endless series of skirmishes occupying nearly a decade: skirmishes that consumed the evenings, weekends and holidays of the four or five core members of the Coalition.

Though useful, the Liaison Committee was a source of increasing frustration for the Coalition members who, above all, wanted to "Save the Stein." This frustration came to a boil in 1982 when, after promising that no decision on an access route would be made for the 18 months of the study process, the Regional Manager of the Forest Service unilaterally announced that timber logged from the Stein would be hauled out via the lower valley, exactly the route which the Coalition opposed. Promises had been broken and one of the stalwarts of moderation on the committee, Dr. Roger Freeman, withdrew in protest in April 1982. Other participants followed suit.

Without public interest scrutiny, the Stein Resource Folio planning continued unimpeded. The Forest Service sent the present owners of Earlscourt, the Mundalls, a notice of intention to expropriate a right-of-way across the farm for access to the Stein trail. In December 1982, David Thompson complained to the Ombudsman that the ministry was ignoring its own, legally non-enforceable, public involvement guidelines.

With new assurances of good faith from the Forest Service, the committee was reconstituted as the Public Advisory Committee, and the old participants returned, though they now acted as individuals, not as representatives of their organizations. But the power of the new committee was unchanged: it was advisory only, had no decision-making authority, and it still had to accept that logging was going to go ahead. No significant changes were going to come out of that committee, and its members knew it.

The major task of the new Advisory Committee was the completion of the forest ministry's Stein River Resource Folio Plan begun in 1981. The Folio is an extensive catalogue and interpretation of the Stein's natural environment and resources, and also a set of vague guidelines for logging in the valley. When the Folio was finished in 1984, the committee was largely spent. It had clearly served a useful function, allowing interested individuals to monitor important decisions and receive some information not otherwise accessible to them. Yet the whole process was so limited—the result being determined ahead of time—that, in the end, it was more an exercise in public relations than public participation. Now too, the preservation initiative was moving elsewhere.

One of the valley's favourite camping spots, the teepee, a three-hour walk from the head of the trail. (Photo: Dennis Darragh)

Another Stein landmark, the cable crossing. This crossing was upgraded, and two others built, through the initiative of Ken Lay of the Western

Canada Wilderness Committee as part of the construction of the Stein Heritage Trail with the Lytton Indian Band in 1987. (Photo: Pat Morrow)

The disintegration of the Public Liaison Committee in 1982 was a pivotal point in the struggle for the Stein. After five years of meetings and debate, hope for a rational decision was gone. The mountaineers, sport fishermen and naturalists who had sat at the table had always felt compromised by the terms of reference set for the committee by the government. And the representation on the committee had always been as limited as the question being addressed— no Natives, and no general public. A new approach was needed.

From a small group of largely Vancouver-based professionals debating the development plans for the Stein, the Stein cause has, since 1982, emerged as a grass-roots movement of Natives, environmentalists, and concerned citizens generally. Like the Coalition before it, the common ground of the movement is the desire to preserve this last wild river and large watershed in southern British Columbia from any form of industrial development.

In the 1970s, the Stein was often treated as a Vancouver issue, of legitimate concern to people in the Lower Mainland of British Columbia because of its significant role in the regional environmental and recreational geography. In the 1980s, it also took hold as a local and provincial, even national, issue. The terms of debate at these levels were very different from those of the Liaison Committee, in fact, the very opposite of the earlier how-to-log approach. The explicit goal was preservation—no roads, no logging, no mining. Making the argument to justify that uncompromising stance, and building the new constituency to achieve the goal of preservation, were

now the two components of the movement to save the Stein.

The Battle Of The Experts

With the technocratic planning phase in eclipse, the controversy shifted both to a lower grassroots level and to an even higher ground of expert economic argument. Liberated from the shackles of the Liaison Committee, the debate quickly expanded to become an evaluation of the merits of the logging plan in its entirety.

Even before the 1982 walkout, reports that highlighted the heritage and tourism merits of the valley had been published. But it was in 1983 that another stalwart of the Federation of Mountain Clubs, Trevor Jones, launched an economic broadside against the whole Stein logging enterprise. Jones, a Vancouver engineer and avid hiker, is also an ever watchful student of forest planning and economics. In his study, **Wilderness or Logging: Case Studies of Two Conflicts in B.C.**, he argued that logging the valley was still uneconomic: it wasn't profitable to build a bridge across the Fraser River and a road through the Stein's lower canyon to go after a relatively small stand of timber in the mid-valley.

Jones' work brought to light two disturbing aspects of the planning process. First, it revealed deep disagreement over just how much "economic" wood was in the valley. The mixture of wood, so-called Spruce-Pine-Fir, was certainly desirable for the local mills, but because of steep slopes, inaccessibility, and diseased wood, not all the wood could be cut and hauled out economically. On this question, the information was, and remains, controversial. Estimates of the

The Heritage Potential

The largest concentration of aboriginal archaeological sites within the Study Region occurs in this upper Fraser Canyon sub-area. Of the 182 sites identified, the majority occur around Lytton, with a particularly large group of sites around the lower Stein River. Archaeological reports note that the Stein River has a wide range of well preserved site types. Test excavations at the confluence of the Stein and Fraser Rivers date artifacts to approximately 200 A.D. These sites could provide a focus for interpretation of Indian history.

Recreation features in the Lytton area include sport fishing and backcountry hiking . . . This basin [the Stein] has become known as one of the last undeveloped watersheds offering "wilderness" experiences in close

proximity to the Lower Mainland. Lytton also has a number of locational advantages in being situated at the Fraser-Thompson River confluence and on Highway 1 . . .

The apparent economic problems in the region have stimulated a search for new sources of employment. Some interest in developing tourism has focused upon improving access and recreational facilities, and providing historical attractions. The location of the region and the quality of recreation resources suggest that accessible leisure opportunities are possible for a large tourist market associated with the Lower Mainland and Highway 1.

Province of British Columbia Provincial Secretary, Heritage Conservation Branch, *Lillooet-Fraser Heritage Resource Study, Vol.1*, March 1980, p. 114.

The sands of the Fraser River, keeper of gold nuggets and ancient pipes, near the ferry landing. (Photo: Greg McIntyre)

The Ministry Calculation

Crossing the Fraser River

If development occurs and the timber is removed via the mouth of the valley, which of the options identified should be used to move timber across the Fraser River?

. . . The ferry at Lytton is the least expensive option, followed by a bridge at Lytton, followed by the North Bend road (low level) . . . Having said all this, if the ferry is feasible and the Thompson River bridge available, the Lytton ferry would be my recommendation. This option is the least expensive and has the added feature that, if markets or other reasons preclude the full development of the Stein River, the capital sunk in crossing the Fraser River is far less in amount . . .

What is at issue is whether or not the value of the Stein River timber exceeds the heavy costs of crossing the Fraser River and building the first 30 km of road. With a ferry at Lytton, these costs are approximately $3.3 million, excluding hauling costs and any repairs to the Thompson River bridge . . .

. . . The acid test is whether the licensees will develop the valley and bear all costs, except those that reflect savings elsewhere (i.e. ferry savings if a Lytton bridge is built). There would then be no question about subsidies.

Memorandum. From Strategic Studies Branch, Ministry of Forests, Victoria, to Regional Manager, Ministry of Forests, Kamloops Forest Region, January 16, 1985.

[Note: As of the date of publication of the present book, the timber companies have not agreed to cover all access costs, as the method and financing of the Fraser River crossing is still undetermined.]

The ferry crossing to the "west side" of the Fraser River. (Photo: Greg McIntyre)

quantity of economically available wood range from a low of less than 2 million cubic metres (m³) to a high of 4 million cubic metres. Proponents of logging use the higher figure, but in 1983 Jones cited Forest Service documents and concluded that there was an available volume of at most 2.3 million cubic metres.[1] Using updated government figures in 1987, Jones showed that the volume of timber available for logging was only 1.97 million cubic metres.[2] As the Ministry of Forests stated in 1986, the "total inventory [is] around 2 million cubic metres."[3] At the proposed cutting rate of 125,000 cubic metres per year, this translates to only 16 years of logging and employment.

Not only are industry claims of timber volumes and employment inflated, argues Jones, but their public assertion that only nine percent of the valley **area** will be logged means, in reality, cutting at least 90 percent of the **quantity** of timber that is economically accessible once a road has been built. This nine percent also represents the heart of the watershed.

Jones' second task was calculating the costs to the taxpayer of logging the Stein. Studies on road access had been done for the Public Liaison Committee and concluded that logging was "marginal even under good market conditions."[4] Jones reviewed the costs for road construction, reforestation, and Forest Service management to produce a fuller calculation of the public costs of the proposal, and then compared them with the economic benefits. His conclusion was that, overall, the provincial government stood to lose over $10 million if logging was carried out at 1982 market prices.

In the wake of this surprising analysis, other studies followed quickly. British Columbia Forest Products independently prepared a financial analysis and placed it before the reconstituted public advisory committee. It concluded that, using 1984 prices, the sales from logging would amount to $64.07 per cubic metre, and the costs would come to $62.66, producing a net profit of $1.41 per cubic metre. This amounted to a 3 percent margin of profitability—less than the company would get if it put its money into a bank savings account!

Other studies came to more pessimistic conclusions. One economic evaluation was released in 1985 by the Simon Fraser University Natural Resources Management Program. It agreed closely with Jones' earlier work, concluding that the logging project involved a net loss of $12 million. Another study in that same year, done by the Vancouver-based Institute for New Economics, evaluated the proposal from the viewpoint of the long-term interests of the local communities. It concluded that the environmentally disruptive, one-time character of the logging proposal was not appropriate to the emerging structural needs of the local communities for greater economic diversification and resource sustainability.

The Forest Ministry's Strategic Studies Branch issued a five-page memorandum to the Kamloops Regional Manager to help to resolve the economic controversy. The memorandum, while offering explanations to counter suggestions that logging would be subsidized, was itself inconclusive on the economic merits of the proposal. The Stein is on the west side of the Fraser River and thus not connected to any highway route except by the motorless reaction ferry which is pushed across the river by the flow of the current. To get access to the valley, the memo rejected the proposal for building an expensive bridge across the Fraser River. It proposed instead to install an improved ferry—its justification being that it was a cheaper investment to write off should lumber markets collapse after the valley had been roaded but only partially logged.

On such advice, the Ministry announced in February, 1985 that road-building up the valley would begin as soon as possible in preparation for logging.

Local Opposition

Until the summer of 1985, the Stein issue had not caused much controversy among the residents of the local towns and Indian bands. Given its limited terms of reference, the Liaison Committee effectively prohibited the Indian bands from participating unless they were willing to compromise their land claim interests. They did not participate, but had been working on their own. In 1983 and 1984, the Lytton and Mt. Currie bands sponsored "Living Alternatives," a wilderness hiking program in the Stein for local Native and non-Native youth. At the same time, the Nlaka'pamux prepared their comprehensive land claim, which included the Stein, and submitted it to the federal government for negotiation in December 1984.

With the February announcement of road-building, local activity accelerated. A Stein Action Committee was formed by non-Natives from Lytton and Lillooet. Both the Lillooet Tribal Council and Lytton band formally proclaimed their opposition to the logging plans. In Vancouver, a grass-roots campaign took off that led to the formation later that year of the now 2000-strong Stein Wilderness Alliance. Meanwhile, the Western Canada Wilderness Committee expanded its educational campaign by producing new newspapers and posters, and holding benefit dances and public debates.

The boldest strategy of all was something quite extraordinary, a strategy designed to raise the profile of the issue while also giving people a first-hand experience of what was at stake in the Stein. Together, Native and non-Native groups agreed to hold a large summer festival high in the Stein alpine meadows.

The first "Voices for the Wilderness" festival in the

Poster announcing the founding meeting of the Vancouver-based Stein Wilderness Alliance, shortly after the first Stein Voices for the Wilderness festival, 1985. Graphic artist: Patricia Walker

135

Bring Us To Our Home

You know, long time ago the Indians used to gather up and there used to be lots of peoples. But now, the White people kinda cut that off so we don't know each other no more. Just lucky to know Jimmie here.

But before, we was all related 'cause we used to get together quite often and see each other. But the White man didn't like that. He said that was no good. If he see us do it again, we go to jail. So we never have big times like this.

Now today, you know, I get amongst lot of White peoples. They're coming back

Louis Phillips in Lytton above the confluence of the Thompson River (not in photo) with the Fraser. Note the gorge of the Stein in the background. (Photo: Pat Morrow)

to it with the Indians now, after couple hundred years of trying to cut it off . . .

This is good country, you know. This Indian country's good country. Before the

White man come, you know, this is where the Indians used to live . . . This is the real life. Indian life is out here. There's nothing new for us Indians. When you bring us out here, you bring us to our home. Just like you bring us to our home when you bring us and see our country again . . .

Comin' up in a helicopter, I see a road pretty near up top here. Only 'bout a quarter mile and it get up on top. Well, when they get up here, what's gonna be left of our good country . . . ?

So now when they spoil the country where the older peoples used to go and get their living, it kinda hurts the Indians' feelings. You know, it's not doin' a bit of good to cheer them up. It's hurtin' them to see these peoples come in here . . . and spoil our country. And then they call us down—"just being Indians, that's all."

But what would they do . . . ? And now they fells the timber and they go and tear the ground out, taking the logs out, and where are our animals going to go? Our martens, our bears . . . ?

And even us, where are we going to go?

Louis Phillips, Nlaka'pamux elder, speaking at the Voices for the Wilderness festival in the Stein Valley's alpine meadows, August 1985.

summer of 1985 was a massive piece of organizing. The Western Canada Wilderness Committee prepared and disseminated its first special Stein newspaper to introduce the person-on-the-street to a valley few had ever heard of. The Lillooet Tribal Council, the sponsor of the gathering, put together the difficult logistics for the mountainous get-together. On the Labour Day weekend, only six months after the ministry announcement, over 500 people made the climb to the top of the Stein. Through a spruce forest at the end of a logging road in Texas Creek on the outside of the Stein ridge, over boulder fields, along high ridges and alpine meadows, a steady stream of people made their way to a unique event. Among the hikers were Natives, non-Natives, groups of young people, grandparents, tourists from Japan, people with babies, and a blind man being led up the trail. It was an eclectic pilgrimage.

Joe David was one of the pilgrims. His people, the Nuu-cha-nulth Indians of the west coast of Vancouver Island, were involved in their own battle to prevent logging on Meares Island near Tofino. They had blockaded the island, declared it a Tribal Park, and finally won a court injunction to stop Macmillan Bloedel from clear-cutting the island's ancient forest pending the resolution of their land claim over the island:

"As I climbed this wonderful mountain, I was overwhelmed, very overwhelmed to see this place, to know there were hundreds ahead of me," he told a fireside gathering that night. "I was filled with love, to know people here and everywhere were taking responsibility all over this continent."

The circle of teepees at the 1986 Stein Voices for the Wilderness festival at the confluence of the Stein and Fraser Rivers. (Photo: Martin Roland)

With the good attendance at the festival, and the front-page news that followed, the profile of the Stein issue jumped dramatically. The Lytton band now stood opposed to any road-building in the valley, the owners of Earlscourt were preparing to go to court to block the proposed expropriation of a logging road right-of-way over their farm, and conservationists were organizing for a showdown. Meanwhile, the Ministry of Forests wrote to the local mill, Lytton Lumber, which had originally been excluded from a share of the timber in the valley. They were offered a small piece of the action by the Ministry—and told that they were expected to "help to smooth the way for this development."[5] In October, road contractors walked the proposed right-of-way flanked by protestors. The contract was awarded; confrontation was looming.

Studies, More Studies

Suddenly, a very different issue surfaced. On the evening news, people across the country saw Haida elders standing in the rain on a muddy road in their bright red ceremonial dress, being arrested by the RCMP for blocking logging trucks on Lyell Island in the South Moresby region of the Queen Charlotte Islands. The convergence in 1985 of three issues—Meares, Stein, and Moresby—rapidly pushed up the political thermometer in the province. To cool things down, the provincial government convened an eight-member Wilderness Advisory Committee of foresters, miners, academics and, belatedly, one environmentalist.

The committee was charged with resolving in three months what the government had been unwilling to resolve for a decade. Its composition and limited terms of reference were ridiculed by editorial writers across the country. But the futures of some two dozen remaining wilderness areas were at issue in a province once synonymous with wilderness abundance, and the conservationist response was enormous. The committee took written submissions and held hearings across the province, from the Lytton community hall to the Hotel Georgia ballroom in Vancouver. A moratorium on road-building into the Stein went into effect during its deliberations.

The recommendations of the committee were released in March, 1986. Its proposal for the future of the Stein was unremarkable except in one respect. Its own economic study of the issue, undertaken by an economic consultant, Gary Bowden, concluded that logging would be marginally profitable—if lumber prices were good over the next two decades and if reforestation costs were excluded from the costs of logging. Despite his conclusion, the committee felt that the issue was "very much a difficult and close question"

A Claim To Land

Our chief concern, which is in fact very simple—the valley is Indian land—we have been in continuous occupancy and use since time immemorial. We have never ceded, sold, nor lost this land in conflict . . .

It would be unjust to give us distant, barren or unusable land. There is no land that we have used more intensively than the Stein Valley. If we are to realize a modest share of our traditional lands, of what was ours before [White] settlement, it should be land we value, that we have used and which has not been exploited nor occupied by others. It should include the Stein Valley.

This does not mean we wouldn't share with those who would use it for acceptable and reasonable purposes. We share, we've shared 'til it hurt! There must be something to share, however. We look to others for support here, as we have supported them.

We fear that the province, realizing that notwithstanding their obstinance, aboriginal title exists, are taking pre-emptive measures. They may well be trying to strip this land before any [land-claim] settlement is considered. There are other valued Native lands in the province under similar pressure. The timing, urgency and frequency of these attacks on land [which] we have a high degree of interest in, are such as to exceed mere coincidence . . .

The fact that the provincial Government chooses not to recognize aboriginal title matters not one iota. They have been wrong before.

From "The Lytton Indian Band Position Respecting the Development of the Stein," Submission to the Wilderness Advisory Committee, January, 1986.

Native boy in headdress. (Photo: Bryan K. Evans)

Rediscovery youth preparing a pelt. (Photo: Thom Henley)

1986 Lillooet Timber Supply Area Options Report

	Status Quo	Basic Forestry	Intensive Forestry	Improved Timber Utilization	Stein River
Net Land Base	308,000	308,000	347,000	308,000	291,000
Available Mature Inventory (m³)	14,683,000	14,683,000	15,232,000	15,577,000	14,107,000
Long Run Sustained Yield (m³/yr.)	444,000	458,000	524,000	485,000	416,000
Sustainable Rate of Harvest (m³/yr.)	542,000	542,000	701,000	669,000	521,000
Period (yr.)	40	40	10	10	40
Utilization Level [1] (cm DBH)	17.5	17.5	17.5	12.5[2]	17.5
Direct Employment Generated [3] 0-20 yr. (person years)	325	275	395	379	307
Stumpage Revenue [4] 0-20 yr. ($/yr.)	780,500	780,500	947,500	908,600	737,000
Silvicultural Costs [5] ($/yr.)					
0-20	507,000	2,190,000	5,050,000	507,000	507,000
21-150	379,000	1,080,000	1,304,000	433,000	369,000

1. Lodgepole pine is 12.5 cm DBH throughout all options.
2. Except Dry Belt Fir
3. Based on 0.6 person yrs./1000 m³ as estimated from Statistics Canada employment data.
4. Based on $1.44/m³ as estimated from volume billed in the Lillooet TSA for the period 1984-86.
5. Costs of silviculture are those associated with field projects only. Fixed overhead costs are not included.

Ministry of Forests, Kamloops Forest Region, *Lillooet Timber Supply Area Options Report*, 1986, p. 26.

The 1986 Forest Service Options Report. This table compares the benefits and costs of logging the Stein with those of improved timber utilization and increased reforestation.

Of special interest is the small loss in timber volumes projected as a result of withdrawing the Stein from the forest land base.

The forest canopy at **Klemeen.** *(Photo: Gary Fiegehen/Robert Semeniuk)*

and that logging the valley was economically "marginal to Government and to BCFP [British Columbia Forest Products]." Nevertheless, it recommended that "the valley should be logged so as to preserve jobs at the Boston Bar and Lytton Lumber mills." There was one important caveat: "[A] road should not be constructed through the Stein River Canyon without a formal agreement between the Lytton Indian Band and the Provincial Government."[6]

The effect of the report was tangible and immediate. First, road-building plans were again put on hold until the provincial cabinet had reviewed the report and taken a position on it. Second, the focus of debate shifted again, this time from economics to legal rights. Finally, 180 years after Simon Fraser had laid claim to the lands of New Caledonia for the North West Company, the traditional rights of the Nlaka'pamux could no longer be ignored. The Nlaka'pamux people might finally have a role in deciding the future of at least some of their lands.

While the provincial cabinet reviewed the Wilderness Committee report, the Ministry of Forests completed its regular five-year planning process for the Lillooet Timber Supply Area (TSA), which included the Stein Valley. It released the results in its Options Report in the fall of 1986, and the story it told was shocking even to critics of the industry. It pointed to an enormous level of overcutting in the Lillooet TSA, recommending that the so-called Annual Allowable Cut (AAC) be reduced from the existing level of 800,000 cubic metres/year (calculated for the 1980 TSA Report) to 444,000 cubic metres/year, a reduction in available wood

supply of almost 50 percent. In only six years since the previous report, it also reduced its forecast of the long-run sustained yield from 656,500 cubic metres/year to 444,000 cubic metres/year. The evidence in the report pointed to a history of over-cutting and under-management.

The Options Report also revealed that the annual allowable cut in the Lillooet TSA would fall by only 21,000 cubic metres of wood per year if the Stein were preserved as a park. This was just 5 percent of the TSA's Long Run Sustained Yield. In comparison, for the next decade, the TSA could gain an additional 159,000 cubic metres of available wood with better reforestation (intensive forestry). A further 127,000 cubic metres of wood could be obtained if the loggers were required to take some of the smaller logs to the mill instead of leaving them as waste in the clearcuts (improved utilization). While the preservation of the Stein might lead to the loss of 18 logging jobs, the report concluded that intensive forestry would create 70. In short, with better forest management, 14 times as much wood and nearly four times as many jobs would be available over the next decade than would be lost if the Stein were preserved from industrial development.

It is not necessary to draw any definitive conclusions about the costs and benefits of the Stein logging proposal to see its flaws. Profitability is dependent on maintaining very good lumber prices not for just a year or two, but continuously over many years. As the Ministry's own studies revealed, this is risky. In fact, the hallmark of the logging proposal is uncertainty—in available timber volumes, costs of access,

Pondering the sunlit river. (Photo: Pat Morrow)

Rediscovery

[After 24 hours alone in the Stein wilderness,] we walked back in silence [to the Rediscovery base camp] sweat lodge, and only then were we allowed to talk of our experiences. After a three-round sweat we all went back to camp, where there was a feast of extravagant things . . . That night, we stayed up late singing and talking around the sacred fire. People talked of their lives and I learned things about my friend Pete—whom I have known for almost ten years—that I never even knew. It was a really good experience for everybody. That night we all made a promise to try our best to be back at the same time together again next year.

A couple of days later we set out towards Lytton on our last leg of the trip. We spent one night at Ponderosa Creek, and the next down below the Devil's Staircase. We were at the bottom of the trail by about noon. We went into town and said our goodbyes, wishing we could turn around and do it again.

Story told by Willie Dubroy, a 15-year-old from the Lillooet area. The last of the Stein Rediscovery trips of summer 1987 drew nine Native and non-Native BC teenagers together for 13 days and about 100 kilometres of hiking and camping, from the headwaters of the Stein River to its mouth on the Fraser at Lytton. In the valley, these young people learned wilderness skills, learned about the rich cultural history of the Stein, and learned about themselves.

Rediscovery students in study. (Photo: Thom Henley)

142

future market prices, and even the viability of the Boston Bar mill, which has lost money every year except one since it was purchased by British Columbia Forest Products in 1975.

Given the high initial costs of access and the relatively small volume of economically available timber in the valley, the mill has been understandably reluctant to undertake the initial investment, one of the reasons that the valley remains unlogged to date. Even in 1987, the government kept open the possibility of itself building a bridge across the Fraser River, raising concerns that hidden subsidies were still intended to encourage the industry to go into the valley. Above all, the Options Report demonstrated that improved forest management for the region—reforestation and improved timber utilization—are practical alternatives to logging the Stein.

The Native Claim

While the government was pondering the future of the Stein, the bands were exploring the valley anew. With the assistance of the Rediscovery program from the Queen Charlottes, an expanded wilderness program was initiated in 1986. Its base camp was at Cottonwood Creek, ironically situated in the middle of the first block of timber later proposed to be cut in the valley. In the summer of 1986, as well, the bands and the Western Canada Wilderness Committee had re-cut the overgrown trail which traverses the valley, making the area more accessible than it had been for decades. And each summer, under the stewardship of the Lillooet Tribal Council, the Voices for the Wilderness festival

grew larger, with over 2,000 people attending in 1987. The Stein had become the top environmental issue in the province.

But with an injunction against logging on Meares Island, and a new national park reserve being established on the Queen Charlotte Islands, the Stein had also become the forest industry's symbolic last stand against what it perceives to be the theft of its land base. Economic or not, the Stein must be logged to demonstrate firm industry control over the province's forest lands. With a $200,000 grant from the British Columbia Council of Forest Industries, a public relations campaign began. In storefronts in Boston Bar, Lytton and Lillooet, the industry began organizing its own citizens' lobby on behalf of logging, the so-called "Share the Stein Constituency."

To no one's surprise, in September, 1987, the provincial government announced that, after considering the Wilderness Advisory Committee's report, it would proceed with logging in

The Last Little Bit Of Dignity

What more do these people want? They take our lands. They take our culture, they take away our traditions. They take our language. They've anglicized us. They've tried to fit us into a society that we really don't belong to. Now they're gonna go and strip our land. They're going to take everything that we have.

That's the last little bit of dignity we have, out there in the Stein Valley! If we allow them to go in there they might as well take the last bit of skin that we've got left on our bodies. And after that what else do they want—our lives?

Chief Ruby Dunstan of the Lytton Band, at the Stein Voices for the Wilderness festival, August, 1987.

When You Put Aside Values

We won in South Moresby. That's such a tiny little piece of this Earth and you see how they act like they lost a big piece of it. I don't know where they think they lost it—it's still up there.

Ten years it took so many people to make that happen—really it's kinda sad — but it shows that it could be done, anyway . . . I rode down from the Charlottes yesterday with a guy from Western Forest Products—he's still a little bit mad at me . . . We've known each other for a long time. I think he put it best when he said:

"You put aside the cultural values and the recreational values and the fish and wildlife values and the spiritual values, and it just makes no sense to leave those lands the way they are."

Guujaaw, of the Haida Nation, at the Stein Voices for the Wilderness festival, August 1987.

the valley. Attempting to improve the cost-benefit calculation and make the proposition look more attractive economically, the new proposal suggested that the Stein logs would be floated down the Fraser to the Boston Bar mill, something that had been explicitly rejected in British Columbia Forest Products' 1984 study as it was so technically difficult that it was "not an option." Meanwhile, the announcement kept open the possibility of a subsidized alternative, stating that "a bridge may be considered sometime in the future."[7]

More significant than this not-so-subtle number juggling was the government's decision to override the recommendation that no road be built without the formal agreement of the Lytton Indian band. The government simply claimed that the Band had refused to negotiate.

The retort from the Band was unequivocal. Lytton Chief Ruby Dunstan called the forest minister a liar. No attempt at all had been made to contact her, she claimed, let alone to negotiate a formal agreement. Confrontation loomed again. The government promised to reconstitute the public advisory committee, then signed a letter approving British Columbia Forest Products logging plan without any consultation at all. Fish and Wildlife authorities expressed opposition to the road plans, and were excluded from discussions, as was the federal Department of Fisheries.

The bands confirmed their opposition to any destruction of the valley in a ceremonial signing of a strongly-worded "Stein Declaration." They also prepared to go to court, hoping to build on the precedent established by the Meares Island case to halt logging pending the outcome of their land claim over

144

The Force That Brought Life

Belatedly we may be moving to rejoin the community of living beings from which we have so long alienated ourselves and of which we have so long been a mortal enemy. Some of us at least are beginning to revolt against the killer beast that modern man has become. Those of you who are here today belong to the new awakening. You are not here simply to save the Stein wilderness, but because you know in your hearts and in your guts and, yes, perhaps finally with the mind as well, that to save the Stein is a step toward saving the living world itself. You have the power now, the real power that derives not from money and the machine, but from the force that brought life into being on this planet . . . Bless you all.

Farley Mowat, a message delivered at the Stein Voices for the Wilderness festival, August 1987.

The 1988 Stein Voices for the Wilderness festival, at St. George's farm, held a commanding view of the Stein gorge across the Fraser. The first large side creek, Stryen (Last Chance) Creek, is on the left. With everyone's attention focused on the stage, the rays of the setting sun catch the small ridge separating the Stein and Fraser watersheds. (Photo: Greg McIntyre)

145

A view from the north
ridge at Cottonwood
Creek looking towards the
valley's headwater
glaciers. This is the same

perspective (though lower
in elevation) as the
accompanying "geoscape"
map. (Photo: Pat Morrow)

This unusual perspective
of the watershed presents
the reverse view from that
of standard maps. North
is on the bottom, rather
than the top, of the map.
The perspective looks to
the prominent headwater
mountains and glaciers

along the southern and
western ridges of the
valley, with the lower and
more gentle northern
ridges in the foreground.
On the left (east) is the
Fraser River, Kumsheen,
and the town of Lytton.
On the right (west) is the
Coast Range. Vancouver
lies beyond the top of the
image. The entire
watershed is drawn here
to precise perspective,
scale and detail.
(Painting: Stephen Fick)

S. FICK

Stein Spirituality

. . . However difficult it is to convey, it must still be understood that although the archaeologic sites within the Stein have special spiritual significance alone, they do not stand in isolation from one another or their surroundings. Rather they form focal points in a network or flux or web of spiritual power that pervades this watershed. These sites provide a map which the initiated can learn to follow to a spiritual maturity and strength unavailable elsewhere, and a key to the spiritual possibilities which have always existed within the Stein watershed. Without the intact, living, loving arms of the Stein which surround them, these sites become nearly meaningless, and are little more than antiquities for museums.

In truth, ancestors still sing in the Stein, using words which have remained unchanged throughout centuries. In truth, there is laughter on the breeze, and each tree, each stone, is alive. That the ancestors have always protected the Stein, and always will, is true; and the Stein, in turn, protects all. As various committees attempt to weigh trees against fish, and fish against deer, and deer against man against tree again, and **all** against money; it is laughter sweeping through the ages down the canyons which can be heard.

No archaeologic site within the Stein stands alone, no more than does any tree or stone or pool: rather these are centers from which ripples of spirituality spread outward in concentric circles. The long-standing tree people with their lofty spirits, the nimble deer people, the shambling bear people, the cool swimmers, the soaring flyers with their unbridled spirits: all contribute to the whole intact entity, wilderness Stein, whose spirit, in water, flows on to us all.

Roads cannot be constructed so as not to violate archaeologic sites, because these sites have no boundaries, but instead serve as focal points in a continuum. To the initiated, the Stein fairly bristles with a spiritual power which would be lost with the construction of the first kilometre of road into this wilderness. The Stein basin is, in a way, a vessel which contains limited awareness, knowledge, and power. The proposed road is the leak which could drain this watershed . . .

John McCandless with Napoleon Kruger, Lillooet Tribal Council, Lillooet, British Columbia.

Sunset over the 1988 Stein Voices for the Wilderness festival. (Photo: Greg McIntyre)

147

Photo of Stein Declaration.

the valley. Civil disobedience now loomed on a grand scale, as literally thousands of newcomers had visited the Stein since the logging plan was announced only two-and-a-half years earlier.

But the story does not end here, and it may yet be resolved without a Meares or Moresby-style confrontation. After persistent pressure from the Lytton band, the Ministry of Forests agreed late in 1987 to sit down to negotiate. Again, however, the ministry attempted unilaterally to limit the terms of reference of the discussions to the details of a road-building agreement. Mindful of the past 180 years, the Natives refused, wanting to open up larger questions including alternatives to logging the Stein, the heritage and environmental values at stake, and, finally, entitlement to land.

Night-time procession of Rediscovery students at the 1987 Stein Voices for the Wilderness festival. (Photo: Bryan K. Evans)

*A member of the
Rediscovery procession.
(Photo: Jeff Gibbs)*

Better Jaw Than Saw

Forests Minister Dave Parker and the Indian bands opposed to the government's logging plan for the Stein Valley are not yet talking the same language but at least they are still talking.

They should continue to talk until they understand each other, for a negotiated agreement would be far preferable to the kind of confrontation Mr. Parker had seemed intent on seeking before he agreed to listen to the bands' concerns about the destruction of their heritage in the valley.

The minister has yet to commit himself to follow the recommendation of the government's wilderness advisory committee, which said no logging road should be built into the valley without the consent of the Lytton band.

Mr. Parker still needs to be persuaded to consider the Stein timber in a wider context.

It is legitimate to consider, for example, whether improved forestry practices could provide sawmills in the area with adequate wood supplies and eliminate the perceived need to log in the Stein watershed. That is an alternative Mr. Parker didn't want to discuss with Indian representatives at their last meeting. He should look into it more thoroughly.

Editorial, *Vancouver Sun*, 11 April 1988, p. B2.

PART

IV

THE JOURNEY AHEAD

Stormy day on the northern ridge. (Painting: Stephen Fick)

Native child by alpine lake. (Photo: Thom Henley)

On March 13, 1985, the **Bridge River-Lillooet News** reported what many had been expecting for a decade: **Forestry Approves Stein Logging Road**. This was anti-climactic for the citizens of Lytton and Lillooet, for on the same page was a more prominent headline emblazoned in red across the top: **Waterland Says: No Need to be Overly Concerned**. The forest minister was, however, not referring to the Stein controversy, but to the very survival of the Lillooet mill.

Evans Products, the Florida-based forest company, had just filed for protection from its creditors under Section 11 of the United States bankruptcy laws. This multinational company owned the local Lillooet mill, and was the town's major employer. Many wondered if history was repeating itself, yet again. Another bust. So began the most recent phase of the Stein controversy: with the irony of a local forest industry, seemingly in danger of collapse, being offered southwestern British Columbia's last large wilderness watershed at a bargain price.

The 1985 announcement also marked the beginning of the Stein preservation movement. Its juxtaposition with a financial crisis in the forest industry highlights the concerns which drive the movement to this day. For the struggle over the Stein River is not just an isolated conflict of special interests; it is the inevitable product of an industry—indeed of a society—out-of-balance with the world which supports it. For more and more people, the character of this society is in question. Our economy, our political institutions, our way of thinking about the world must change if we are finally to make peace, not just with the Stein and the people of Kumsheen, but with the planet.

Making Forestry Sustainable

Technical solutions exist to the problems exemplified by the Stein issue, but they have not been implemented. Already identified by the Ministry of Forests in its 1986 Options Report, the problems and solutions begin in the woods. Government regulations specify that only logs over 17.5 centimetres (7 inches) in diameter need be hauled to interior mills. Today, smaller trees, broken logs, and less valuable species are left on the ground because they don't return as much profit when hauled to the mill as do the big logs. This so-called "high-grading" leaves large amounts of usable wood strewn about the landscape to rot or to be burned as slash. The alternative to this wastage is closer utilization of the cut wood, that is, requiring that smaller stems be brought in as well. Reducing the mandatory haul-log size to 12.5 centimetres (5 inches) would produce approximately six times as much wood for the Lillooet TSA as would logging the timber in the Stein.

A second solution is improved reforestation. While the industry is concerned about the "alienation" of the Stein from the forest base, another kind of forest land withdrawal occurs on even the best forest lands: large areas of the province's forest lands do not sustain new forest growth after cutting. This often occurs because of inappropriate cutting techniques (large scale clearcutting on steep hillsides, for instance), soil erosion, or from a failure to replant or tend new seedlings.

High-Grading

That the high-value end of the supply is being depleted becomes an inescapable conclusion when the species and locales of present operations are considered. And relaxed utilization standards have aggravated this problem by allowing larger areas to be cut to attain the same timber volume. In effect, the long-established trend to take the best first has been accelerated.

British Columbia Ministry of Forests, *Summary Report, 1984 Forest and Range Resource Analysis,* Victoria: Queen's Printer, p.24.

Waste Not, Want Not

Imagine 320,000 pickup trucks full of firewood, stretched bumper-to-bumper on the Trans-Canada Highway from Vancouver, through Calgary, into Saskatchewan. That's how much timber Canada's second-largest logging company left to rot in the B.C. rainforest last year. On one of British Columbia's richest timber claims, MacMillan Bloedel Ltd. wasted almost one-quarter of the Crown timber it cut in recent years, data from the company's reports show . . . MacMillan Bloedel is not the only company wasting usable wood.

Christie McLaren, "Quest for profit leaves coastal timber to rot," *The Globe and Mail,* Toronto, 12 December 1987, p.A4.

Waste wood left as slash in the Queen Charlotte Islands, at Yakoun Lake. (Photo: Clinton Webb)

Mining Our Forest Resource

We are cutting more wood each year than the unmanaged forests are growing. Political decisions have set harvest rates at these artificially high levels, and we are, in fact, robbing the inventory which should belong to our children. We are temporarily maintaining employment levels at the expense of jobs which our sons and daughters and their children should rightfully have. We are mining our national forest resource . . .

Prior to the recent federal-provincial agreements that have been signed, Ottawa talks about $700 million it has put back into forestry in the previous five years—to put that in perspective, in the same period it has taken some $10 billion out of forestry in tax revenue, or, in simple terms, for every dollar received, the government reinvested seven cents. For a comparison, it has put over $3 billion into one enterprise—the C.B.C. Indeed, more has been put into Canadair than back into forestry in the last eight years.

"Strategy for Survival," Presentation to the National Forest Congress, Ottawa, 10 April, 1986, in *Silviculture*, Summer 1986, pp. 14-17, 29.

The Global Web Of Life

[Part of a global pattern, the loss of virgin forests and ecosystems in British Columbia reflects some of the same causes, and has similar effects, as deforestation in other countries.]

Just as we are learning the value of these tropical ecosystems, they are disappearing. Scientists estimate the rate of deforestation at 1% to 2% annually. Every minute more than a hundred acres (40 hectares) of tropical forest are wiped out or seriously degraded. Every day more than 240 square miles (620 square km) fall before the bulldozer, the chainsaw, and the axe. An area the size of Great Britain is destroyed annually.

Millions of plant, animal, and insect species which have evolved over hundreds of millions of years face extinction as their habitats are levelled. Nearly half of the tropical rain forests have been destroyed in the last two centuries. The remainder—about 3.5 million square miles (9 million square km)—could be gone in the next 50 years. The extinction rates of the present are a thousand times those of the past tens of millions of years. We are literally destroying the resource base that is vital for the future survival of our species as well as the web of life on our planet.

Millions of native people and their extraordinary cultures are on the verge of physical and cultural extinction due to the deforestation of the lands they have inhabited for thousands of years. Their knowledge of living sustainably in the forests and of the medicinal value of obscure plants is being lost forever.

Financing Ecological Destruction, Washington D.C., 1987, pp.4-5. A publication of 20 international conservation organizations concerned about World Bank lending policies in Third World countries.

Every year the planet's remaining forest cover is diminished by an area the size of Great Britain.

These lands are considered Not Satisfactorily Restocked (NSR) land. Between 1979 and 1984, the amount of NSR land in the province increased **annually** by an average of 58,900 hectares (225 square miles). In the Kamloops Region which encompasses the Stein, 16,200 hectares of land were added to the NSR total in that period; 6,000 hectares more than the area of the Stein which is planned for logging.[1]

Comparison with other countries reveals the potential which exists for improvement in reforestation and better management of our forests. Finland plants 50 percent more trees per harvested hectare than we do.[2] Compared with how New Zealand, Finland and Sweden fertilize, thin, space, and weed their forests, we hardly tend our forests at all. As a result, these competitors realize much greater value from their timber lands than we do, and, in so doing, put less pressure on other forest lands.

These two changes—closer utilization and better reforestation—are part of a need to shift the forest industry from an **extensive** to an **intensive** economic strategy. Extensive forestry, the kind practised in British Columbia, depends on the continuous consumption of a high volume of virgin timber. This means non-stop road-building as the industry moves from one valley to the next. This cut-and-run approach, which is especially common in Third World rainforests which often do not regenerate at all after clear-cutting, has led to a global road-building binge. On these roads, industrial development probes ever further into the world's shrinking forest wilderness, causing so much disruption that many see road-building as one of the gravest environmental threats to the globe today. The Stein is one instance of this problem.

The alternative is intensive forestry: getting more return from a smaller geographic area. This involves a change from techniques of conquest and timber "mining" (such as clearcutting large areas) to those of nurture (such as selective logging and better tending of the forest crop). It implies a range of more environmentally efficient practices that are less dependent on expensive machinery, and rely more on human labour. This is a desirable objective in itself for communities such as Lytton and Lillooet that are cash poor and have many unemployed. As one expert has noted, there is so much work to be done that silviculture "in all its diverse forms—planting, spacing, thinning, fertilization, stand protection—has the potential of creating a new sub-industry within the province's forest industry."[3]

Making a limited resource base more productive also reduces the pressure to consume remaining wilderness areas. In California, it has been demonstrated that an improvement in forest productivity of only three to four percent would free up enough land to cover all new wilderness designations proposed in the state by the federal Congress.[4] Professor John Walters, then of the University of British Columbia's Faculty of Forestry, estimated that only 13 million hectares of intensively managed forest land could produce 84 million cubic metres of forest products annually.[5] This is more than have been produced in any year prior to 1987 on the province's estimated potentially productive forest land base of 26 million hectares. As the British Columbia forests ministry concluded for the Lillooet Timber Supply Area in 1986, improved reforestation and intensive forestry could increase the yield by some 60 percent. Local mills would benefit immediately.

Significant improvements can also be made at the other end of the forestry process—in the mill. One of these is to increase the amount of lumber which is recovered from the timber going through the saws. Like many older mass-production mills in the province, the British Columbia Forest

Jobs In The Woods

There is a possibility of easing rural unemployment through expanded silviculture programs. This has the effect of stabilizing rural communities . . .

As mills are modernized and new processes developed the number of employees required will drop and the skill levels will increase. The same effects will be felt in harvesting as operations are increasingly mechanized.

Silviculture will be mechanized more slowly. It will remain labour intensive for some time. Silviculture operations therefore offer a double benefit: job opportunities for some displaced workers as well as for new young employees; and a more competitive wood supply which will contribute to the overall competitive position of the Canadian forest industries.

Alexander Edwards, "Creating meaningful employment through effective silviculture," *Silviculture,* November 1986, pp. 24-25.

Value-Added

At the base of the Pattullo Bridge, amid the lumber stacks and saw-chip mounds that dot the industrial shoreline of the Fraser River in New Westminster, Robert Landucci has been practising value-added manufacturing for the last 10 years. His company, Landucci Lumber, employs 62 people and has a monthly sales volume of $2 million. The company produces small runs of high-quality finished products such as railings, screenings, and window frames designed to meet the specific needs of customers . . .

Despite Landucci's obvious success, he speaks like an outsider trying to break the shackles of a conservative industry. "You go to Japan or Germany or the United States, and this is happening," he says, "but they think I'm crazy here. People in British Columbia, especially those connected with the major mills, have got a preconceived notion about value-added manufacturing. It's considered almost illegitimate. But this is the answer to our problems in the B.C. lumber industry."

Where the industry once exploited the advantage of a seemingly endless timber supply, says Landucci, it must now gain maximum benefit out of a smaller quantity of what he calls "the best quality softwood in the world. You have to sell by the piece now, not by the thousands of board feet, and when the industry realizes this, it will have made the transition."

Landucci is [not] alone in his approach . . . In Abbotsford, Kenneth Stobbe and David Hurd run what amounts to a roadside stand in log homes, selling to passersby on the Trans-Canada Highway. "The market is unlimited," says Stobbe. "We don't even need to advertise—the traffic is enough. We're working with Japanese, Germans, Americans. They just don't have the fir trees we still have.

"Two loads of logs here will keep five people busy for two months. In a mill, how long would it take? Two hours? We're paying the same stumpage as the big mills do, but we're providing maybe five times the employment per unit of wood."

This graph shows the large increase in the provincial annual allowable cut since sustained yield became official provincial policy in 1945.

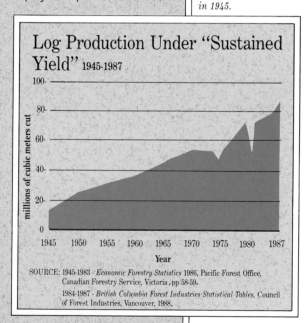

Log Production Under "Sustained Yield" 1945-1987

SOURCE: 1945-1983 - *Economic Forestry Statistics 1986*, Pacific Forest Office, Canadian Forestry Service, Victoria, pp 58-59.

1984-1987 - *British Columbia Forest Industries Statistical Tables*, Council of Forest Industries, Vancouver, 1988.

R. Michael M'Gonigle and Edward Alden, "Wilderness Epitaph," *Equinox*, September/October 1986, p. 56. Reprinted with permission of *Equinox Magazine*, (c) 1986, Telemedia Publishing Inc.

Products mill at Boston Bar has traditionally had a low recovery factor, meaning that there is much wastage as the timber is cut. One expert recently estimated that the mill continues to lose so much of the wood currently being cut into lumber that improving recovery would offset much of the volume which the Stein is intended to provide to the mill.[6]

Finally, there exists the oft-repeated call for value-added processing—making furniture, not two-by-fours. Over 75 percent of British Columbia Forest Products Boston Bar output still goes out as rough-cut construction grade lumber for the American and, more recently, overseas markets. Western hemlock is one of the staples of the mill, but is considered a low grade softwood in British Columbia, and is sold as two-by-fours and pulp. To British Columbia Forest Products, one of the attractions of the Spruce-Pine-Fir stands in the Stein is that they would improve the product mix. The Japanese, though, value the pale fine-grained hemlock, and cut the lumber up to make door and window frames, moulding, and interior trim. The products re-manufactured from these two-by-fours sell in Japan for five times the price paid to local companies for the lumber.[7] Even basic techniques such as treating or kiln-drying this lumber would add value to the product. Modernizing the sawmill by increasing both its capacity to process more lumber and its ratio of machinery-to-labour (that is, increasing its labour productivity) is no answer if the goal is just to produce more construction grade rough lumber with fewer employees. This just leads to bigger cut volumes and more layoffs, as happened across British Columbia between 1980 and 1985 when the cut went up, even as 20,000 jobs were lost.

Genuine long-term solutions require greater efficiency in the use of the forest resource—less wastage in the woods, more benefits from the wood that is processed through the

Surveying the forest of the mid-Stein—traditional territory and coveted timber. (Photo: Leo deGroot)

Community-Oriented Tourism

Community-oriented policies have taken hold in several locations including Oregon . . . There the Eugene area's "Buy Oregon" project resulted in $2 million worth of new business for local firms in its first year . . . and the project has since been adopted state-wide. Thus we can see evidence of communties taking a more direct role in determining their economic destiny.

Part of this rise in community consciousness has been a growing awareness of the local heritage, both natural and cultural, which has created the local way of life . . .

To take advantage of this interest in local character and employment, the tourism industry needs to become a facilitator of community aspirations as well as a business. The industry has the opportunity because, as the tourism market has matured, more tourists are looking for authentic experiences and local flavour; so the conservation and marketing of genuine local or regional characteristics will help provide the distinctiveness and intimacy that more tourists are seeking . . .

Peter Murphy, "Community-Driven Tourism Planning." In *Tourism as a Generator for Regional Economic Development, Proceedings of the First Annual Advanced Policy Forum on Tourism, Whistler, B.C. May 1987.* Anne Popma and Ann Pollack (editors), 1987, pp. 71-73.

157

Protection Of Our Rivers Must Be A Priority

Don't kid yourself that you're doing it right now . . . We have to beware of the 'Great North' syndrome—the belief that there's an inexhaustible amount of wilderness in Canada . . . Right now we're at the end of the North American frontier. We're making the final, irreversible decisions that will determine the environment that . . . will exist in these countries. If the old frontier represented conquering wilderness, the new frontier, I think, means conquering civilization . . . The U.S. is down to a handful of rivers that are really worth saving. . . Less than two per cent of 3.2 million miles of river in the lower 48 states retain outstanding wilderness values . . . Who's to say that same point won't apply to [Canada] in 10 or 15 years' time?

Roderick Nash, Professor, University of California at Santa Barbara, addressing a Vancouver audience in 1986. Quoted in "Protection of our rivers must be a priority," *Vancouver Sun*, 23 September 1987, p.B3.

Plantations Are Not Sustainable

All nations will be in equal poverty if we denude our forests . . . We have in the Northwest [of North America] perhaps the last chance in the world to learn how to grow a sustainable forest. No one has ever done it . . .

Everything from the giant 800-year-old Douglas-fir decomposing on the forest floor for four centuries, to the tiny creeping vole whose droppings transmit nitrogen-fixing bacteria to seedling roots, play important roles in the natural regeneration of forests.

Those processes are not being replicated in plantations whose soils are becoming increasingly compacted and whose trees have been subjected to herbicides and pesticides that play havoc with delicate ecosystems . . .

Chris Maser, quoted in "Spare That Old Growth," *Vancouver Sun*, 9 March 1988, p.B1.

Plantation forest at the University of British Columbia Research Forest. (Photo: Richard Chester)

mill. A more efficient and sustainable forestry requires making a greater commitment to the environment, to the local communities, and to the employees, than the industry has, so far, been willing to make. To attempt to justify the continuation of past practices with the claim that they protect jobs is misleading in light of the industry's recent history. This is especially true given the availability of more resource-efficient and labour-intensive alternatives. In fact, without such changes, forestry in the Fraser canyon will simply exhaust the supply, and go the way of the other boom-and-bust industries which preceded it.

Making Room For Wilderness

With more sustainable forestry, much room exists for preserving wilderness as well. This is certainly the solution for the Stein. The benefits are great. Many of these are non-monetary, meaning they cannot easily be quantified in money terms. The cultural value to the Nlaka'pamux of preserving the Stein is inestimable. Its value as a sanctuary for the non-Native peoples of Vancouver and the Lower Mainland is tremendous as well, even for many who will never visit it but take comfort in knowing that it is there. In fact, the valley's "existence value" (as economists call the pleasure many people have merely in knowing that the valley is preserved) might be significant if it were ever calculated.

The Stein's value as a wildlife and scientific preserve is also great, particularly since it is now the last complete watershed in the area. Reforestation of logged areas is experimental today, using a relatively narrow genetic stock of replacement trees. To conduct such an experiment, the preservation of a natural reference point is imperative. If silviculture fails, or the global climate changes, the diversity of the wilderness would be the only insurance we would have for maintaining a broad genetic base for future forests.

Representative Ecosystems Diminishing Rapidly

Essential ecological processes and life-support systems depend upon the genetic materials of the world's living resources, as do breeding programs for plants, animals and microorganisms . . .

. . . Thus, although Canada has a strong capability in tree improvement, the preservation of intraspecific variation, particularly in the form of naturally evolved, locally adapted populations, must be viewed as a critical strategy in the conservation of Canada's forest resources. To illustrate the point, we might ask whether we shall have adequate genetic resources if the climate shifts over the next 70 years as predicted.

Protected areas are established for several reasons, including preservation of special habitats, unique sites and communities and representative examples of natural ecosystems. They serve as irreplaceable sites for scientific investigation and education, as well as having aesthetic qualities that become apparent once visited. For all this, there are still very few protected areas that fulfill the needs of forestry. Even in British Columbia, where there is a seeming abundance of protected areas, the Association of B.C. Professional Foresters has urged the establishment of a system of forested ecological areas noting that opportunities for their selection are diminishing rapidly . . . Nevertheless events in British Columbia support the view that the forest sector has much to gain from a more systematic approach to protected areas, and has much to do to achieve it.

D.F.W. Pollard, Senior Policy Advisor, Canada Forestry Service, "The World Conservation Strategy and the Forest Sector in Canada," *The Forestry Chronicle*, October 1987, p.367.

Teaspoon Creek, a cool and magical oasis, awaits the traveller within a few hours of entering the valley. (Photo: Dennis Darragh)

Future Recreation

The types of recreational activities which are expected to increase in popularity will be unstructured activities which stress individualism, self-fulfilment, improvement of personal skills and satisfaction of personal needs (Hicking-Johnston, 1981). Recreational pursuits which focus on human energy (as opposed to mechanized equipment) are also expected to increase in popularity (Van Doren, 1981). These predictions suggest outdoor recreational activities such as hiking, skiing, canoeing, sailing, windsurfing, and bicycling will likely experience continued growth. Recreational activities that . . . are situated "close to home," i.e. local and regional facilities, will likely be in greater demand in the future.

The Future: Some Assumptions,
A Background Paper for the Four Mountain
Parks Planning Program, Parks Canada Paper 25,
Ottawa, 1981.

Wilderness provides insurance not just of the genetic diversity of trees, but also of wildlife: road access to a valley increases hunting tremendously. The mix of wildlife in a mature, unlogged natural ecosystem such as the Stein is very different from that in a disturbed valley. Here again, the Stein Valley could serve as a benchmark against which to measure wildlife population and habitat changes in neighbouring valleys, and as a refuge for (and even exporter of) species whose habitats have been damaged or populations over-hunted in the surrounding valleys.

These non-economic values of preservation are by far the most important ones. But wilderness preservation increasingly makes sense in traditional economic terms as well. For the Stein, many calculations show logging the valley to be a poor business proposition, involving government subsidies, high market risks, and the likelihood of great financial losses. Under these conditions, doing nothing at all in the valley would make more sense economically. But this is not the alternative to logging, as preservation of the valley would actually provide significant economic opportunities.

Despite Lytton's boom in the 1930s and 1940s, based to a great degree on tourism, the opportunities offered to the region by wilderness-based "adventure tourism" are not appreciated today. This is one of the fastest growing segments of the travel industry. For the last ten years, it has been growing by 17 percent per year in British Columbia, [8] accounting in 1987 for over 570 businesses (excluding fishing, hunting, and alpine skiing operators) in the province.[9] The sale of adventure travel products alone generates nearly $60 million annually.[10] Low impact wilderness tourism will not replace logging in British Columbia, but could certainly supplement a more sustainable forest industry, and in the process diversify local economies.

Family of hikers climbing
to the first Stein Voices for
the Wilderness festival.
(Photo: Pat Morrow)

While a desire for wilderness retreats is a global tourist trend, it is especially important for a province that advertises itself as "SuperNatural BC." In the Visitor '87 travel survey to British Columbia, interest in "visiting the Queen Charlotte Islands" and "heritage activities" led all other vacation categories.[11] To foreigners, Native cultural heritage and natural open spaces are characteristics associated with Canada. Consultants estimate that over 35 million North Americans are in the market for an adventure/recreation trip,[12] and that an increasing proportion of them are coming to British Columbia from distant American states, and overseas.[13]

In this light, the comparative advantage of the Stein is its complete character—as a wild river, intact watershed, and focus of Native culture—close to the large cosmopolitan centre of Vancouver and to the American market. In the United States, visitors to some parks that were once wilderness, such as Yellowstone, now camp on poured concrete pads. Hut-to-hut tourism, wildlife observation stations, a lodge on the ridge accessible from Duffey Lake Road (near to the Whistler resort), a Native Interpretation Centre at the mouth of the Stein—all these offer great potential for an environmentally sustainable tourism, a permanent alternative to a few years of clearcut logging. With local management of the Stein tourist industry, this valley behind the gorge across from Lytton could well become the focus for the whole community's cultural and economic revival.

An interesting parallel exists here with the situation of the forest industry. In both tourism and forestry, distinct products are desirable for economic success. As a tourist resource, a roaded and clearcut Stein Valley would be as indistinct as a knotty two-by-four on the lumber market. However, its preservation as an intact wilderness watershed with living cultural and spiritual traditions would ensure that its unique ecological and economic attractiveness endures. Indeed, the biggest problem preservationists might face a couple of decades from now would not be the threat of logging in this "unused" area so close to Vancouver, but having it loved to death, as is now happening to popular wilderness areas in the United States.

The Stein is but one valley. There are other environments throughout the province, the country, and the globe that face similar threats and opportunities. For reasons that are economic and non-economic, what is required is not just the preservation of the Stein, but of a true "wilderness mosaic" here and abroad. In British Columbia, this demands that the best 10 or 15 percent of the land, not four or five percent, be formally preserved in parks and designated wilderness. Such an expansion would, however, affect only one or two percent of the productive forest base, certainly no threat to the industry. Wilderness demands simply do not compare to the losses currently incurred to Not Satisfactorily Restocked land, hydroelectric reservoirs and rights-of-way, and highways. As one critic commented, "for the forest industry to remain adversaries of those who recommend a balanced parkland system in BC is like chasing chipmunks around the front porch while the wolverines are in the larder."[14]

Confronting The Goliath

In theory, a practical solution exists to the Stein controversy. With a two-pronged policy of reorienting the forest industry and preserving wilderness, all the interests—industrial, Native and environmental—can be met. Sustainable forestry and a wilderness mosaic are certainly reasonable and rational objectives. Yet, they seem to be unattainable. In British Columbia and internationally, road-building, clearing of the remaining virgin forests, damming of the last wild rivers,

The System Is Not Right

To Dan Hanuse, president of the Truck Loggers' Association of B.C. ". . . British Columbia has to address the sunset of the tenure system whether it's in ten years or twenty years. The system is not right for a free society, where someone gets tenure forever and ever by simply renewing their lease. It just can't go on; we can't hide the fact that there is no competition for a public resource. This has been going on for forty years."

The crux of the entire discussion on B.C. forests is a single fact: a handful of corporate giants hold 93% of the total allowable annual cut while only 7% is made available to competitive bidding among small contractors . . .

Frank O'Brien, "Forests Under Review," *The Truck Logger*, April/May 1986, pp. 6-10.

Rushing mountain stream. (Photo: Gary Fiegehen/Robert Semeniuk)

and disruption of Native cultures have all escalated in recent years. Reforms from the decade of environmentalism have simply not turned the tide of ecological decline. Something more basic is needed, and the Stein has become a rallying point for both sides in that bigger battle.

At issue from the Stein watershed to the Amazon basin is not just how we manage the land base, but who ultimately controls it. To suggest new policies is to confront that seemingly insuperable obstacle which has buffetted Kumsheen for 150 years—control by remote economic interests. One author, Bill Wagner, recently reported that 20 companies control 99.8 percent of all Tree Farm Licences, and 91.4 percent of the licences in remaining areas. Four interlinked groups of companies control 93.2 percent of the allocated public forest cut in the province. These groups are so close to each other that they are "corporately cooperative" rather than competitive.[15] Moreover, the corporate creation, the British Columbia Council of Forest Industries, with its big budget and ready access to government officials, is a powerful advocate of public policies that reflect private business objectives.

Not one of the four multinational groups mentioned by Wagner is based in British Columbia. As is also true for so many resource-based Third World countries, the profits from the deforestation of the provincial landscape leave the region, while the environmental costs stay. In Sweden, the government nets between $20 and $50 per cubic metre for its sale of standing timber.[16] In British Columbia, the price paid in 1986-1987 averaged $2.88/cubic metre; in the Kamloops region, it averaged $1.56.[17] In that year, the expense of running the Ministry of Forests, $417 million, exceeded the revenues paid into it by the industry by $170 million![18]

The support given to these large corporations was evident when the Forest Service initially allocated the entire Stein cut to British Columbia Forest Products, now controlled by the New Zealand forestry giant, Fletcher Challenge. (The company was renamed Fletcher Challenge Canada Limited in September, 1988.) The family-owned local mill in Lytton, Lytton Lumber, fought for months to get a portion of that cut. Yet the Lytton mill has been conscientious over the years in supporting the local community. It employs more Native people than the British Columbia Forest Products' mill, does its banking at the local bank, and even stayed open through the recession of 1981-82 when the Boston Bar mill closed down. Historically, it has been more efficient in the woods and in the mill, having a higher lumber recovery factor and providing a more specialized product.[18] Such companies should naturally be the allies of preservationists concerned about efficient resource allocation. But Lytton Lumber is squeezed for timber (and pays more for it) because so much of the local land base has been allocated to the multinationals. So when the Forest Service finally allocated 20 percent of the cut to this mill right outside the Stein, with the stated expectation that the company would "smooth the way for this development," the mill owner and his forester took up the cause.

This situation of control of the land base by large, distant corporations has had predictable consequences for the forests. Although extensive logging began in British Columbia about the turn of the century, it was not until 1945 that a policy of "sustained yield" was proposed. Even as it was implemented, however, larger and larger tracts of timber fell under the control of fewer and fewer corporations. Sustained yield has never become a reality. In 1980, the first comprehensive provincial Resource Analysis undertaken by the Forest Service concluded that the old stands of virgin timber had been so overcut that a "falldown" in supply would be inevitable as we run out of old-growth before the second-growth is ready to cut.

Despite the sustained yield policy, in the years since 1945 the cut has gone up and up. By the 1980s, the limitless resource had become a statistical mirage. As the guru of the province's forest economists, University of British Columbia's Professor Peter Pearse, put it: "Using the industry's own cost factors, we found that only a fraction—about a quarter—of the old-growth inventory that the Forest Service claims to be available could be harvested at a profit."[19]

Facing this falldown, the industry defends its territory tenaciously. The greatest threat seen by industry is not wastage, inadequate reforestation, or lack of value-added processing, but the demands of environmentalists and Native bands. As a result, new forestry practices and new parks are achieved (if at all) at a snail's pace, and only after much unnecessary acrimony. Profitable or not, logging the Stein Valley has now become a rallying point for the entire industry.

Instead of improved forestry and reconciliation, the talk is of "multiple use." For Kumsheen, this means logging not nine out of ten local valleys, but ten out of ten. The principle of multiple use, as it is applied today, means industrial use everywhere first. The concept of "multiple use without resource extraction" advanced for the Stein by the Federation of Mountain Clubs is incomprehensible to the industry and its professional foresters. They allow no room, not even intellectually, for non-industrial development for different types of recreational and cultural usage, and wildlife protection. These are seen as secondary usages, to be permitted only as an afterthought to logging. This explains the assertion that there will be "multiple use" in the Stein because the companies plan to log only nine percent of the valley area. What this means, in reality, is that the company

The Stranglehold Of Corporate Tenures

To create wilderness . . . the government cannot reduce a licensee's allowable cut by more than five per cent. This is why license holders can argue that there is a high cost in terms of lost jobs and incomes if land is set aside for wilderness or other purposes. It is not because we are running out of timber, it is because it is all spoken for under long-term renewable licenses and committed to support long-term yield plans. There is almost no opportunity even to withdraw timber in one area and replace it with timber in another.

Peter Pearse, "The Tenure System's Main Faults: Lack of Competition, Over Allocation of Timber," *Forest Planning Canada*, 1987, p.25.

plans to build roads the entire length of the main river, up its side hills and major creeks, take nearly all of the desirable timber, and irrevocably disrupt the whole valley environment.

Such is the appetite of the industrial goliath we have created in the past century, a giant which now resists rational redirection. The provincial government is of little help. With the exception of the three-month hearings of the Wilderness Advisory Committee, the so-called public participation process from 1976 to date was premised on the inevitability of logging and was given no authority to decide otherwise. Full power and discretion was retained by the Forest Service. Even the 1988 discussions between the Native bands and the Ministry have stalled on this issue.

The existing structure of control infects the very way in which people think about British Columbia's forests and associated resources. The official stewards of the forests, Registered Professional Foresters, have been repeatedly criticized for allowing, indeed supporting, the waste of the forest resource. Yet, instead of encouraging innovation and imagination within their ranks, foresters remain the staunchest advocates of staying the course. They have even launched investigations of those few of their members who have dared to investigate and report on abuses.[14]

Other professionals, such as many contract archaeologists, seem no longer able even to appreciate, let alone speak out for and defend, the heritage values of the province. For an archaeologist to talk of an area's spiritual integrity is, at best, incomprehensible to other archaeologists. At worst, it is professional suicide. Instead, as paid contractors to a mining or forestry company undertaking the mandatory impact assessment, they count the artifacts, map and classify them, collect samples, and then pronounce on how many might be destroyed by the road-builders.

Legislative reforms that do take place are small. Under intense pressure from the United States, the government has reluctantly increased the royalties payable to it for Crown timber, an important step that should encourage some improvements in utilization. At the same time, though, more and more of the provincial forest base is to be turned over to forest companies as Tree Farm Licences, giving them virtual ownership rights. This process makes the creation of new parks and wilderness areas, and the settlement of Native land claims, more expensive and more difficult to achieve legally. Even new regulations permitting the creation of wilderness areas under the Forest Act leave the Ministry of Forests with complete discretion regarding when to add, and when to delete, new areas. Meanwhile, the existing park system is being opened up to active mining and logging through the creation of Recreation Areas scattered throughout parks like the Kokanee where industry has made past claims.

The Costs Of Reform

As the history of Kumsheen and the present danger to the Stein demonstrate, the institutions brought by White society have been successful in removing resources from local communities, but in return they have failed to provide community and ecological stability. High-grading the best trees, and leaving scarred and charred hillsides behind are more immediately profitable than instituting practices which would sustain the forests and provide more local employment. More diversified uses of the forest base (through wilderness tourism, for example) would also benefit, not the forest industry, but local entrepreneurs and Native bands.

Though rational and just, the needed changes confront entrenched patterns of extraction, and an over-extended structure pushing beyond natural limits the world over. To achieve solutions, the movement to preserve the Stein, of necessity, looks beyond the status quo.

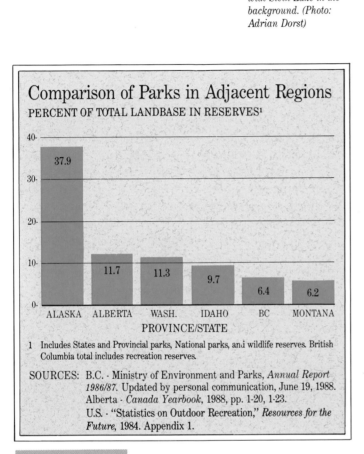

Comparison of Parks in Adjacent Regions
PERCENT OF TOTAL LANDBASE IN RESERVES[1]

PROVINCE/STATE	Percent
ALASKA	37.9
ALBERTA	11.7
WASH.	11.3
IDAHO	9.7
BC	6.4
MONTANA	6.2

1 Includes States and Provincial parks, National parks, and wildlife reserves. British Columbia total includes recreation reserves.

SOURCES: B.C. - Ministry of Environment and Parks, *Annual Report 1986/87*. Updated by personal communication, June 19, 1988.
Alberta - *Canada Yearbook*, 1988, pp. 1-20, 1-23.
U.S. - "Statistics on Outdoor Recreation," *Resources for the Future*, 1984. Appendix 1.

This chart compares the natural areas set aside in several jurisdictions.

A stately Douglas-fir tree, with Stein Lake in the background. (Photo: Adrian Dorst)

Isolated In The Cosmos

As scientific understanding has grown, so our world has become dehumanized. Man feels himself isolated in the cosmos, because he is no longer involved in nature and has lost his emotional "unconscious identity" with natural phenomena . . . No river contains a spirit, no tree is the life principle of a man, no snake the embodiment of wisdom, no mountain cave the home of a great demon. No voices now speak to man from the stones, plants, and animals, nor does he speak to them . . . In spite of our proud domination of nature, we are still her victims, for we have not even learned to control our own nature . . . Our present lives are dominated by the goddess Reason, who is our greatest and most tragic illusion. By the aid of reason, so we assure ourselves, we have "conquered nature."

But this is a mere slogan.

Carl Jung, *Man and His Symbols*, New York: Dell, 1964, pp. 85, 91.

In the modern city, the natural world exists some place out there beyond the freeway. Oblivious to its environment, the city is nonetheless sustained by a stream of wealth extracted from that natural world. Our forests, minerals and other natural resources, and the communities which have long existed in equilibrium with them, are the victims of our centralized industries and what we call "progress." Rivers flowing since geologic time, climax forests and complex ecosystems, 7000 year-old cultures of balanced inhabitation—all fall before the forces of consumerism, centralized economic growth and territorial expansion.

The Stein is but one contemporary example of this worldwide pattern. The trends are not encouraging—wilderness, old-growth forests, wild rivers, and indigenous Native cultures within these natural areas have declined to a point nearing extinction today. Every year, the rate of this decline accelerates to keep up with the ever-quickening pace of that economic growth which sustains imperious urbanized centres at the expense of local economies and the environment. The cause-and-effect relationship is direct. Says the 1987 United Nations World Commission on Environment and Development: "The annual increase in industrial production today is perhaps as large as the total production in Europe around the end of the 1930s. Into every year, we now squeeze the decades of industrial growth—and environmental disruption—that formed the basis of the pre-war European economy . . . There are thresholds that cannot be crossed without endangering the basic integrity of the system."[1]

If the citizenry and its leaders in British Columbia and around the world do not yet understand the consequences of our way of life or appreciate the significance of the ecological decline we face, it is perhaps because we are already so far removed from nature. Vancouver sits in the south west corner of a large province, and exploits the forests and minerals of a vast territory most have never seen, let alone explored. To the urban dweller, the province's wilderness is but an abstraction; to the forest industry, environmental activists are an inconvenience and a threat. With industry and government so unresponsive, achieving a balance with nature requires fundamental changes in our institutions and attitudes. This is the profound lesson to be learned from the Nlaka'pamux and the Stein.

The Structure Of Extraction

Political economists have long characterized the modern economic world as one where peripheral territories supply cheap resources to an industrial core, which then processes them at a profit. This so-called dependency theory is used by scholars worldwide. Significantly, it was first postulated in the 1930s by a Canadian, Harold Innis, as a way of explaining Canada's development based on furs and fish, timber and minerals. British Columbia's economic history is an especially clear demonstration of this theory. After 200 years of "development" by White society, British Columbia remains dependent on primary resource exports for its capital. This dependence has led to the so-called "staples trap" where the provincial economy does not diversify and become self-sustaining, but remains dependent and unstable, relegated to

A Rediscovery trip camped on the north ridge. (Photo: Leo deGroot)

being an economy of "hewers of wood and drawers of water."

The history of Kumsheen since 1808 has been a history of this process in operation. From the serious depletion of the fur-bearing animals in the 1820s, to the upheaval of the 1858 Gold Rush, through two railway construction booms-and-busts, to the eventual demise of the mixed farm and tourism economy built up in Lytton in this century, to today's dangerous over-dependence on the forest industry—all these have repeatedly reduced a once self-sustaining community to one dependent again and again on the wishes and whims of outside companies and markets.

With the resources provided by rural and Native communities like Kumsheen, wealth has poured into the centre of White society—into corporate office towers, swelling bureaucracies, booming cities, and rising levels of consumption and waste. Keeping this centralized system of wealth creation intact, whatever the costs, is a goal which unites the system's apparently disparate beneficiaries. On environmental issues such as the Stein, or on Native issues of land entitlement, there is little to distinguish between the attitudes of the Forest Service manager, the president of British Columbia Forest Products, and the provincial head of the International Woodworkers of America. This consensus has been very evident throughout the 15 years of negotiations over the future of the Stein.

The Structure Of Nurture

The current worldwide pattern of resource over-exploitation has evolved because, under pressure from an

Land And Ethics

Our educational and economic system is headed away from, rather than toward, an intense consciousness of land. Your true modern is separated from the land by many middlemen, and by innumerable physical gadgets. He has no vital relation to it; to him it is the space between cities on which crops grow. Turn him loose for a day on the land, and if the spot does not happpen to be a golf links or a 'scenic' area, he is bored stiff . . . The 'key log' which must be moved to release the evolutionary process for a [land] ethic is simply this: quit thinking about decent land-use as solely an economic problem. Examine each question in terms of what is ethically and esthetically right, as well as what is economically expedient. A thing is right when it tends to preserve the integrity, stability, and beauty of the biotic community. It is wrong when it tends otherwise.

Aldo Leopold, *A Sand County Almanac*, New York: Oxford University Press, 1949, pp.223-226.

The Pattern Of Dependency

1. Rapid influx of entrepreneurs upon discovery of the resource (many mineral stakes, small mills or sawmills);
2. Centralization and concentration by large corporations buying out small operators or by anyone expanding the scale of their operation to become as "cost-efficient" as possible;
3. Rapid use and depletion of the resource base, facilitated by ever more efficient harvesting and processing technologies that maximize the return to capital (if not to the local labour force);
4. The slow retreat or abrupt withdrawal of the industry leaving the local community or provincial government to make do with a much-diminished resource base and seek out some new industry for the area.

Darcy Case-Davis, Report to the Institute for New Economics, Vancouver, 1985.

Planning Is Cheaper Than Repair

In looking at our resources, our waste, and our past mistakes, we have arrived at a list of recommendations based on four basic assumptions:

1. That "sustained yield" is the only acceptable forest management, and that it means a sustained yield of all resources, from fish to water to trees.

2. That sustained yield can only be guaranteed if the local community is involved in resource-use planning . . .

3. That logging will incur either planning expense ahead of development or environmental costs afterwards. We found that planning is cheaper than repair. Thus, good ecology equals good economics.

4. That full and proper utilization of all resources will allow us to decrease our volume production of wood fibre and maintain economic stability at the same time.

RECOMMENDATIONS:

That a resource committee, comprised of six local resource management agencies and six local residents, be formed and charged with all resource management . . .

That a system of "rural woodlots" be instituted . . .

That all stumpage from the Slocan P.S.Y.U. [Public Sustained Yield Unit] be reinvested into the Slocan P.S.Y.U . . .

That in order to utilize the decadent cedar, private logs, woodlot logs, and thinnings, a small "product mill" be set up in the Valley . . .

That the Valhalla Range on the west side of Slocan Lake . . . be designated as a no-road access nature conservancy area . . .

Slocan Valley Community Forest Management Project, Undated (1974, approximately), pp.xiii-xiv.

Hugging a tree in the Stein Valley. (Photo: Leo deGroot)

expanding core economy, communities have not been able to provide protection for their local resource base. In the face of this top-heavy (and top-down) structure of power, numerous grassroots movements have sprung up which advocate a social re-balancing. These movements have a common objective: to empower local communities to pursue a sustainable future in their own places under their own direction. Wilderness preservation, Native self-determination, the preservation of the family farm, "appropriate technology," Green politics, bioregionalism, and even liberation theology point to the need for basic change, and all require one thing as a prerequisite—increasing community power. At root, this requires a local veto over measures that threaten local sustainability, an approach exactly opposite to the disenfranchisement which both the Nlaka'pamux and the White community have long endured at Kumsheen.

What this community control might look like has been a topic of debate for more than a decade. One outstanding example of alternative forest planning, the **Slocan Valley Community Forest Management Project**, came 15 years ago from a local citizens' group in the Kootenay area of British Columbia. It called for a community forestry, developed by, managed by, and benefiting, local interests.

The contrast of such an approach with traditional approaches can be seen by considering reforestation. Today, reforestation consists of low-cost, one-shot planting by a migrant contractor working for a large forest company. It has not been very successful. True stewardship of the forest base can best develop where local organizations are given long-term responsibility for the nurture—planting, thinning, and cultivation—of forest lands. With local businesses working in logging and reforestation, with local management, and with local control over timber allocations, royalties and

expenditures, community forestry would provide greater local returns and better resource management.

Community approaches are useful in tourism as well. Tourism can be a demeaning form of local servitude to the big-city tour operator. This is what the international Native magazine, **Cultural Survival**, calls "the tourist trap."[2] But tourism can also contribute to a diversified cultural and economic life as it did so well in Lytton in the 1930s and 40s. Archaeological and wilderness tourism offers such increased potential today.

The Haida are taking advantage of this very potential with their innovative "Haida Watchmen" program that monitors tourist activities in the Queen Charlotte Islands. The Watchmen co-exist with, and build on, the local Rediscovery program which has for a decade brought Native and non-Native youths out into the wilderness for physical and spiritual training. A Rediscovery program is now also being implemented in the Stein, providing an excellent base for local management of the various forms of tourism which might emerge there. Here again, spiritual and economic values not only co-exist, but reinforce each other. Moreover, the "co-management" regime which the Haida are evolving with the federal government for the South Moresby Park Preserve could become a model for managment in other areas. For governments, the message is clear: subsidies for an outmoded infrastructure of extraction should give way to investments in a new infrastructure of stewardship.

In addition to rebalancing political power between the core and periphery, a new economics is called for. Citing the ever-growing number of global environmental and economic problems, the United Nations World Commission on Environment and Development called in 1987 for a new global economics of Sustainable Development. Grassroots

Governor Douglas' Plans For Modern Times

. . . In my Despatch, No.4, of the 9th of February last, on the affairs of Vancouver's Island, transmitting my correspondence with the House of Assembly up to that date, there is a message made to the House on the 5th of February 1859, respecting the course I proposed to adopt in the disposal and management of the land reserved for the benefit of the Indian population at this place, the plan proposed being briefly thus:—that the Indians should be established on that reserve, and the remaining unoccupied land should be let out on leases at an annual rent to the highest bidder, and that the whole proceeds arising from such leases should be applied to the exclusive benefit of the Indians . . .

Copy of Despatch from Governor Douglas of British Columbia to the Right Hon. Sir E.B. Lytton, the namesake of Lytton village, dated 14 March 1859. In *Papers Related to the Affairs of British Columbia*, London: Eyre and Spottiswoode, 1859.

The New Paradigm

Sustainable development is development that meets the needs of the present without compromising the ability of future generations to meet their own needs . . . In its broadest sense, the strategy for sustainable development aims to promote harmony among human beings and between humanity and nature. In the context of the development and environment crises of the 1980s.., the pursuit of sustainable development requires:

- a political system that secures effective citizen participation in decision-making;
- an economic system that is able to generate surpluses and technical knowledge on a self-reliant and sustained basis;
- a social system that provides for solutions for the tensions arising from disharmonious development;
- a production system that respects the obligation to preserve the ecological base for development;
- a technological system that can search continuously for new solutions;
- an international system that fosters sustainable patterns of trade and finance, and
- an administrative system that is flexible and has the capacity for self-correction.

Report of the World Commission on Environment and Development (United Nations), *Our Common Future*, New York: Oxford University Press, 1987, pp. 43, 65.

The Executive View

It is hard to avoid the evidence that the B.C. forest sector is an industrial basket case . . . We limp from crisis to crisis. The fashionable "problems" of the day never get solved; they are merely replaced by others.

It might help if we faced the fact that the B.C. forest industry is founded on a myth. This myth, which has been around for 40 years, is that we have a rational, reasonable forest policy expressed in a carefully constructed set of laws and regulations.

Central to the creation of this myth was the belief that large, integrated forest corporations were best suited for the job of building and running the province's forest industry. They were the only ones, it was argued, with the stability and financial resources to undertake the investments in processing plants and provide the continuity in forest management . . . As it turned out, this has not been the case . . .

The senior executives and directors of the province's major forest corporations have provided very little evidence that they have any long-term concern for the future of the industry . . . What many of them have indicated . . . is that when the quick profits and capital gains have been realized they will sell out and return from whence they came.

Ken Drushka, "B.C.'s Forests: Condition Critical," The *Truck Logger*, January 1987, pp.10-15.

environmental and development activists call this "eco-development." Again, the essence of the needed change lies in the stable, self-sustaining community. With the ecological problem universal in scope, this is the meaning of the catchphrase "Think Globally; Act Locally."

Sustainable development requires that local communities once again have control over their resources and their economic destiny. This cannot be achieved by holding a local referendum on the future of the Stein, or by letting local companies, rather than foreign ones, liquidate the resource base for the overseas market. Instead, what is needed is a long process of putting political and economic institutions into place at the local level which actually allow sustainability to take root. Simply closing the Boston Bar mill is no solution for local residents without a commitment to replace it with other, more resource-efficient institutions.

The range of alternative possibilities is great. Locally-owned, smaller-scale businesses are necessary to create the economic dynamism missing in one-industry resource towns like Lytton and Lillooet. Local resources could be used by these businesses to produce both goods for local consumption as well as high-valued, specialized products for export. This is the difference between two-by-fours for sale to the mass housing market and handbuilt log houses for local use and for export to the United States, Germany and Japan; it is the difference between camper vans in every valley, and archaeological wilderness programs run from a Native Interpretation Centre and a Stein Lodge. At the depth of the Depression in the 1930s, when local farms were producing world class apples for England and beans for the general

store, when tourists were coming from Vancouver to admire the orchards and the scenery, the variety of businesses and local products available in Lytton, and the richness of the community life, far exceeded what is there today.

With resource management rooted in the democratic local community, eco-development ultimately means striking a balance between Natives and non-Natives, between the needs of one region and the demands of another, between the luxuries of one generation and the necessities of generations to come.

Wisdom, Wilderness And Survival

Achieving this will not be easy. If a stable, locally-controlled community were to be established at Kumsheen, it would be the first since Simon Fraser laid his claims to the wilderness there 180 years ago. The task is great, taking us into territories not yet entered by White society in its conquest of British Columbia. Yet it is possible, and has already begun in places like South Moresby in the Queen Charlotte Islands.

A key ingredient is Native land title. Today Native land claims are considered a threat to the modern economy, not its salvation. This is so because real local control, Native or non-Native, raises the spectre of re-allocating lands now being exploited on a short-term basis by non-local interests. The potential to challenge this short-term extractive system has been the main attraction which Native land claims have had for environmentalists. However, because of the uncertainty which they harbour about the political implications of Native claims, environmentalists have been viewed with skepticism by Native leaders.

But the two interests are actually different aspects of an even larger movement, something which is clear when we

Empowering Vulnerable Groups

[Native] communities are the repositories of vast accumulations of traditional knowledge and experience that link humanity with its ancient origins. Their disappearance is a loss for the larger society, which could learn a great deal from their traditional skills in sustainably managing very complex ecological systems. It is a terrible irony that as formal development reaches more deeply into rain forests, deserts, and other isolated environments, it tends to destroy the only cultures that have proved able to thrive in these environments.

The starting point for a just and humane policy for such groups is the recognition and protection of their traditional rights to land and the other resources that sustain their way of life—rights they may define in terms that do not fit into standard legal systems. These groups' own institutions to regulate rights and obligations are crucial for maintaining the harmony with nature and the environmental awareness characteristic of the traditional way of life. Hence the recognition of traditional rights must go hand in hand with measures to protect the local institutions that enforce responsibility in resource use. And this recognition must also give local communities a decisive voice in the decisions about resource use in their area.

Report of the World Commission on Environment and Development, *Our Common Future*, New York: Oxford University Press, 1987, pp.114-116.

That's Vancouver, That's New York

Ecosystem cultures [are] those whose economic base of support is a natural region, a watershed, a plant zone, a natural territory within which they have to make their whole living. Living within the terms of an ecosystem, out of self-interest if nothing else, you are careful. You don't destroy the soils, you don't kill all the game, you don't log it off and let the water wash the soil away. Biosphere cultures are [those] that begin with early civilization and the centralized state; are cultures that spread their economic support system out far enough that they can afford to wreck one ecosystem, and keep moving on. Well, that's Rome, that's Babylon. It's just a big enough spread that you can begin to be irresponsible about certain local territories.

Gary Snyder, *The Old Ways*, San Francisco: City Light Books, 1977, pp.26-27.

To Whom The Land Also Belongs

If you were to apply the notion of social contract to a Native concept of land ownership, what you will find is that Native people are only one party to the contract. These trees, those rocks, the deer, that fish swimming around, they're all parties to the contract.

And that's why Native people say we could never sell, we could never surrender the land, because it doesn't belong to us. If you're going to have a sale, you're going to have to go ask the deer, you know, consult the trees over there. You have to consult the rocks, see if it's okay with them, see, 'cause we're only one party to the contract.

And that's the reason Native people say, 'We'll be glad to share with others.' Inasmuch as Europeans find it hard [to understand], 'I wonder what's wrong with these native people, they can't understand this buying and selling of land,' well it's just as hard, you know, for native people to understand: 'I wonder why these people are dealing with land as though it was just another commodity, when it belongs to everybody, it belongs to those trees, it belongs to those animals.'

Leroy Littlebear, of the Blackfoot people, at the Stein Voices for the Wilderness festival, August 1987.

Tired hiker asleep on her packs, her face blackened in the traditional method for passing by Devil's Lake. (Photo: Leo deGroot)

Local Native youth building a cabin at the Rediscovery base camp near the junction of Cottonwood Creek and the Stein River. (Photo: Thom Henley)

The Rediscovery base camp. (Photo: Lin Yip)

reflect on Kumsheen and the Stein. The long tenure of the Nlaka'pamux people at the "centre of the world" is a pretty good basis for a claim to land. But this longevity is itself the result of a cultural wisdom learned and passed on by the community living in that place. In our search for more durable institutions, protecting the source of that traditional wisdom is the fundamental justification for the Native claim. This is also what wilderness advocacy is all about.

In his classic book, **Small is Beautiful**, E.F. Schumacher comments that the "task of our generation, I have no doubt, is one of metaphysical reconstruction . . . for it is our central convictions that are in disorder."[3] The movement which advocates such a reconstruction turns again to those victims of our economic growth—to wilderness and the aboriginal understanding of that wilderness—for guidance. The special relationship of traditional Native peoples to nature—their spiritual metaphysic—is an often-mentioned but little-understood phenomenon.

To aboriginal peoples, Nature is power. Above all, Nature is **spiritual power with physical effects**. The Sioux called the power of nature **wakan**, the Algonquin **manitou**, the Nlaka'pamux **hah-hah**. The essence of the natural world is an intangible field of force, and reverence for it is common to aboriginal cultures. The experience of this spiritual form of the world comes from direct personal contact with wild nature unmediated by the intrusion of human artifice. The campsite by the logging road is not wilderness, and it is not enough. In Teit's phrase, isolation "in the wilder parts" is required.

With tribal peoples, rituals in the wilderness are indispensable to gaining awareness, personal strength and power. Time spent there has been of great practical value for Native people, producing a range of sophisticated and successful traditional medicines, ingenious technologies,

A Sacred Valley

In 1961, I was fortunate enough to be hosted by Andrew and Sarah Johnny while I conducted site survey on the west bank of the Fraser River. Andrew Jr. and I became fast friends as we explored the banks of the river and chatted with elderly Thompson people, with Andrew as interpreter. As a student of Professors Wayne Suttles and Carl Borden, I was well steeped in the ethnography of the Thompson, and had studied and restudied the works of James Teit and others. So while I had the typical young man's conviction that I knew it all (well, most all), I found a wealth of unpublished information that I had not the skills to document. It all contributed, however, to an attitude towards the Native Peoples of North America that has stayed with me over the years.

The Johnny family lived near the mouth of the Stein River, a traditional village area. There were signs of archaeological sites everywhere; even to a relative novice the importance of the area was obvious. Even more fascinating was the Stein River and the valley, an area I began to see as far more than a river in a magnificent setting. Without being explicit, my Thompson friends began to educate me into the true significance of the Stein, a place where their young men and women had been sent for years to participate in the age-old Guardian Spirit quest.

It is hard for a Western person, trained to think in a philosophy spawned of Near Eastern regions, to fully appreciate the bonds forged between people and nature. I saw and appreciated the beauty in the unspoiled Stein valley; but, what I could not fully comprehend at first was the intimate relationship that comes from seeing the environment in terms of interacting spirits, spirits that are thought to influence our actions and future. Although nominally Christian, my hosts in the Stein still felt the tug of a religion that had no building we call a church, had no hierarchical arrangement of clergy, and had no written word to codify religion. Yet, only on rare occasions, would they allow the mask to fall away, and reveal something of their true feelings towards the land and the Stein Valley, feelings that I have not the skill to communicate in a medium so formal and foreign as written English.

Clearly, to my Thompson friends the Stein was more than a beautiful valley, a place for roots and berries, a place to hunt deer and mountain goat. It was sacred. It embodied a religion far older than Christianity, one that preached the oneness of humans and the spirits that surround us.

Archaeologists have worked hard to make our society understand that the prehistoric past is important and worth saving. As a people we appreciate our heritage, providing that the cost is not too high. And when it comes to the tangible remains of past societies we claim to have the answer to the bulldozer and the developer: Simply put, it is give us the time and finances to excavate a sample before it is lost forever. That may work with tangible remains such as village sites. Yet, I know of no way to mitigate the impact of "civilization" on sacred places that do not

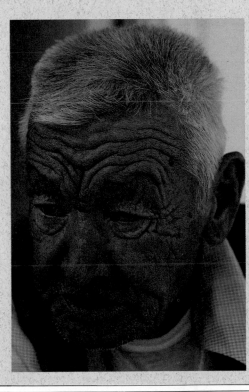

depend on the focus of a church or of statues to Pharaohs. It is an enormous problem that we have yet to solve despite our mechanical sophistication. To couch it only in terms of recovering arrow heads is clearly unsatisfactory.

What are the compromises? If the traditional mitigation techniques are unsatisfactory, and in this case I must believe they are, then another option should prevail. Places like the Stein Valley, important as they are to the cultural heritage of Canada's Native Peoples, should be protected. Surely there are enough natural resources in a Province so blessed as British Columbia that society can afford to set aside culturally critical areas. We now accept the need to preserve the range of mountain goats or certain plants. Why cannot we accept the importance of areas that have deep, long lasting religious significance to our people?

Professor David Sanger, Archaeologist, University of Maine, letter to author, June 1988.

Andrew Johnny, father of Lytton Band Chief, Ruby Dunstan. The Johnny family lives near the Stein trailhead. (Photo: Pat Morrow)

Low water in the Stein River in autumn. (Photo: Martin Roland)

Christianity And Nature Power

Question:

But you're a Christian now, and you believe in God. How do you square that with your Indian belief in Nature Power?

Answer:

You've read the Bible. Look at the beginning of any of them—Matthew, Luke and the others. Almost the first thing Jesus did, he went out into the wilderness, forty days and forty nights, and just like an Indian, fasted and lived by himself. Well, he heard a voice; it talked to him, tempted him. Only after that experience, in the wilderness, did he have all that power to help the people, just like an old Indian.

Louis Phillips, Nlaka'pamux elder, Summer 1983.

Toward A New Culture

Today, descendants of the two distant worlds that met in mutual wonder in British Columbia over 200 years ago face future centuries together. It is worth considering which of those two cultural traditions will ultimately be seen as having been best adapted—the indigenous system, which sustained a stable, comfortable and creative human environment for tens of thousands of people over many thousands of years, or the industrial newcomer, which manages to keep millions of people in luxury today, but at tremendous cost to the environment. Perhaps we could learn some lessons from prehistory about how people can achieve stable cultural systems.

Knut R. Fladmark, *British Columbia Prehistory*, Ottawa: National Museums of Canada, 1986.

healthy diets, and self-actualized individuals. The strength of a shaman is grounded in time spent in the wild. For modern society too, fullness as a human being still demands that we be allowed to experience ourselves not just as manipulators of an environment we do not directly inhabit, but as spiritual beings who are integral parts of the world around us.

Such is the wisdom we lose as we continue to push aside Nlaka'pamux culture and transform the sites of their power into mere roadside artifacts or logging clearcuts. We pass a death sentence on the Stein from the helicopter and the boardroom, never experiencing that which we destroy.

A deeper level of knowledge is essential for the survival of a world so out-of-balance with the life forces which sustain it. Our political and economic institutions must come back down to earth. As individuals too, we must again be able to experience that direct connection with the natural world which instills a reverence for life.

The possibility for such renewal still resides in the undisturbed Stein Valley. Over the generations, philosophers have tried to convey this awareness to a deafened world. But we can really only know the meaning of what they say when we hear it directly from the wilderness, from the Stein and the few remaining places like it.

For that, wilderness must survive.

The waters of Elton Lake rushing down towards the Stein River below. (Photo: Kevin Oke)

E P I L O G U E

A s Lytton Indian Band Chief Ruby Dunstan points out, controversies centred around appropriate resource management are as old, intricate and endless as the Stein Valley itself. It follows that the present conflict will have no easy resolution.

Within the collective memory of both the Nlaka'pamux and Lillooet Peoples is the certain knowledge that the ancestors were willing to fight to defend their homeland against exploitation. Continuing responsibility for proper management of traditional lands is a legacy which indigenous peoples cannot easily relinquish.

At no time during the past 10,000 years, however, has an outsider appeared at the door to the Stein who was so ruthless, relentless, and totally lacking in respect for natural systems as the one currently proposing to "harvest" the timber in this watershed. This newcomer to the Valley possesses an awesome capability to destroy; and established communities of plants, animals, birds and fish, along with those intricate patterns of resource use practised by the Native inhabitants over millennia, now face extinguishment.

The present consciousness of this "global intruder" dictates that as long as any wilderness remains anywhere, industry is duty-bound to mount a fresh attack on one unprotected flank or

Beaver pond. (Photo: Leo deGroot)

White Mountain heather.
(Photo: Kevin Oke)

another. If the natural systems at work today in the Stein
Valley are to be given the opportunity to continue, the vigilance
of the Lytton and Mt. Currie Indian Peoples and their allies
needs to be unceasing.

The flurry of activity at the Stein has recently grown to a
frenzy. Deeply rooted and stately groves of pine, spruce and fir
sway slightly as a BC Forest Products corporate helicopter
clatters by. Where once an alert and thoughtful People carefully
chose their steps along the Stein trail, choppers now ferry an
army of survey crews, road engineers, company archaeologists,
and public relations personnel who seek to make this planned
invasion palatable.

At stake are the glittering forests of the Stein: the vault of
several hundred years of sunlight banked in slow old growth.

Also at stake is the spiritual and cultural heritage of the
Lytton and Mt. Currie Indian Peoples, along with those
patterns of sustainable resource management learned and
practised since the dawn of Creation.

But perhaps what is most in jeopardy are our own fledgling
minds.

In a few short centuries humankind has conceived a colossus
of tools: from bone hook to bulldozer, from bow-and-arrow to
atom bomb. Unfortunately the tremendous capacity of these
new tools to destroy is unmatched by humankind's present
capacity of restraint. The Lytton and Mt. Currie Indian elders
say that if we do not learn to use our tools properly, these same
tools will eventually abuse us with unthinking severity. And
that this has happened more than once in the past.

The global newcomer, however, has yet to come to even a
cloudy comprehension of restraint.

The one resource which has been neglected in the rush to
wrest riches from the various promised lands is, ironically, also
the most valuable. This is the point-of-view of the indigenous

peoples who have crafted sustainable systems of resource management fitted to specific locales over thousands of years. This is the eloquent, and time-tested perspective of the so-called "savage" whose thinking has always been suspect because it did not mirror that of the global intruder. These are the place-specific songs, prayers and rituals directed toward deer, cedar tree, salmon, rock, cloud . . . and physical and cultural survival.

These are also the bounds of decency which all humankind needs to observe if we are to spend any length of time in the Stein Valley or elsewhere on this planet. This is restraint.

In distinct contrast, the global intruder pretends to be a god. He surveys the landscape to its furthest horizons, imposes his vision at tremendous cost to natural systems, and accumulates and calculates profit. Nothing is beyond possibility. There are no bounds. Everything must add up.

Sadly, indigenous peoples have had to become very familiar with this state-of-mind, since in the eye of the global newcomer Native peoples are simply another part of a primitive landscape to be developed.

In the past century indigenous people have had to witness the unthinking exploitation and rapid depletion of the natural resources which have sustained their cultures from "time-out-of-mind."

Under the threat of incarceration these same peoples have been forced to stand quietly by as their families and communities were disrupted, their children taken unwillingly from their homes and relocated in distant schools where they came face-to-face with the practice of "civilization."

These children were beaten for speaking in their own languages. And in the residential schools they were forbidden to eat traditional foods lovingly sent by parents and grandparents: the berries, mushrooms, fish and game abundant within their own homelands.

All of this occurred, whether consciously or unconsciously, in a calculated effort to circumvent established systems of land use implemented by Native peoples which would not have allowed the stripping of natural resources from the face of the planet at a net cost to future generations.

A more hopeful and positive pathway than that which the global intruder has thus far chosen still lies untrodden. Long overdue is the close observation and emulation of those respectful and intimate relationships which indigenous peoples have carved with their surroundings.

This is the type of opportunity, rapidly diminishing globally, which still remains in the Stein Valley.

I believe this is why the elders say that what is in the greatest jeopardy in the Stein Valley is the one thing on earth which can be changed: our own minds. It is the continuing wish of the Lytton and Mt. Currie Indian Peoples that the struggle at the Stein will prove a seed sown in what they still hope may become the fertile mind of humankind.

Because, the elders say, if this should fail, so will all else.

John McCandless, *Stein Coordinator;*
Lytton & Mt. Currie Indian Bands

Footnotes

Chapter 1

1 W. Kaye Lamb, editor, *The Letters and Journals of Simon Fraser, 1806-1808*, Toronto: Macmillan, 1960, p.87.

2 James Teit, "The Thompson Indians of British Columbia," *Memoir of the American Museum of Natural History*, 1(4), 1900, p.178.

3 W. Kaye Lamb, *The Letters and Journals of Simon Fraser, 1806-1808*, p.86.

4 Linguistic transcriptions of Native terms used throughout are from manuscripts by either Randy Bouchard, British Columbia Indian Language Project, Victoria, British Columbia or James Teit.

5 James Teit, unpublished ethnographic fieldnotes (1898-1918), American Philosophical Society, Philadelphia. (Microfilm copy at the Provincial Archives of British Columbia, Victoria).

6 Ibid.

7 James Teit, "The Lillooet Indians," *Memoir of the American Museum of Natural History*, 2(5), 1906, p.202.

8 James Teit, "The Thompson Indians," p.167.

9 James Teit, "The Lillooet Indians," p.240.

10 James Teit, unpublished ethnographic fieldnotes.

11 James Teit, "Traditions of the Thompson River Indians of British Columbia," *Memoirs of the American Folk-lore Society*, Vol.6, 1898, p.111.

12 James Teit, "Mythology of the Thompson Indians," *Memoir of the American Museum of Natural History*, 8(2), 1912, p.320.

13 James Teit, "The Thompson Indians," p.337.

14 James Teit, Marion K. Gould, Livingston Farrand and H. Spinden, "Folk-Tales of Salishan and Sahaptin Tribes," *Memoirs of the American Folk-Lore Society*, 11, 1917, p.12.; James Teit, "Traditions of the Thompson River Indians of British Columbia," p.20.

15 Charles Hill-Tout, "Notes on the N'tlaka'pamuq of British Columbia, a Branch of the Great Salish Stock of North America," 1899. Reprinted in Ralph Maud, editor, *The Salish People*, Vol.1, Vancouver: Talonbooks, 1978, p.94.

16 Louis Phillips, personal communication, June 1988.

17 James Teit, unpublished ethnographic fieldnotes.

18 Arnoud Stryd, personal communication, 1985.

19 Knut Fladmark, *British Columbia Prehistory*, Ottawa: National Museums of Canada, p.52.

20 Ibid., p.137.

21 Arnoud Stryd and Morley Eldridge, "Excavations at the Kopchitchin Site (D1Ri6) North Bend, B.C.," Report to the Heritage Conservation Branch, Victoria, British Columbia, 1985, p.18.

22 Ibid., p.137.

23 Harlan Smith, "Archaeology of Lytton, British Columbia," *Memoirs of the American Museum of Natural History*, 2(3), 1899, p.131.

24 David Sanger, "A Burial Site Survey of the Shuswap, Thompson and Lillooet Area of South Central British Columbia." Manuscript prepared for the National Museum of Man, Ottawa, 1961.

25 James Baker, "Site Survey in the Lytton Region, B.C., 1973," Heritage Conservation Branch, Victoria, 1974.

26 Mike Rousseau, "Thompson-Okanagan Impact Assessment, 1979: Final Report," Heritage Conservation Branch, Victoria, British Columbia, 1979.

27 *Lillooet-Fraser Heritage Resource Study*, Heritage Conservation Branch, Victoria, British Columbia, Vol.1, 1980, p.85.

28 Ian Wilson, "Stein River Haulroad Heritage Resources Inventory and Impact Assessment," Report prepared for British Columbia Forest Products Ltd., Boston Bar, British Columbia, 1988 (1985).

29 M.L. Parker, "Preliminary Dendrochronological Investigations in the Stein River Valley, Tree Age, Size, and Modification by Aboriginal Use." Contract report prepared for Western Canada Wilderness Committee, Vancouver, March 1988.

30 Katharine Howes and Pat Lean, "An Interview with Inga Teit Perkin, Daughter of Noted Ethnologist James A. Teit, November 25, 1978," *Nicola Valley Historical Quarterly*, 2(2), 1979, p.4.

31 Letter from James Teit to Edward Sapir, July 25, 1919. Canadian Ethnology Service, Canadian Museum of Civilization, Ottawa.

32 Wendy Wickwire, "The Contribution of a Colonial Ethnographer: Charles Hill-Tout, 1858-1944," *Canadian Folklore Canadien*, 1(1-2), 1981, pp.62-67.

Chapter 2

1 James Teit, "The Thompson Indians of British Columbia," *Memoir of the American Museum of Natural History*, 1(4), 1900, p.319.

2 Ibid., pp.312, 318.

3 Ibid., p.318.

4 Franz Boas, "The Religion of American Indians," in George W. Stocking, editor, *A Franz Boas Reader*, Chicago: University of Chicago Press, 1982 (1910), p.259.

5 Jay Miller, "Numic Religion: An Overview of Power in the Great Basin of Native North America," *Anthropos*, 78(3-4), p.341.

6 James Teit, "The Thompson Indians of British Columbia," pp.317,321.

7 James Teit, "Notes on Rock Painting in General," Newcombe Family Papers Add. MS. 1979, Vol. 23, Provincial Archives of British Columbia, Victoria, 1918.

8 Ibid.

9 Ibid.

10 Louis Phillips, personal communication,

11 Randy Bouchard and Dorothy Kennedy (1985), "Indian Land Use and Indian History of the Stein River Valley, British Columbia." Appendix One of: *Stein River Haulroad Heritage Resources Inventory and Impact Assessment Permit 1985 - 20*. Report prepared by I.R. Wilson Consultants Ltd. for British Columbia Forest Products Ltd. (Revised February 1988), pp.118-119.

12 James Teit, "The Thompson Indians of British Columbia," p.345.

13 Louis Phillips, personal communication, 1985.

14 James Teit, "The Thompson Indians of British Columbia," p.338.

15 Marshall Sahlins, *Stone-Age Economics*, Chicago: Aldine Publishing Co., 1972, pp.17, 34.

16 James Teit, "The Thompson Indians of British Columbia," p.238.

17 Archibald McDonald, "Thompson's River District Report," 1827, in E.E. Rich, editor, *Simpson's 1828 Journey to the Columbia*, London: The Hudson's Bay Record Society, 1948, p.231.

18 David Sanger, "A Burial Site Survey of the Shuswap, Thompson, and Lillooet Area of South Central British Columbia." Manuscript prepared for the National Museum of Man, Ottawa, 1961, p.20.

19 James Teit, "The Thompson Indians of British Columbia," p.193.

20 Ibid., p.192.

21 Charles Hill-Tout, "Notes on the N'tlaka'pamuq of British Columbia, a Branch of the Great Salish Stock of North America." Reprinted in Ralph Maud, editor, *The Salish People*, Vancouver: Talonbooks, 1978, (1899), p.58.

22 James Teit, "The Thompson Indians of British Columbia." p.194.

23 Letter from T.L. Thacker, Little Mountain, near Hope, British Columbia, to Harlan Smith, 24 March, 1923. In Harlan Smith, unpublished notes, Archaeological Survey of Canada, Canadian Museum of Civilization, Ottawa.

24 Willy Justice, personal communication, 1985.

25 Mary (Millie) Williams, In Randy Bouchard and Dorothy Kennedy, "Indian Land Use and Indian History of the Stein River Valley, British Columbia." 1988 (1985), p.183.

26 Nancy Turner, Laurence C. Thompson, M. Terry Thompson, and Annie York, "Knowledge and Usage of Plants by the Thompson Indians of British Columbia," Forthcoming, Royal British Columbia Museum, Victoria.

27 Trinita Rivera, "Diet of a Food Gathering People, with Chemical Analysis of Salmon and Saskatoons." In Marian Parker, (editor) *Indians of the Urban Northwest*, New York: AMS Press, 1949, pp.34-35.

28 Willy Justice, Raymond Dunstan, Adam Klein, personal communication, 1985.

29 Nancy Turner et al., "Knowledge and Usage of Plants by the Thompson Indians of British Columbia."

30 Nancy Turner, *Food Plants of the British Columbia Indians, Part 2, Interior Peoples*, British Columbia Provincial Museum Handbook No. 36, Victoria, 1978, p.26.

31 James Teit, "The Lillooet Indians," p.240.

32 Nancy Turner et al., "Knowledge and Usage of Plants by the Thompson Indians of British Columbia."

33 Willy Justice, Hilda Austin, personal communication, 1985.

34 Andrew Johnny, Willy Justice, personal communication, 1985.

35 Randy Bouchard and Dorothy Kennedy, "Indian Land Use and Indian History of the Stein River Valley, British Columbia," p.123.

36 Willy Justice, personal communication, 1985.

37 Willy Justice, personal communication, 1985.

38 Adam Klein, personal communication, 1985.

39 Louis Phillips, personal communication, 1985.

40 Nancy Turner, *Plants in B.C. Indian Technology*, Handbook No.38, British Columbia Provincial Museum, Victoria, 1979, pp.76, 85.

41 Adam Klein, personal communication, 1985.

42 Louis Phillips, personal communication, 1985.

43 Nancy Turner, *Food Plants of the British Columbia Indians*, 1978, pp.146-147.

44 James Teit, "The Thompson Indians," p.230.

45 Louis Phillips, personal communication, 1985.

46 Andrew Johnny, personal communication, 1985.

47 Ron Purvis, personal communication, 1985.

48 Ron Purvis, unpublished manuscript in the author's possession, Lillooet, British Columbia.

49 Stein Basin Study Committee, "The Stein Basin Moratorium Study," Report submitted to provincial Cabinet's Environment and Land Use Committee, Victoria, 1976, p.20.

50 Willy Justice and Andrew Johnny, personal communication, 1985.

51 Richard Mayne, *Four Years in British Columbia and Vancouver Island*, London: John Murray, 1862, p.101.

Chapter 3

1 Wilson Duff, *The Indian History of British Columbia, Vol.1*, Anthropology in British Columbia Memoir No.5, Victoria: British Columbia Provincial Museum, 1964, p.55.
2 James Teit, "The Thompson Indians of British Columbia," p.176.
3 John Work, "Answers to Queries on Natural History, Fort Colvile, 1 April 1829," Colvile District Report for 1829, Hudson's Bay Company Archives, Winnipeg.
4 Simon Fraser, in William K. Lamb (editor), *The Letters and Journals of Simon Fraser, 1806-1808*, Toronto: Macmillan, 1960, p.84.
5 James Teit, "The Thompson Indians of British Columbia," p.245.
6 Archibald McDonald, "Thompson's River District Report 1827." In E.E. Rich (editor), *Simpson's 1828 Journey to the Columbia*, London: The Hudson's Bay Record Society, 1947, p.227.
7 James Teit, "The Shuswap," Memoir of the American Museum of Natural History, 2(7), 1909, p.607.
8 Aimee August Shuswap elder, Neskainlith Indian Reserve, near Chase, British Columbia, personal communication.
9 Robin Fisher, *Contact and Conflict, Indian-European Relations in British Columbia, 1774-1890*, Vancouver: University of British Columbia Press, 1977, p.40.
10 Calvin Martin, *Keepers of the Game: Indian-Animal Relationships and the Fur Trade*, Berkeley: University of California Press, 1978.
11 James Teit, "The Thompson Indians of British Columbia," p.354.
12 Governor James Douglas, *Diary*, 14 September 1860, Provincial Archives of British Columbia, Victoria.
13 Rolf Knight, *Indians at Work*, Vancouver: New Star Press, 1978, p.131.
14 G.P.V. Akrigg and Helen B. Akrigg, *British Columbia Chronicle 1847-1871*, Vancouver: Discovery Press, 1977, pp.96-97.
15 *British Colonist*, 16 May 1859, p.3.
16 *British Colonist Supplement*, 16 May 1862.
17 Andrew H. Yarmie, "Smallpox and the British Columbia Indians, Epidemic of 1862," *British Columbia Library Association Quarterly* 31, 1968, p.15.
18 Letter and sketch map sent by Gold Commissioner Henry M. Ball to Governor Douglas, 20 October, 1860, Provincial Archives of British Columbia, Victoria.
19 *British Colonist*, 12 January 1863, p.3.
20 Robin Fisher, *Contact and Conflict*, pp.160-165.
21 Randy Bouchard and Dorothy Kennedy, "Indian Land Use and Indian History of the Stein River Valley, British Columbia," 1988 (1985), p.138.
22 *Inland Sentinel*, 30 November 1882, p.2.
23 Ibid.
24 *Inland Sentinel*, 12 March 1885, p.1.

Chapter 4

1 Roger Freeman and David Thompson, *Exploring the Stein River Valley*, North Vancouver: Douglas and McIntyre, 1979, p.27.
2 Ministry of Forests, *Stein River Resource Folio Plan*, August 1984, pp.45-49.
3 Stein Basin Study Committee, "The Stein Basin Moratorium Study," Victoria, 1976, p.33.
4 Ministry of Forests, *Stein River Resources Folio Plan* 1984, pp.45-49.

Chapter 5

1 Hans L. Roemer, Jim Pojar and Kerry R. Joy, "Protected Old-Growth Forests in Coastal British Columbia," unpublished document, 1988, p.14.
2 Frederick J. Swanson et al., Unpublished data on file at the School of Forestry, Oregon State University, Corvallis, cited in George W. Brown, *Forestry and Water Quality*, Corvallis: O.S.U. Book Stores, Inc., 2nd ed., 1983, p.23.
3 Alan N. Chatterton, "Stein River Mainline—Geologic Hazards," November 1985, British Columbia Forest Products Ltd.: Resources Planning Group, Crofton, British Columbia, Map 1.
4 Ibid., p.27.
5 Ministry of Forests, *Stein River Resources Folio Plan* 1984, p.19.

Chapter 6

1 *Bridge River-Lillooet News*, 13 January 1949.
2 James K. Burrows, "A Much-needed Class of Labour: The Economy and Income of the Southern Plateau Interior Indians, 1897-1910," *BC Studies*, 71, 1986, pp.27-46.
3 *Bridge River-Lillooet News*, 27 April 1967.
4 Ibid., 23 May 1934.
5 Ibid., 27 September 1946.
6 Ibid., 5 January 1961.
7 Ibid., 5 January 1961.

Chapter 8

1 Trevor Jones, *Wilderness or Logging? Case Studies of Two Conflicts in B.C.*, Vancouver: Federation of Mountain Clubs of British Columbia, 1983, p.10.
2 Trevor Jones, *The Stein—A Case for Preservation*, November 1987, pp.7-8.
3 British Columbia Forest Service, Kamloops Forest Region, *Lillooet Timber Supply Area Options Report*, October 1986, p.16.
4 F. Nyers, *Review of the Fraser River Crossing at Lytton*, British Columbia Forest Service, 1978, p.7.
5 Letter from A.B. Robinson, Regional Director, Kamloops Forest Region, Ministry of Forests, to Chris O'Connor, Lytton Lumber, Lytton, 11 October 1985.
6 Wilderness Advisory Committee, *A Wilderness Mosaic*, 1986, Victoria: Queen's Printer, pp.42-43.
7 Ministry of Forests and Lands, Press Release, "Backgrounder—Stein Valley," 2 October 1987, p.2.

Chapter 9

1 Peter Pearse, Andrea Lang, and Kevin Todd, "The Backlog of Unstocked Forest Land in British Columbia and the Impact of Reforestation Programs," *The Forestry Chronicle*, December 1986, p.519.
2 F.L.C. Reed, "Reshaping Forest Policy in British Columbia." Prepared for The Vancouver Institute Saturday Evening Lecture Series, February 16, 1985, Table 2, "Comparison of Annual Silvicultural Treatments in Finland and B.C.," p.15.
3 John Doyle, "Silviculture Solutions," *The Truck Logger*, April/May 1988, p.10.
4 Peter Emerson and Gloria Helfand, *Wilderness and Timber Production in the Natural Forests of California*, Washington D.C.: Economic Policy Department, The Wilderness Society, 1983, p.xi.
5 John Walters, Forestry professor, "A Silvicultural and Political Strategy for the Association of B.C. Professional Foresters," unpublished document, University of British Columbia Faculty of Forestry, February 1984, pp.8-10.
6 Larry Pocock, Y.C. Trading Corp., White Rock, British Columbia, Consultant, "Notes of Tour of BCFP's Boston Bar Sawmill—December 1987," submitted to the Institute for New Economics, Vancouver, British Columbia, January 1988. And personal communication.
7 Frank O'Brien, "Less is More," *The Truck Logger*, December/January 1988, p.104.
8 D.P.A. Group Inc., *Economic Impacts of the Adventure Travel Industry in British Columbia*, study prepared for the Outdoor Recreation Council of B.C., January 1988, pp. 2-3, 7.
9 MacLaren Plansearch Corp. Tourism Research Group/Lavalin, *Adventure Travel Market Analysis*, draft final report, prepared for the Outdoor Recreation Council of B.C., February 1988, p.4-1.
10 Ibid. p.7-1.
11 Marktrend Marketing Research Inc., B.C. Research, and Economic Planning Group, *Visitor '87: A travel survey of visitors to British Columbia*, prepared for Ministry of Tourism, Recreation, and Culture, March 1988, p.91.
12 MacLaren Plansearch, *Adventure Travel Market Analysis*, p.7-1.

13 Marktrend, *Visitor '87*, p.105.
14 John Woodsworth, "Parks: How many are too many?" In *Parks in British Columbia*, Peter Dooling (editor), Vancouver: University of British Columbia, August 1985, pp.56-63.
15 Bill Wagner, "An Emerging Corporate Nobility? Industrial Concentration of Economic Power on Public Timber Tenures," *Forest Planning Canada*, 4(2), 1988, p.14.
16 A. P. Meristem, "A Comparison of the Forest Economy of Sweden and B.C.," *Forest Planning Canada*, 3(2), 1987, p. 17.
17 Ministry of Forests and Lands, *Annual Report 1986/87*, 1988, pp.48-49.
18 Ibid. pp.42-43, 45
19 Lew McArthur, Lytton Lumber. Interview, July 1985.
20 Peter Pearse, "The Tenure System's Main Faults: Lack of Competition, Over-Allocation of Timber," *Forest Planning Canada*, 3(4), 1987, pp.25-26.
21 A. Hopwood, F. Marshall, and D. Smith, "Discipline, Ethics, and the Forestry Profession in British Columbia," *Forest Planning Canada*, 4(1), 1988, pp.14-25. See also p.13, p.26.

Chapter 10

1 World Commission on Environment and Development, *Our Common Future*, Oxford, New York: Oxford University Press, 1987, pp.31-33.
2 "The Tourist Trap: Who's Getting Caught?," *Cultural Survival Quarterly*, 6(3), 1983, pp.3-35.
3 E.F. Schumacher, *Small is Beautiful: Economics As If People Mattered*, New York: Harper & Row, 1973, pp.93-94.

189

BOOK PROJECT SUPPORTERS

Preparation of this book was undertaken under the auspices of the Institute for New Economics and was made possible by the work of the Stein Wilderness Alliance, in particular Alistair Blachford, Gordon White, Joanne Fleming, Linda Glennie, Cecile Helten, Brian den Hertog, Jean Hamilton, Anita Brochocka, Jennifer Nener, and Jackie Garnett. Their fund-raising efforts supported the research, writing, cartography, collecting of photographs, and graphics production. Their support relieved the Institute of an unbearable financial burden, allowing the authors and contributors to concentrate on presenting the story of the Stein in as complete a manner as they could. The support of the following individuals is gratefully acknowledged:

(Photo: Murray Webb)

Deborah Aaron, Norman Abbey, Dr. Raja T. Abboud, (Mrs.) Dorothy M. Aberdeen, Judith Lynn Abrams, R. & M. Abramzik, ACDC Design Ltd., H. Adamowicz, Edith Adamson, Neil Aitken, Alex & Ruth, Frances Allen, Karen Alvaro & Robert Greenlee, Pat Amighetti, Alice V. Anderson, Mrs. H. (Elizabeth) Anderson, Mary K. Annis, Sharon Antoniak, Dr. Saul Arbess, Ian H. Armstrong, Kit Lia Ashera, Kenneth I. Ashley, Emil Augustin, W.K. & H.A. Bachmann, Ronald L. Bacon, L. Bailey & B. Grainger, Bob & Sandi Baker, Wilf Bangert, Cathy Bannink, M. Bardwell, Ralph Barer, Steve Barer, John Barling, P.C. Barre, Lucy Bashford, Fredrick Bass, Henry Bauld, Don Bayliss, Rob Bayliss, R.L. Beadle, Martin Beck, Jillian D. Begg, Donald & Gisele Bentley, Richard Berger & Miriam Dyak, Audrey Berns, R. & D. Billas, Heinrich Binder, Patricia Bingham, Alistair Blachford, David de Ploget Blacoe, Marianne Blanchet, Gayle & Doug Blenkhorn, David Blissett, Edna & John Blyth-Crotch, Marc Bombois, Anne Bosch, Donna M. Bourne, Loni & Christopher Bowers, Marion Boyle, Randy J. Boyle, H. Layton Bray, David & Pat Breen, D. Brenner, Irene Brereton, G. Brewster, Joyce & Peter Brittany, Anita Brochocka, Glen Brown, Robert A. Browning, Francis M. Brunette, Bunny, Jeffrey Burrows, Karl Bury, Steve Bushell, S.M. Butcher, Bill & Margaret Caird, Sandy Cairns, Kathryn Campbell, Margaret Campbell, Mrs. Gaile V. Campbell, Joan Carlisle-Irving, A. Carson, Ralph Cartar, D. Cartwright, Catbalue Goldsmith, Don Cavaghan, Native Education Centre, Steve D. Chambers, Michael Chechik, Vivian Chenard and Walter Schibli, Nancy A. Chiavario, Mrs. Dorothy Chichik, Daniel Chowne, Hugh & Carolyn Cleland, Barbara Clemes, Robert Climie & Randy

Julian, Dr. & Mrs. R.A. Cline, Gloria & David Cohen, (Mrs. W. R.) Patricia N. Collinson, Caroline Cook, David & Sally Cooper, Grant Copeland, Leanne Corcoran, Robert L. Coupe, Janet E.Q. Cousins, Joan Cowley, Peter & Jenny Coy, E. Mary Craig, Pleasance Crawford, Creative Contemplative Society, Carol Critchley, Beryl J. Cunningham, Barbara Curran, Dah Sing Bank Ltd., Sean & Carmen Daly, Connie Dancette, Alice Davies, Herb Davies, A. de Cosson, J. De Jong, Thomas De Marco, Susan Elizabeth DeBeck, Brian DenHertog, Sharon Dennie & Sara Fujibayashi, Patrick R.G. Denonville, F.E. Devito, Mrs. Leslie Diamond, Eberhard & Sarah Diehl, Larry Dill, Robert Dill, Darko Dimitrijevic, Pete Dixon, Marnie Dobell, Shelly Donald, Carl Douglas, Graham Dowden, Michael & Sharon Down, Anna M. Driehuyzen, Robert Drislane, Dr. Peter Charles Drummond & Phyllida M.B. Drummond, Peter Dunlop, Gail & Terence Dyson, Dr. Jan Easton, Bill Edmonds & Family, Peter Edwards, Gillian S.E. Elcock, C.M. Elgar, Mr. & Mrs. Frank English, Merritt B.C., John H. Esling, Brian D. Evans, R.D. Fairbairn, The Gladish Family, E.M. Farrer, Mary Farris, Enzo Federico, Robin Fells, Mrs. Freda F. Fennell, Stephen E. Field, Findlater's, F.M. Finlay, Dr. Stanley J. Fisher, Aline La Flamme, Robert & JoAnne Fleming, Frank & Pat Fornelli, Dennis Forsgren, Roy & Jacqueline Forster, Bristol Foster, Angus H. Fraser, Lili Frinton, Trudy M. Frisk, Ken Gamey, Jacqueline Garnett, Lee Gass, M. Gawlak, Dr. A.C. Gedye, John Gellard, S. Gerigh, Byran, Carol & Thomas Gibson, Michael Gilfillan, David Gill, Linda Glennie, Benoit Godin, Ray C. Goiffon, Niel Golden, Rene Goldman, Mike Gordi, Rachel Gourley, Doug Graeb & Joan Frost, Jeanette Wong Graf, Maetel Grant, Anita & Wayne

Gray, Great Outdoors Equipment Ltd./Chris & Carol Boothroyd, Mr. Norman Greaves, Gerry Green, Greenpeace Canada, Lee Grenon, Jane & Robert Grey, Amund Groner, Rolf Grut, Dr. Eve Gulliford, Bruce Hainer, A.C. Hall, Philip Hall, D.C. Hallaran, William Hamilton, Dorothy Hamilton, George & Dixie Hamilton, Jean A. Hamilton, Thelma L. Hamilton, Roger Hare, Enid Harris, Julia & Ted Harrison, R. Patrick Harrison, Susan S. Harrison, Mickey Jean Harrop, John Hart, Barbara Hartley, Henry Hawthorn, Peter Herd, Jason A. Herz, Franz J. Hess, Phillip and Margaret Hewett, Thomas Hickman, Ashley & Wendy Hilliard, Greta Hiscock, Rosemary & Eric Hoare, R.E. Hodge, Doc Hodgins, Hilda Hoenisch, Inge Hohndorf, Peggy Hornbrook, Robert B. & Gayel A. Horsfall, Lee D. Horvat, Wayne Hoskins, Eve Howden, Ron Howe, Lyn Howes, J.B. Howie, Marcia Huber, Peter Humphrys, Kathleen Hunt, Peter Huron, Viki Inskip, Interworld Electronics & Computer Industries Ltd., Ronaye Ireland, Esther James, Stuart & Jean Jamieson, Beth Jay, Glyn L. Jenkins, Ivan Johnson, Cate Jones, Trevor Jones, Patrick J. Julian, Randy Julian, David Kaetz, Ray Kamer, Jo Kehoe, Wes Kenzie, Walter & Marie Kerchum, Michael Kerr, Brian Kiessling, Marc C. Kiessling, S. Ellen King, Sherry King, E.H. Klein, Laura Klein, Lisa L. Kofod, A. & S. Kreutzmann, Brigitta B. Krukenberg, Werner Kurz, Jamie Laidlaw, Juliet & Rick Laing, Kimberley Laing, Peter and Lale, Jeffrey Lammers, Judith Langford, J.L. l'Anson, Francine Laporte, Alexander P. Latham, Ed & Kay Latimer, Ken & Carleen Lay, Francis L. Lea, Bruce R. Ledingham, David & Julie Leffelaar, M. Lefkowitz, Dana Lepofsky & Ken Lertzman, Morley & Joy Lertzman, Sarah L'Estrange, Daniel Lewis, Leonard Libin, Thomas Beck Liddell,

Ms. Emily (Lee) Lightfoot, Paul & Jessoa Lightfoot, Casimir C. & Shelagh Lindsey, D.J. Livingstone, Ruth Loomis, S.D. Lott and J.A. Fricker, Ursula Lowrey, Paul Luykx, Patrick F. Mackie, Allan MacKinnon, Keith & Jennifer MacLeod, Margaret MacQuarrie, Mr. & Mrs. D. MacTavish, Mr. & Mrs. John Macwillian, Lisa Madetoja, Janice & Barry Madill, Eleanor Mae, Paul Magid & Alice Devora, Warren Magnusson & Sharon Walls, Maid of the Mountain, Joanne Manley, Michael Manolson, H. Marcus, David Marmorek & Betty Bronson, T. & E. Marshall, David Martin & Lucinda Jones, Gil Matilla, Anne Mayhew, P.C. McAffrey, Peter B. McAllister, Mr. & Mrs. Neil McAskill, Sheila and Don McConnell, R. G. McDiarmid, Allan McDonell, Lindsey McDonell, Tavish McDonell, Zoe McDonell, Jaimie McEvoy, Kathy McGrenera, L.M. McKenzie, Andrew McLean, James A. McLean, Celeste McLeod, Deanna McLeod, Bessie L. McMurray, Michael McWilliams, Mieneke Mees, Micha J. Menczer, A.C.R. M'Gonigle, Shelagh M'Gonigle, Susan M'Gonigle & Peter Hertzberg, Elaine Michel, Pat Michie, Maureen Milburn, Dr. Edward H. Miller & Nancy L. Miller, Janet Miller, Ron Mills, feather Mills, Bill & Bridget Ann Milsom, Martin & Pawli Model, Ryder Jon Moore, Karen Mo''rcke, Jan More, Wendy Mott, Helen & Alex Muir, Victoria, Mr. & Mrs. James I. Murray, Martin Roy Musser, Robert Kai Asataro Nagata, Wayne Nagata, Michael John Nagy, Roy & Charlotte Nelson, Jennifer Nener, Virginia & Ray Newman, Edmund Nicholson, Marjorie O. Nicol, Thomas Nicol & Julie Mussenden, Christine C. Nicolson, Northwest Wildlife Preservation Society, Olga Nunn, Jim Oakley, Dr. W. Pat O'Brien, Eamonn Gerrard O'Donoghue, Finn & Eileen Ohrling, Mr B. Van Oldenborgh, Sharon Gayle Olsen, Julie

Olson, Kevin O'Neill, Rick O'Neill, J.M. Page, Peter Paterson, A.C. Patterson, H.F. Pearce, Norman Pearson, E. & M. Pechlaner, Joe Percival, Armand Petronio, Daniel & Janet Phelps, Louise & Bus Phillips, M.L. Phillips, Pierce van Loon, Barristers & Solicitors, Don Plenderleith, James & Constance Polomark, Louise E. Poole, Michael Poole, Marta Powell, Rob & Charlotte Powell, Michael Praisley, Sharon Priest-Nagata, Jerilynn C. Prior, Dianne Radmore, Beverly & William Ramey, W.M. Ratcliffe, Mary M. Reaume, Bruce M. Reeves, I. Reinelt, Reinhard Derreth Graphics Ltd., John & Jean Reiter, Craig & Zara Reynolds, Herb Rice & Lee Masters, Linda Richards, Eva & Helmut Rietzler, Joan Rike, L.G. Roberts, Kathy Robertson, Jan Robinson, Hulda Roddan, C.A. Ronayne, Edward, Katherine & Michael Rosnoski, Allyn Ross, K & P Ross, Martin Rossander, Olivia Rousseau, Ian Rowles, Richard Claude Roy, Peter Royce, Gordon Runtz, Craig & Tygh Runyan, Lila Ruzicka, Stuart, Gretchen & Hugh Ryan, Alnoor & Gulzar Samji, Karen Sanford, O.M. Sanford, Trevor and Sarah, Darlene Scarr, John and Ida Schibli, Peggy M. Schmid, John Schreiber, Wilson E. Schwahn, Kathleen Scobie, Bob & Sheillah Scott, Marie Seabrook, Allen Seager, George E. Semper, Rick Seward, Sheep Creek Apiaries, Shpak-Spence, Inc., Chad Deeken & Gwen Shrimpton, Sierra Club of Western Canada, Ritva Silvo, Maureen & Tony Simmonds, Anges Simpson, William, Annerose & Muriel Sims, Rhys E. Smallwood, Terence G. Smith, Risa Smith & Tom Mommsen, Helen Speight, Marty Spencer, C. Spicer, Spike A.T.F. Meares Island, Paul G. Stanwood, Donald R. & Robert Steeves, Michael & Katharine J. Steig, George & Dorothy Stevens, Hilary Stewart, Wayne Still, Beba Stoyka, Linda

Strachan, Keith Surges, C. Suzuki, A.L. Swenson, Emma K. Miller Tansley, John Jamieson Tansley, Robert Tarrant, Dr. Sheilah D. Thompson, Nancy E. Thompson, Diane Thorne, Allan Thornton, Jim Titerle, R.G. Todd, Daryl Torres, Shirley Tremblay, Les Tulloch, A.D. Turner, Douglas & Sheila Turner, Nancy J. Turner, Frederika van Nouhuys Ward, Corrie van Walraven, Cora Alice Ventress, Dr. N.A.M. Verbeek, Hendric and Barbara Verkuylen, Ricki Vogt R.M.T., Allan Voykin, Carole Waddell, Lyn Vander Wal, Jennifer Waldie, Jane Walker, Jim & Kathleen Walker, Jean Wallace & Steve New, Gerald Warner, Susan Watkin, Peter Watson, Peter Watts, Clinton M. Webb, Vera & Tim Webb, Carole Webber, Western Canada Wilderness Committee, Norma Whale, Phil & Pat White, Ronald White, Taoya White, George & Fran Whitney, Dorothy & John Wickwire, E. Williams, Harry Joe Williams, Joan M. Williams, C. & K. Wilson, Judy L. Wilson, W.G. Wilson, Gordon Wirth, Bruce Thomas Witzeol, Vera Wojna, Anna Saskia Wolsak, Stan Wood, N.J. & R.J. Woodham, Bruce & Sylvia Woodsworth, David R. Wright, Anne Yandle, Susan Yates, R.C. Ydenberg, Alan Young, Alan J. Young, Yukon Conservation Society, Linda & Ted Zacks, Peter Zimprich

In Wildness Is The Preservation Of The World

What I have been preparing to say is this: in wildness is the preservation of the world . . . Life consists of wildness. The most alive is the wildest. Not yet subdued by man, its presence refreshes him . . . When I would re-create myself, I seek the darkest wood, the thickest and most interminable—and to the citizen—most dismal, swamp. I enter as a sacred place, a Sanctum sanctorum. There is the strength, the marrow, of Nature. In short, all good things are wild and free. . . .

A town is saved, not more by the righteous men in it than by the woods and swamps that surround it. A township where one primitive forest waves above while another primitive forest rots below,—such a town is fitted to raise not only corn and potatoes, but poets and philosophers for the coming ages. In such a soil grew Homer and Confucius and the rest, and out of such a wilderness comes the Reformer eating locusts and wild honey.

Henry David Thoreau, "Walking," 1853, in *Excursions:*
The Writings of Henry David Thoreau, Vol.9, Boston: Riverside, 1893.